# ULTIMATE TRIAD ARPEGGIOS for Guitarists

By Yohei Nakamura

# Biography

Yohei Nakamura is a Japanese guitarist based in Los Angeles, California. After graduating from Los Angeles Music Academy and Berklee College of Music, Yohei has been touring worldwide with the artists such as Stevie Wonder, Chaka Khan, Brian McKnight and Sheila E..

A list of the artists that Yohei has performed with includes Lady Gaga, Beyonce, Ed Sheeran, Ariana Grande, Babyface, Usher, Pharrell Williams, PJ Morton, Marcus Miller, Ledesi, Richie Sambora, Gary Clark Jr., India Arie, Whitney Houston, Judith Hill, Janelle Monae, Jill Scott, Prince, Steven Tyler, Annie Lennox, Stephanie Mills, Jennifer Hudson, John Legend, Andrea Bocelli, Ne-Yo, Corinne Bailey Rae, Joss Stone, Candy Dulfer, Johnny Gill, Jonathan Butler, Ai and many more.

# Table of Contents

**6/8 Sequence ②**



**6/8 Sequence ③**

# Introduction

Triad is a harmony with three scale notes that are stacked in thirds.
There are four types of triads: **Major triad** (Root, 3, 5), **Minor triad** (Root, ♭3, 5), **Diminished triad** (Root, ♭3, ♭5) and **Augmented triad** (Root, 3, ♯5).

° = diminished triad
+ = augmented triad

The triad is in **Root Position** when the root is the bass note and the third and the fifth are piled up in order.
By moving the bass note of Root Position up an octave, the third becomes the bass note. It is called **First Inversion**.
By moving the bass note of First Inversion up an octave, the fifth becomes the bass note. It is called **Second Inversion**.

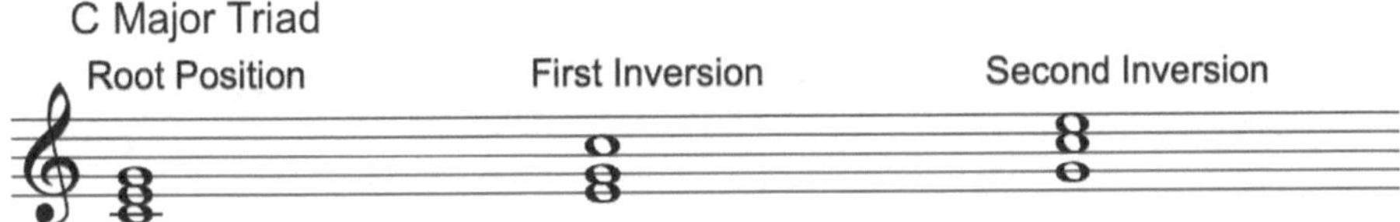


Triad is one of the most fundamental chords but also can be applied to advanced harmony concepts. For example, C major triad could be a part of Am7, Fmaj9, Dm11, F♯7(♭9♯11), etc.

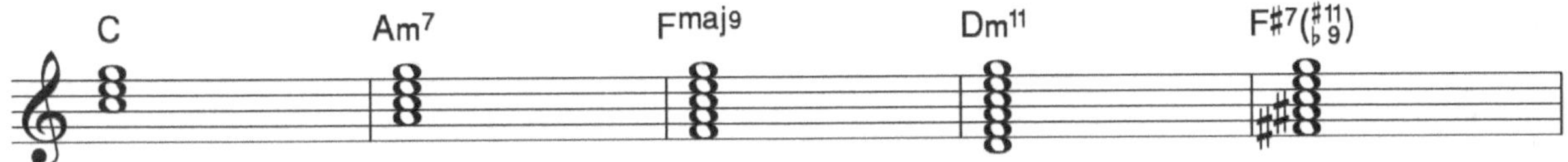


Even a chord which seems to be complicated can be simplified by breaking it down into some triads. For example, within E7(♭9♭13), you can find triads such as D°, E+ and Fm.

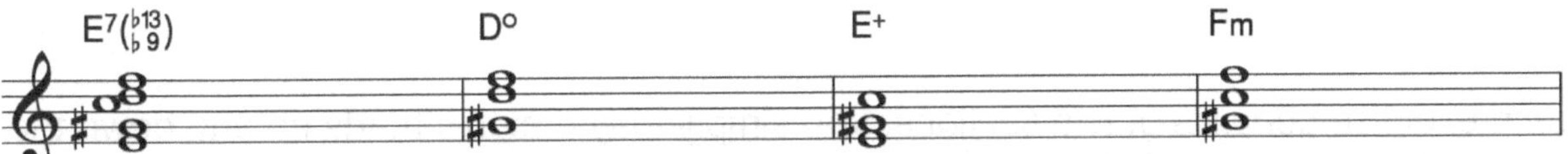

Any triads can be used as an extension of the chords that contain seventh and tensions.
This idea could be applied to not only rhythm playing but also soloing. Playing triad arpeggios within the phrases would make your guitar solo more unique and interesting. As you can play the same note on different strings, each triad arpeggio has several ways to play as well.

This textbook contains a variety of exercises that helps you learn how to play triad arpeggios on the entire fretboard. These are perfect exercises for you to improve your technique and gain a better understanding of the fretboard simultaneously.

In this book, we use the diatonic triads in five different scales: **Major Scale**, **Minor Scale**, **Harmonic Minor Scale**, **Melodic Minor Scale** and **Harmonic Major Scale**.

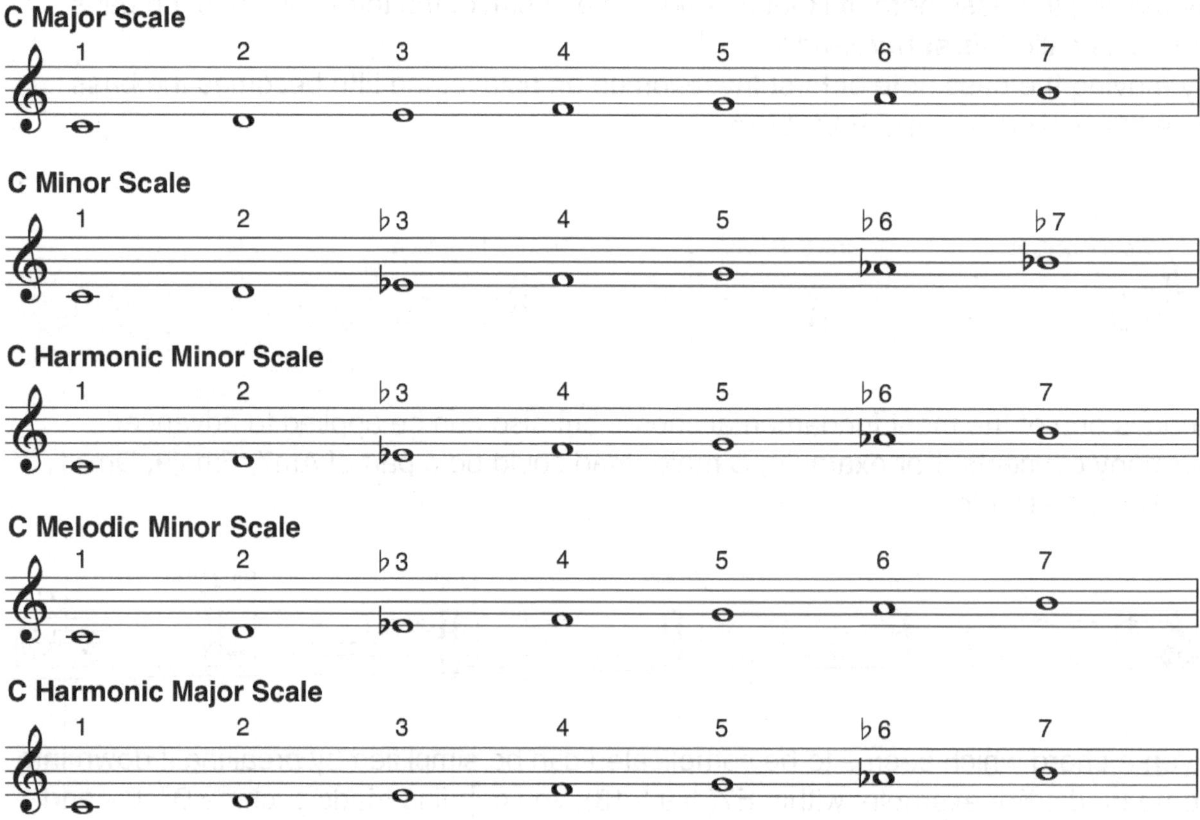


Each exercise consists of two sections. You simply play diatonic triads up and down the neck in the first half. Here is an example with C Major scale.

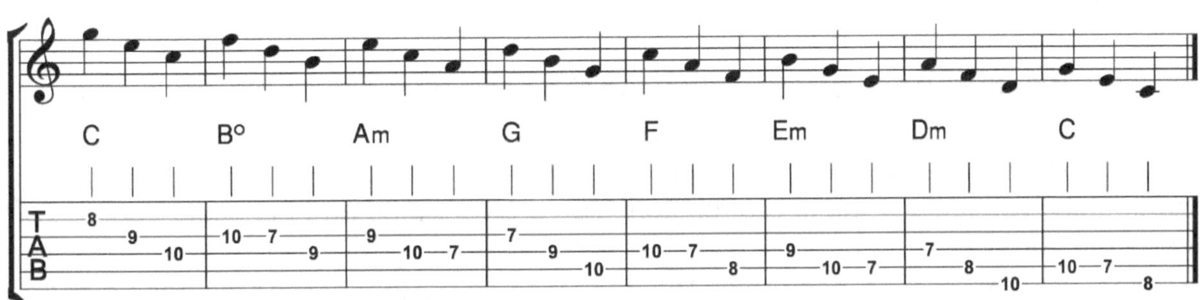


In the second half, you play diatonic triads backwards as you go up the neck, and vice versa. With this method, the inversion changes in cycles as you move on to the next triads. In this example, the first C is in root position. It is followed by B° in first inversion and Am in second inversion. G is back in root position and it keeps changing in the same manner for the following triads.

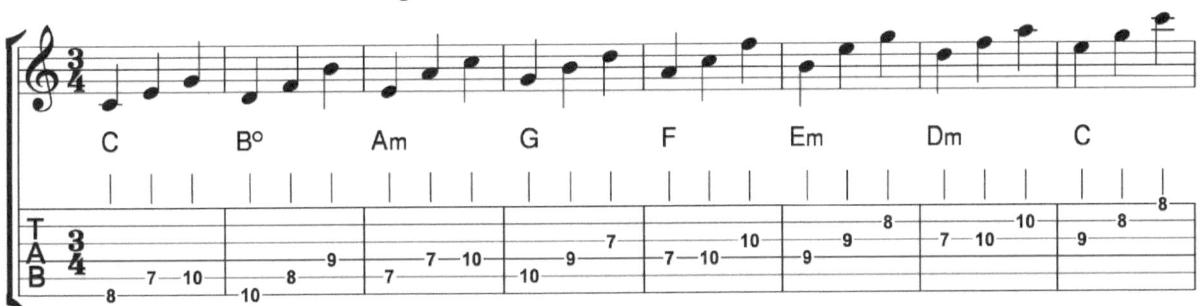

# Practice Tips

## 1. Practice in different keys

Once you get used to each exercise, try to play exactly the same one in different keys. Some exercises might feel more difficult to play in a certain key because your fingers need more stretch in a lower position. I would not recommend you to transpose it by half steps because it is less challenging. "Circle of fifths" is a great way to practice. The key keeps being transposed down a perfect fifth to cover all 12 keys.
C→F→B♭(A♯)→E♭(D♯)→A♭(G♯)→D♭(C♯)→G♭(F♯)→B→E→A→D→G

## 2. Identify the chord relationships and the scale degrees

Do not only follow the numbers on the guitar tabs. Your practice will be a lot more meaningful if you identify the chord relationships of every triad and the scale degrees of every note you play.
For example, Gm (chord tones are G, B♭ and D) could be VIm of B♭ Major scale and the scale degrees are 1, 3 and 6. It could be IIm of F Melodic Minor scale and the scale degrees are 2, 4 and 6. It could also be IVm of D Harmonic Major scale and the scale degrees are 1, 4 and ♭6.

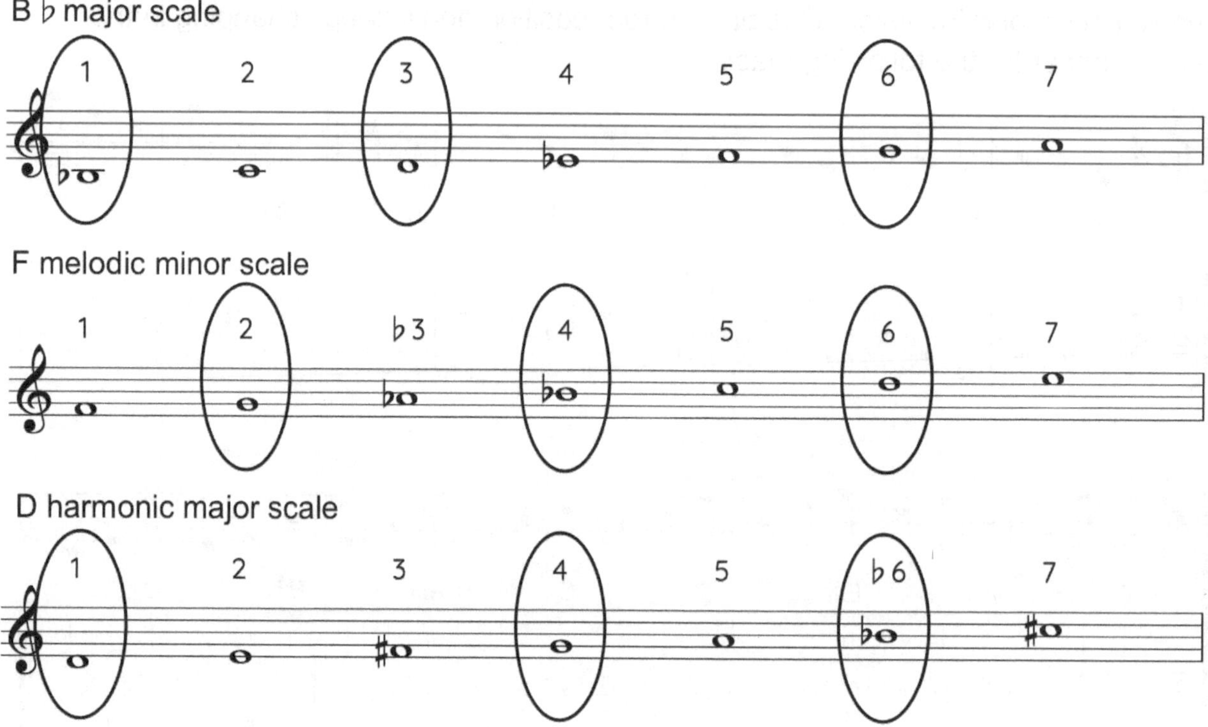

The same triad would have completely different characters based on what key you are in. It is highly recommended to memorize the following formula for the diatonic triads as you practice each scale.

**Major Scale**

I IIm IIIm IV V VIm VII○

**Minor Scale**

Im II○ ♭III IVm Vm ♭VI ♭VII

**Harmonic Minor Scale**

Im II○ ♭III+ IVm V ♭VI VII○

**Melodic Minor Scale**

Im IIm ♭III+ IV V VI○ VII○

**Harmonic Major Scale**

I II○ IIIm IVm V ♭VI+ VII○

### 3. Always use a metronome and practice it over and over

Take each repeat sign over and over. If you can't even play the whole exercise one time through without any mistake or a pause, drop the tempo down and start over. Always start from a slow tempo and gradually speed up. Accuracy is more important than speed.

### 4. Enjoy every step of the learning process

I recommend you to pick at least one exercise a day and use it as a warm up routine before you play anything else. You can choose any exercise in any order. Knowing more triad arpeggios could help you discover new phrasing ideas and chordal approaches.
Your everyday performance would be a lot more fun.
You are getting better by every single note you play!

# C Major Scale 3/4 Sequence
## Root Position

# C Major Scale 3/4 Sequence
# Root Position (Alternative Position)

# C Major Scale 3/4 Sequence
## First Inversion

# C Major Scale 3/4 Sequence
# First Inversion (Alternative Position)

# C Major Scale 3/4 Sequence
# Second Inversion

# C Major Scale 3/4 Sequence
# Second Inversion (Alternative Position)

# F Minor Scale 3/4 Sequence
## Root Position

# F Minor Scale 3/4 Sequence
# Root Position (Alternative Position)

# F Minor Scale 3/4 Sequence
# First Inversion

# F Minor Scale 3/4 Sequence
# First Inversion (Alternative Position)

# F Minor Scale 3/4 Sequence
# Second Inversion

# F Minor Scale 3/4 Sequence
# Second Inversion (Alternative Position)

# B ♭ Harmonic Minor Scale 3/4 Sequence
## Root Position

# B ♭ Harmonic Minor Scale 3/4 Sequence
# Root Position (Alternative Position)

# B ♭ Harmonic Minor Scale 3/4 Sequence
# First Inversion

# B ♭ Harmonic Minor Scale 3/4 Sequence
# First Inversion (Alternative Position)

# B ♭ Harmonic Minor Scale 3/4 Sequence
## Second Inversion

# B ♭ Harmonic Minor Scale 3/4 Sequence
# Second Inversion (Alternative Position)

# E♭ Melodic Minor Scale 3/4 Sequence
# Root Position

# E ♭ Melodic Minor Scale 3/4 Sequence
## Root Position (Alternative Position)

# E♭ Melodic Minor Scale 3/4 Sequence
## First Inversion

# E ♭ Melodic Minor Scale 3/4 Sequence First Inversion (Alternative Position)

# E ♭ Melodic Minor Scale 3/4 Sequence
# Second Inversion

# E♭ Melodic Minor Scale 3/4 Sequence Second Inversion (Alternative Position)

# A♭ Harmonic Major Scale 3/4 Sequence
## Root Position

# A♭ Harmonic Major Scale 3/4 Sequence
# Root Position (Alternative Position)

# A ♭ Harmonic Major Scale 3/4 Sequence First Inversion

# A ♭ Harmonic Major Scale 3/4 Sequence First Inversion (Alternative Position)

# A ♭ Harmonic Major Scale 3/4 Sequence Second Inversion

# A ♭ Harmonic Major Scale 3/4 Sequence
# Second Inversion (Alternative Position)

# D♭ Major Scale 4/4 Sequence ①
# Root Position

# D♭ Major Scale 4/4 Sequence ①
# Root Position (Alternative Position)

# D♭ Major Scale 4/4 Sequence ①
## First Inversion

# D♭ Major Scale 4/4 Sequence ①
# First Inversion (Alternative Position)

# D ♭ Major Scale 4/4 Sequence ①
## Second Inversion

# D♭ Major Scale 4/4 Sequence ①
# Second Inversion (Alternative Position)

# F♯Minor Scale 4/4 Sequence ①
## Root Position

# F♯Minor Scale 4/4 Sequence ①
# Root Position (Alternative Position)

# F♯Minor Scale 4/4 Sequence ①
# First Inversion

# F♯Minor Scale 4/4 Sequence ①
# First Inversion (Alternative Position)

# F♯Minor Scale 4/4 Sequence ①
## Second Inversion

# F♯Minor Scale 4/4 Sequence ①
# Second Inversion (Alternative Position)

# B Harmonic Minor Scale 4/4 Sequence ①
# Root Position

# B Harmonic Minor Scale 4/4 Sequence ①
# Root Position (Alternative Position)

# B Harmonic Minor Scale 4/4 Sequence ①
# First Inversion

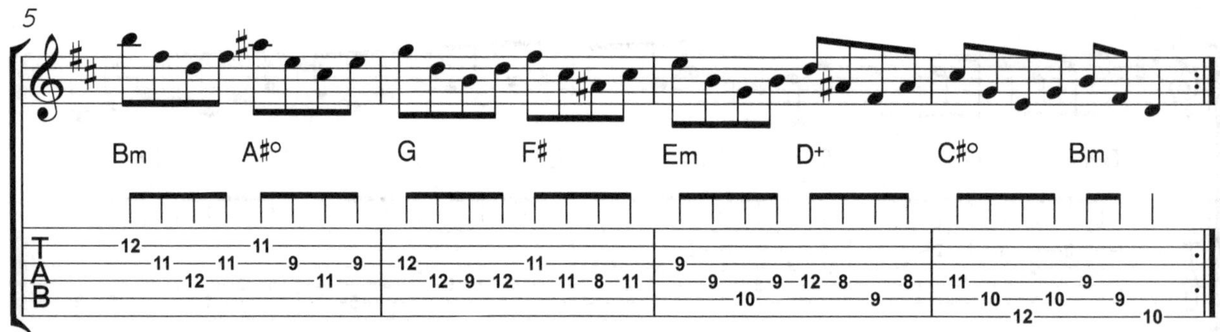


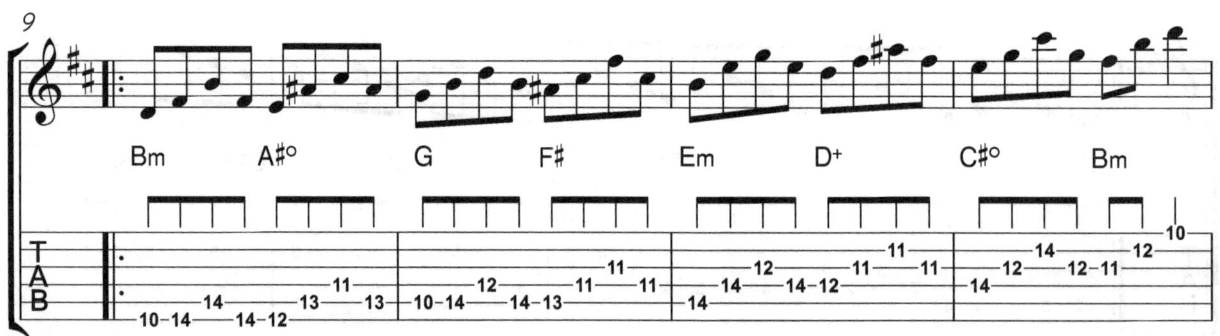


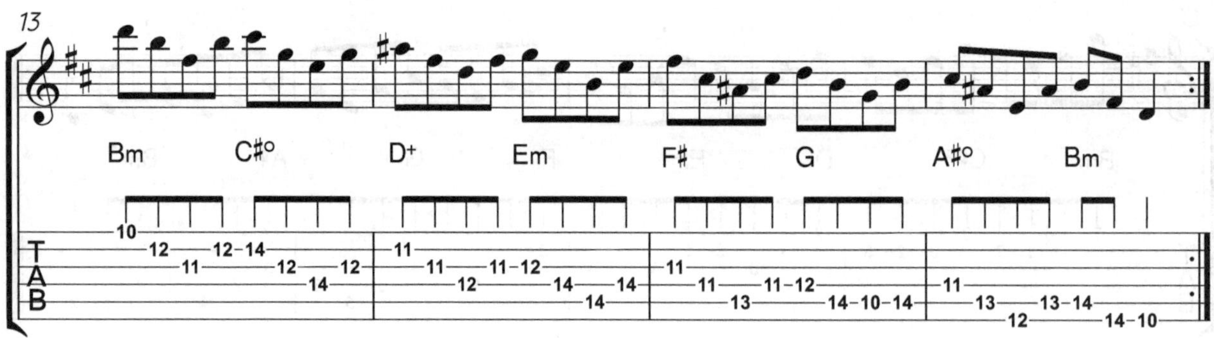

# B Harmonic Minor Scale 4/4 Sequence ①
# First Inversion (Alternative Position)

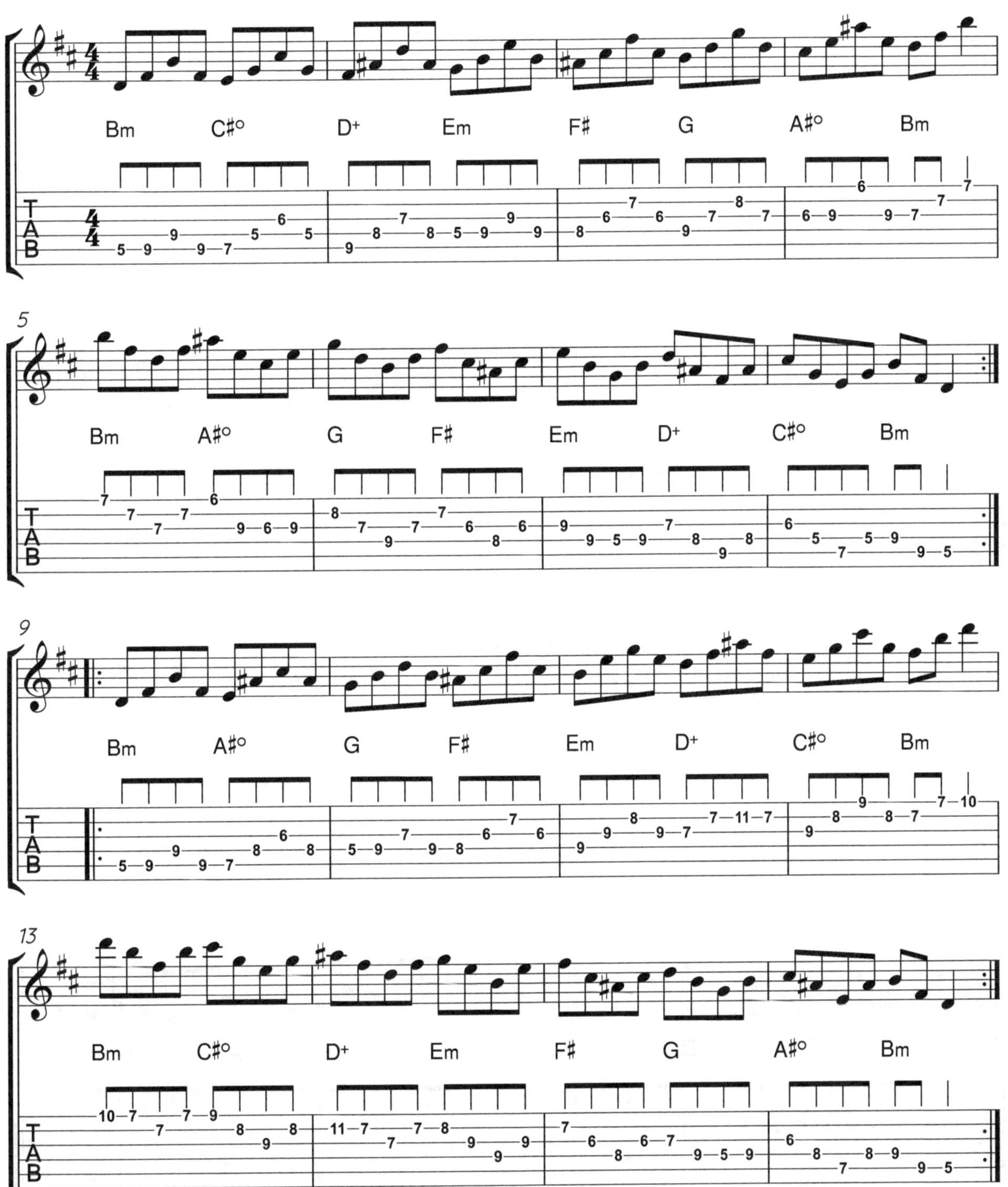

# B Harmonic Minor Scale 4/4 Sequence ①
## Second Inversion

# B Harmonic Minor Scale 4/4 Sequence ①
# Second Inversion (Alternative Position)

# E Melodic Minor Scale 4/4 Sequence ①
## Root Position

# E Melodic Minor Scale 4/4 Sequence ①
# Root Position (Alternative Position)

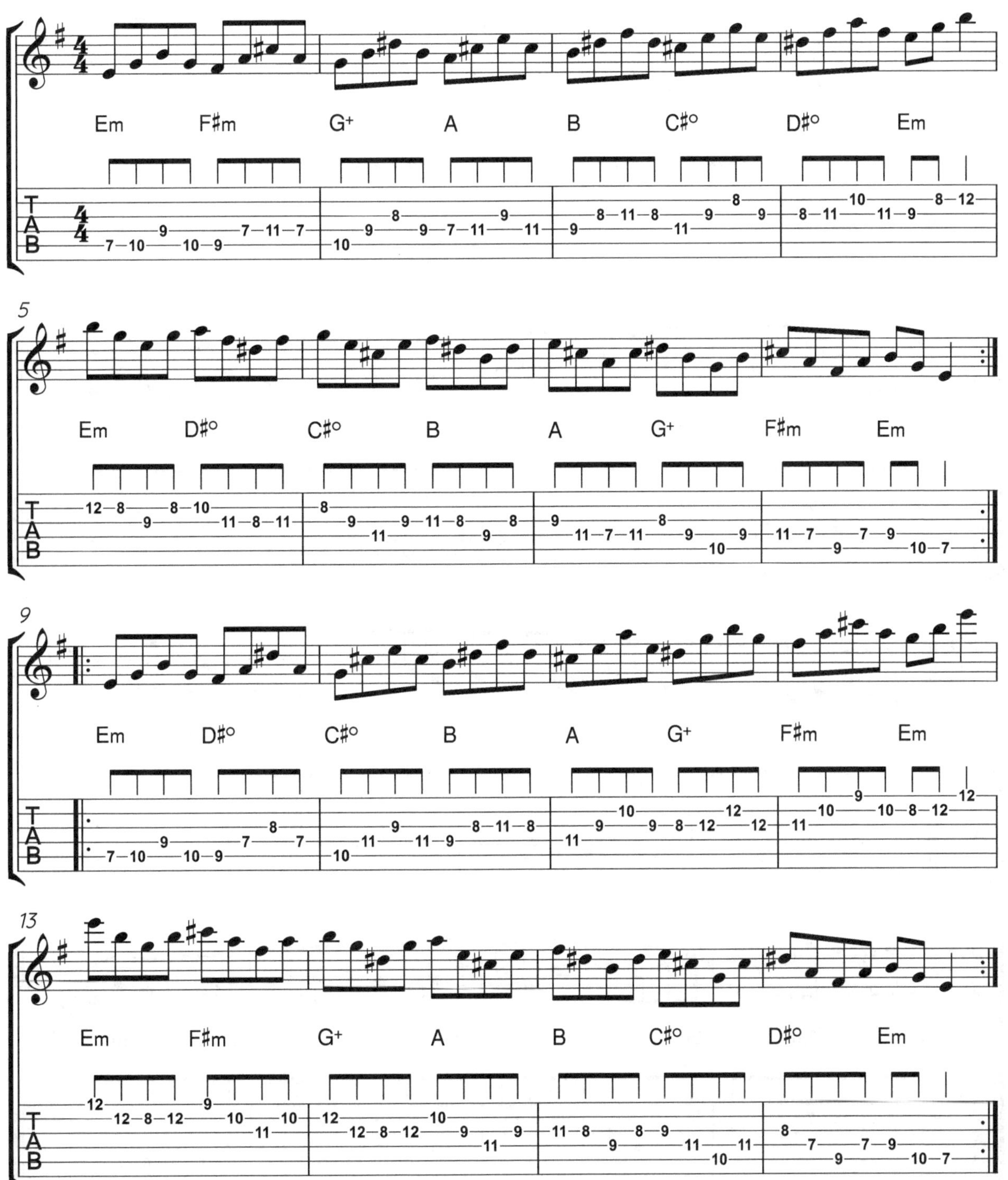

# E Melodic Minor Scale 4/4 Sequence ①
# First Inversion

# E Melodic Minor Scale 4/4 Sequence ①
# First Inversion (Alternative Position)

# E Melodic Minor Scale 4/4 Sequence ①
## Second Inversion

# E Melodic Minor Scale 4/4 Sequence ①
## Second Inversion (Alternative Position)

# A Harmonic Major Scale 4/4 Sequence ①
# Root Position

# A Harmonic Major Scale 4/4 Sequence ①
# Root Position (Alternative Position)

# A Harmonic Major Scale 4/4 Sequence ①
# First Inversion

# A Harmonic Major Scale 4/4 Sequence ①
# First Inversion (Alternative Position)

# A Harmonic Major Scale 4/4 Sequence ①
# Second Inversion

# A Harmonic Major Scale 4/4 Sequence ①
# Second Inversion (Alternative Position)

# D Major Scale 4/4 Sequence ②
## Root Position

# D Major Scale 4/4 Sequence ②
## Root Position (Alternative Position)

# D Major Scale 4/4 Sequence ②
## First Inversion

# D Major Scale 4/4 Sequence ②
## First Inversion (Alternative Position)

# D Major Scale 4/4 Sequence ②
## Second Inversion

# D Major Scale 4/4 Sequence ②
# Second Inversion (Alternative Position)

# G Minor Scale 4/4 Sequence ②
## Root Position

# G Minor Scale 4/4 Sequence ②
# Root Position (Alternative Position)

# G Minor Scale 4/4 Sequence ②
## First Inversion

# G Minor Scale 4/4 Sequence ②
# First Inversion (Alternative Position)

# G Minor Scale 4/4 Sequence ②
## Second Inversion

# G Minor Scale 4/4 Sequence ②
## Second Inversion (Alternative Position)

# C Harmonic Minor Scale 4/4 Sequence ②
## Root Position

# C Harmonic Minor Scale 4/4 Sequence ②
# Root Position (Alternative Position)

# C Harmonic Minor Scale 4/4 Sequence ②
## First Inversion

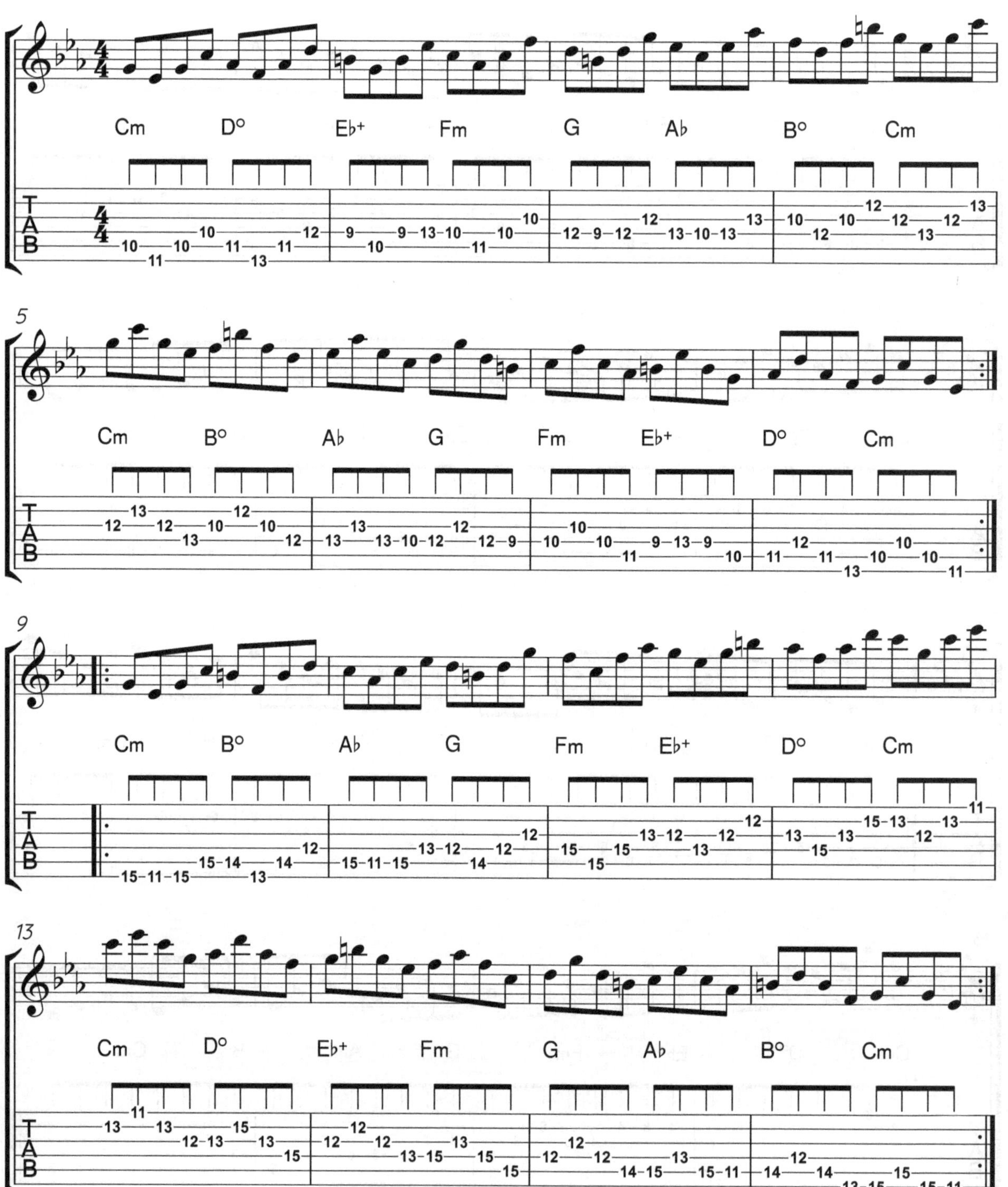

# C Harmonic Minor Scale 4/4 Sequence ②
# First Inversion (Alternative Position)

# C Harmonic Minor Scale 4/4 Sequence ②
## Second Inversion

# C Harmonic Minor Scale 4/4 Sequence ②
# Second Inversion (Alternative Position)

# F Melodic Minor Scale 4/4 Sequence ②
## Root Position

# F Melodic Minor Scale 4/4 Sequence ②
# Root Position (Alternative Position)

# F Melodic Minor Scale 4/4 Sequence ②
## First Inversion

# F Melodic Minor Scale 4/4 Sequence ②
# First Inversion (Alternative Position)

# F Melodic Minor Scale 4/4 Sequence ②
## Second Inversion

# F Melodic Minor Scale 4/4 Sequence ②
# Second Inversion (Alternative Position)

# B♭ Harmonic Major Scale 4/4 Sequence ②
# Root Position

# B♭ Harmonic Major Scale 4/4 Sequence ②
# Root Position (Alternative Position)

# B ♭ Harmonic Major Scale 4/4 Sequence ②
## First Inversion

# B♭ Harmonic Major Scale 4/4 Sequence ②
# First Inversion (Alternative Position)

# B ♭ Harmonic Major Scale 4/4 Sequence ②
## Second Inversion

# B ♭ Harmonic Major Scale 4/4 Sequence ②
# Second Inversion (Alternative Position)

# E♭ Major Scale 4/4 Sequence ③
## Root Position

# E♭ Major Scale 4/4 Sequence ③
# Root Position (Alternative Position)

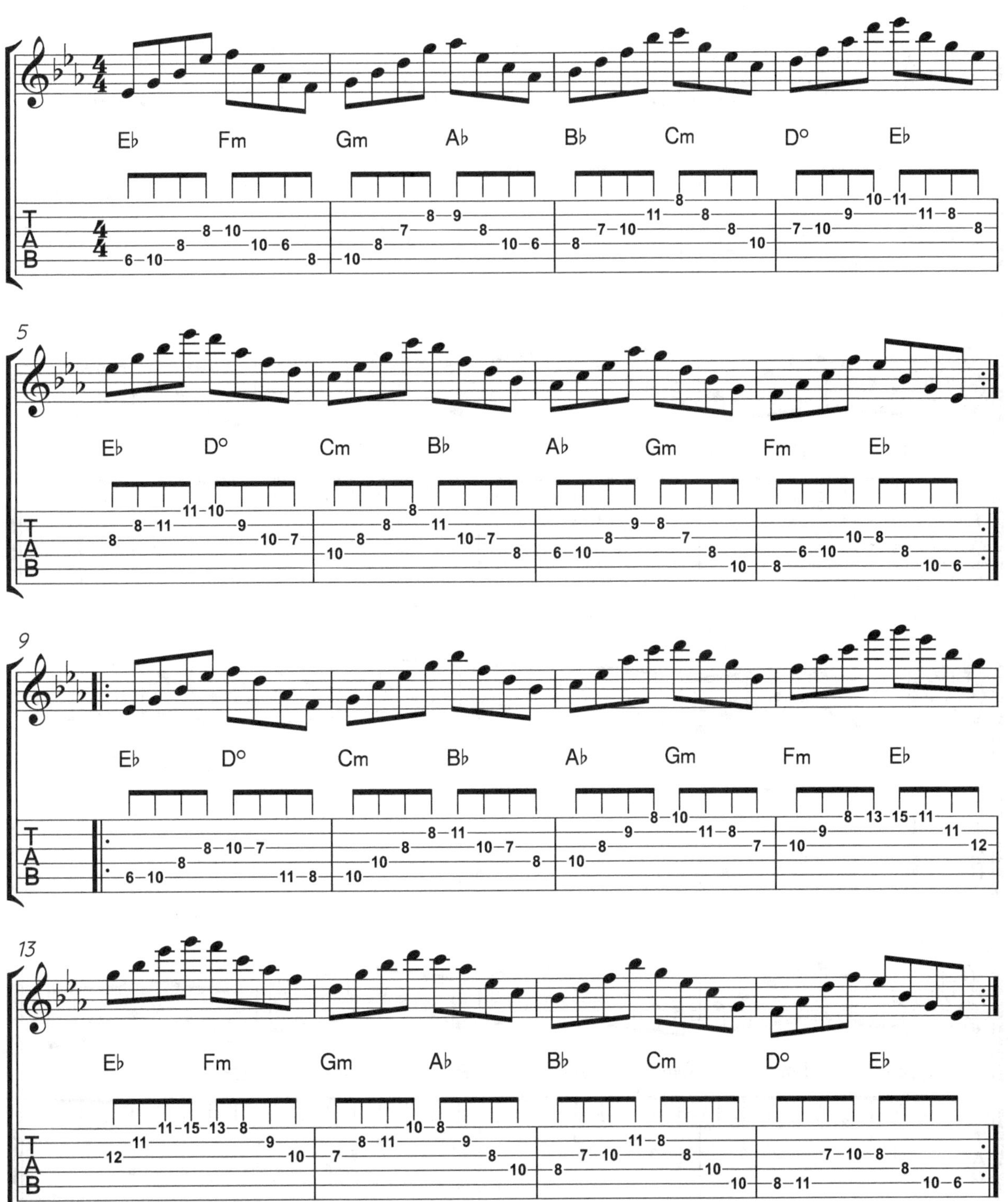

# E ♭ Major Scale 4/4 Sequence ③
First Inversion

# E♭ Major Scale 4/4 Sequence ③
# First Inversion (Alternative Position)

# E♭ Major Scale 4/4 Sequence ③
## Second Inversion

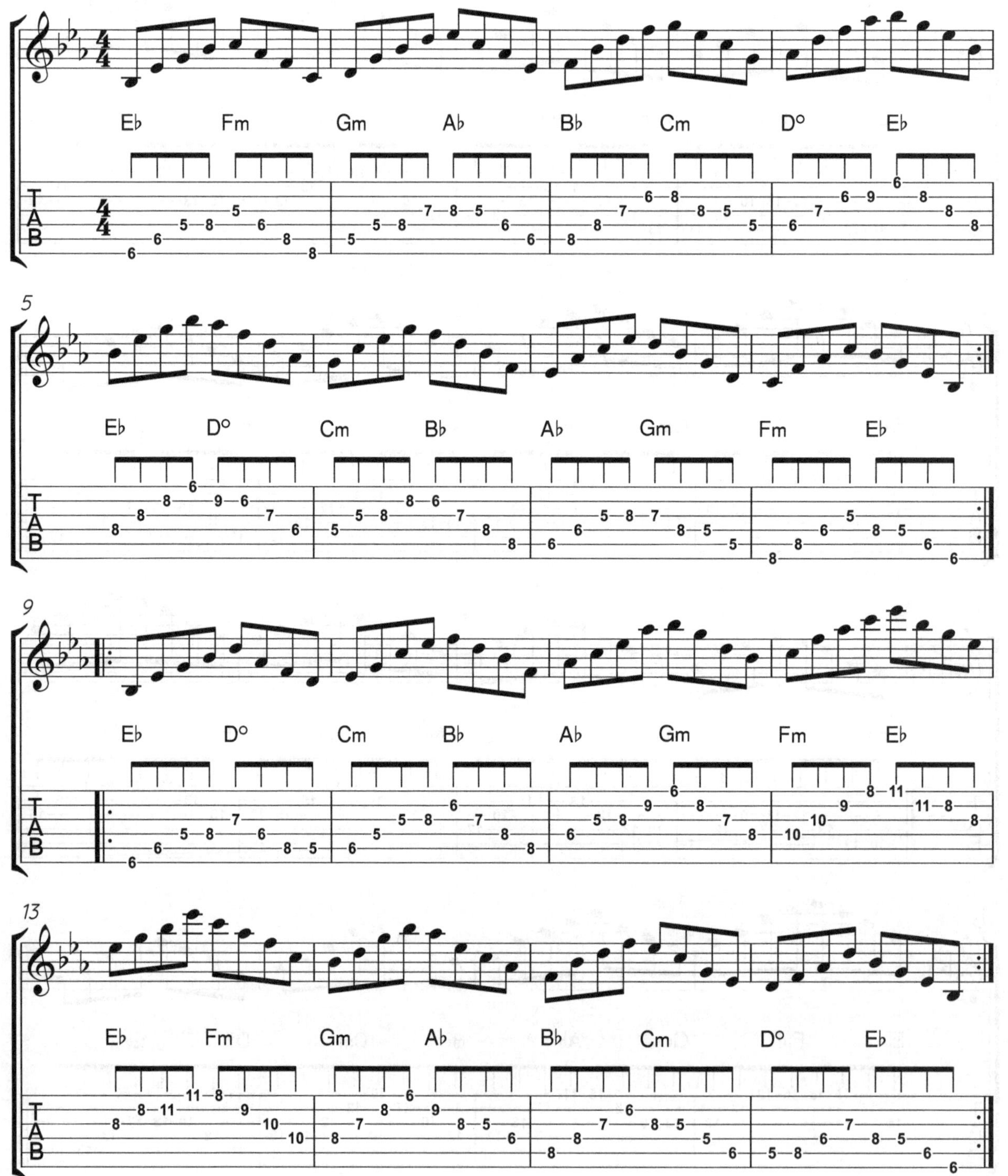

# E ♭ Major Scale 4/4 Sequence ③
# Second Inversion (Alternative Position)

# G♯Minor Scale 4/4 Sequence ③
## Root Position

# G♯Minor Scale 4/4 Sequence ③
# Root Position (Alternative Position)

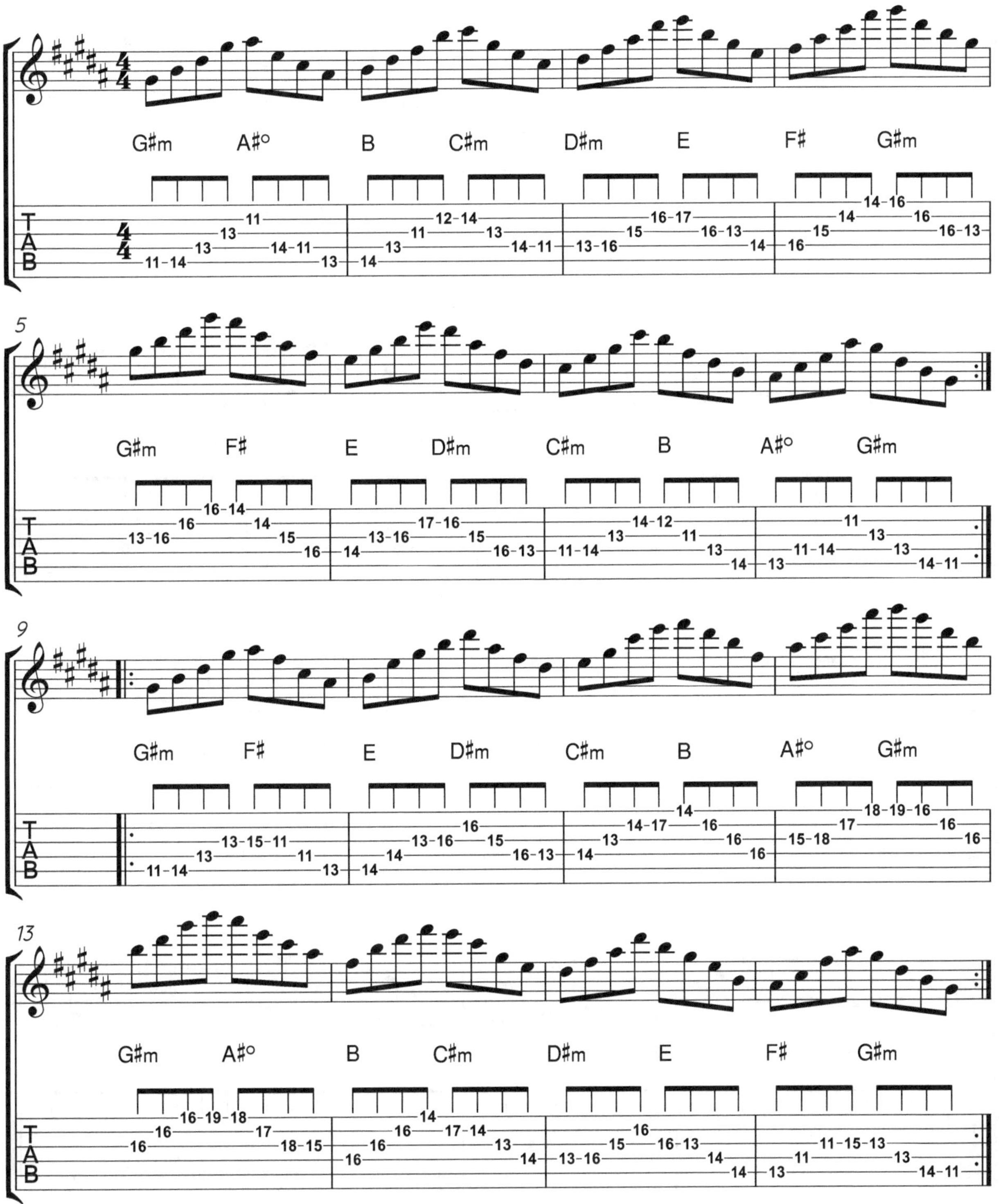

# G♯ Minor Scale 4/4 Sequence ③
## First Inversion

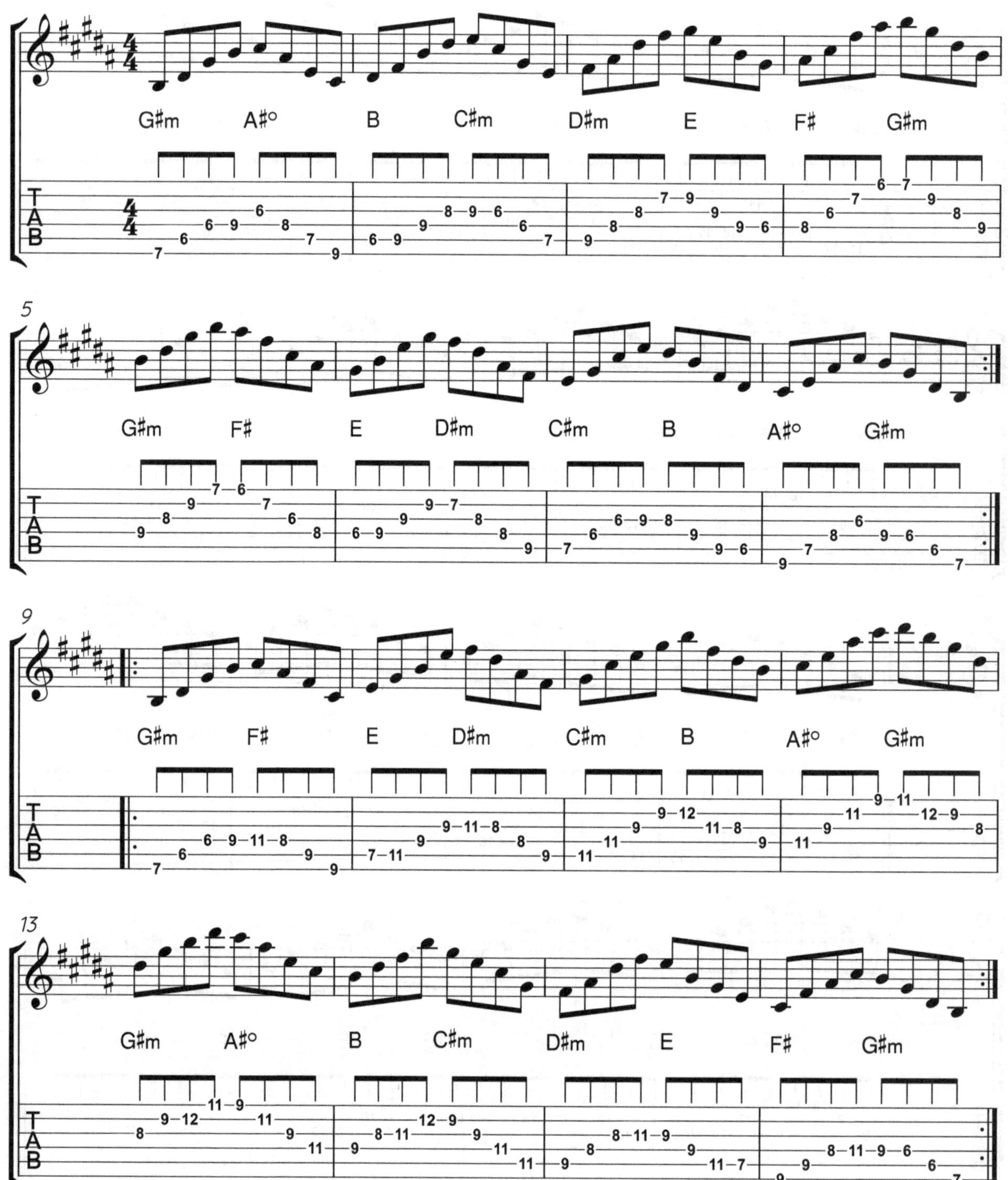

# G♯Minor Scale 4/4 Sequence ③
# First Inversion (Alternative Position)

# G♯Minor Scale 4/4 Sequence ③
# Second Inversion

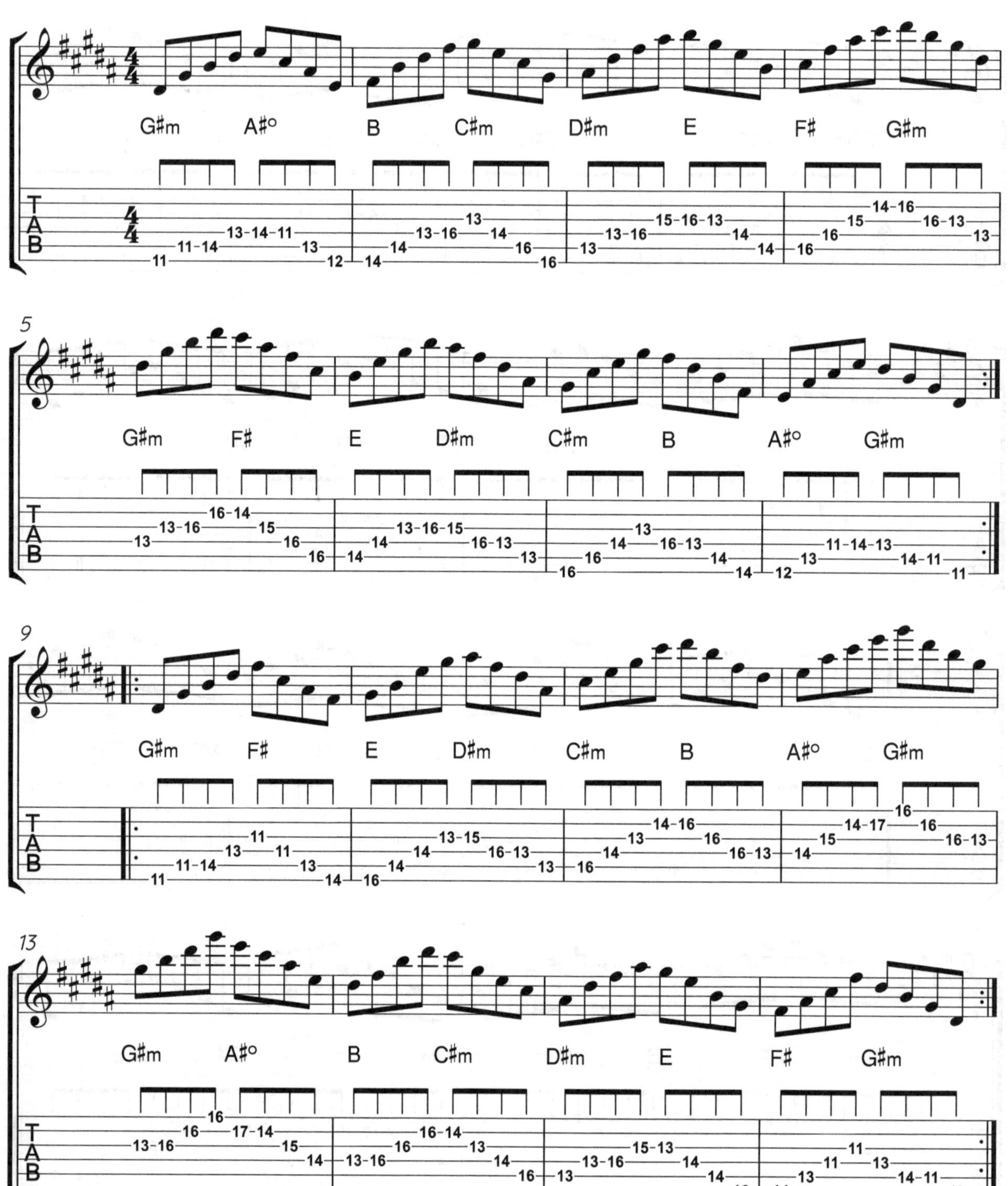

# G♯Minor Scale 4/4 Sequence ③
# Second Inversion (Alternative Position)

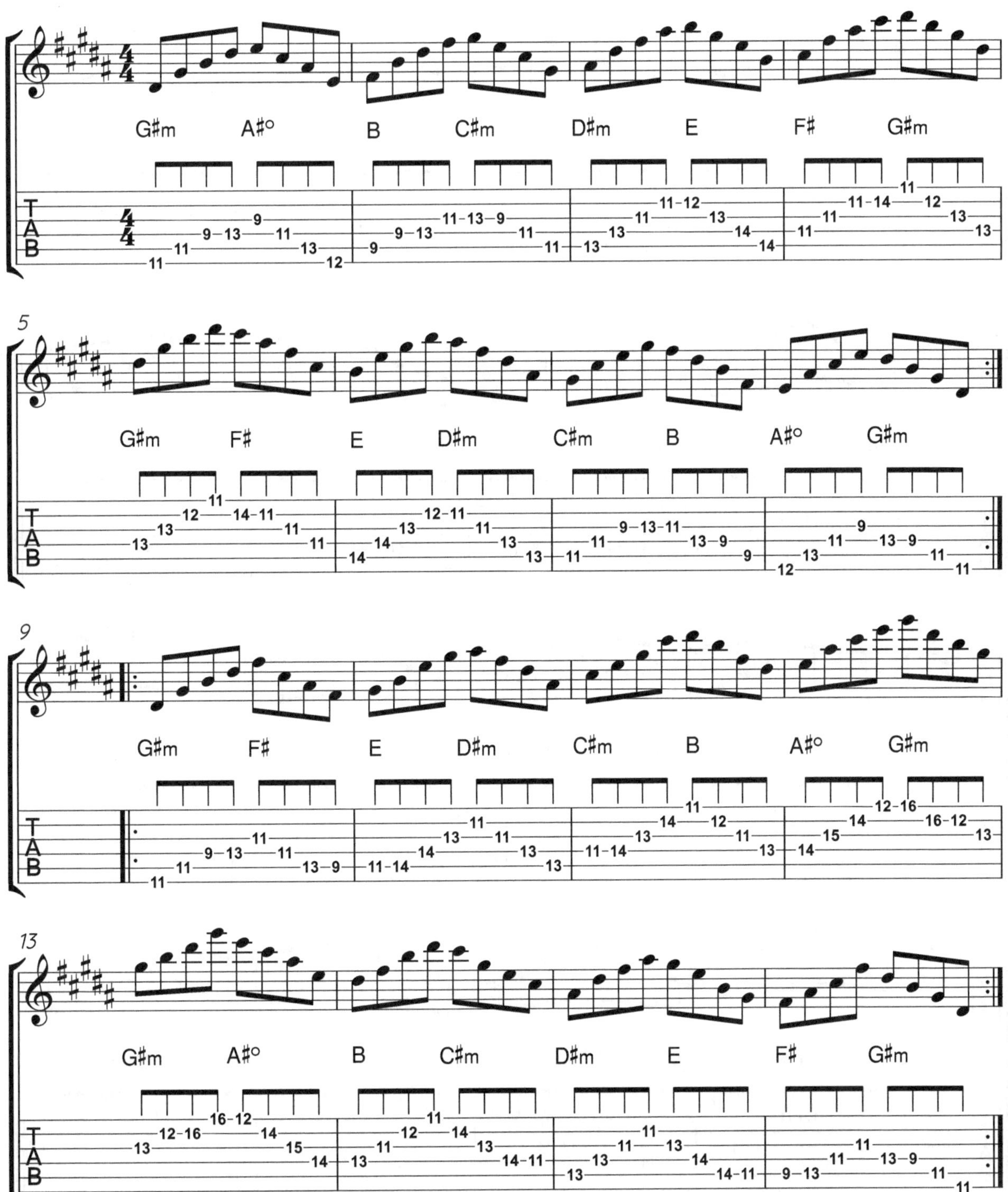

# C♯Harmonic Minor Scale 4/4 Sequence ③
# Root Position

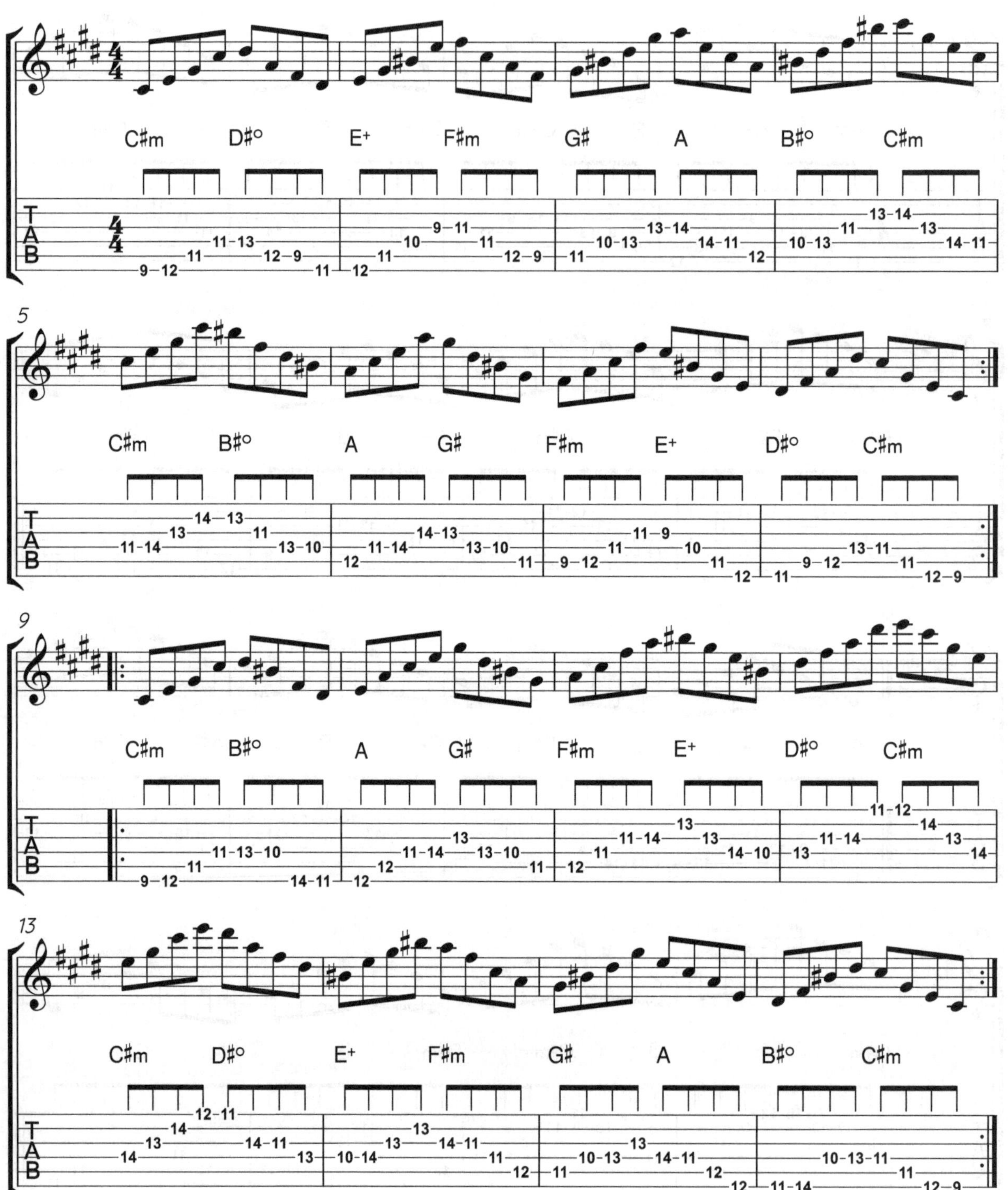

# C♯Harmonic Minor Scale 4/4 Sequence ③
# Root Position (Alternative Position)

# C♯Harmonic Minor Scale 4/4 Sequence ③
## First Inversion

# C♯ Harmonic Minor Scale 4/4 Sequence ③
# First Inversion (Alternative Position)

# C♯Harmonic Minor Scale 4/4 Sequence ③
## Second Inversion

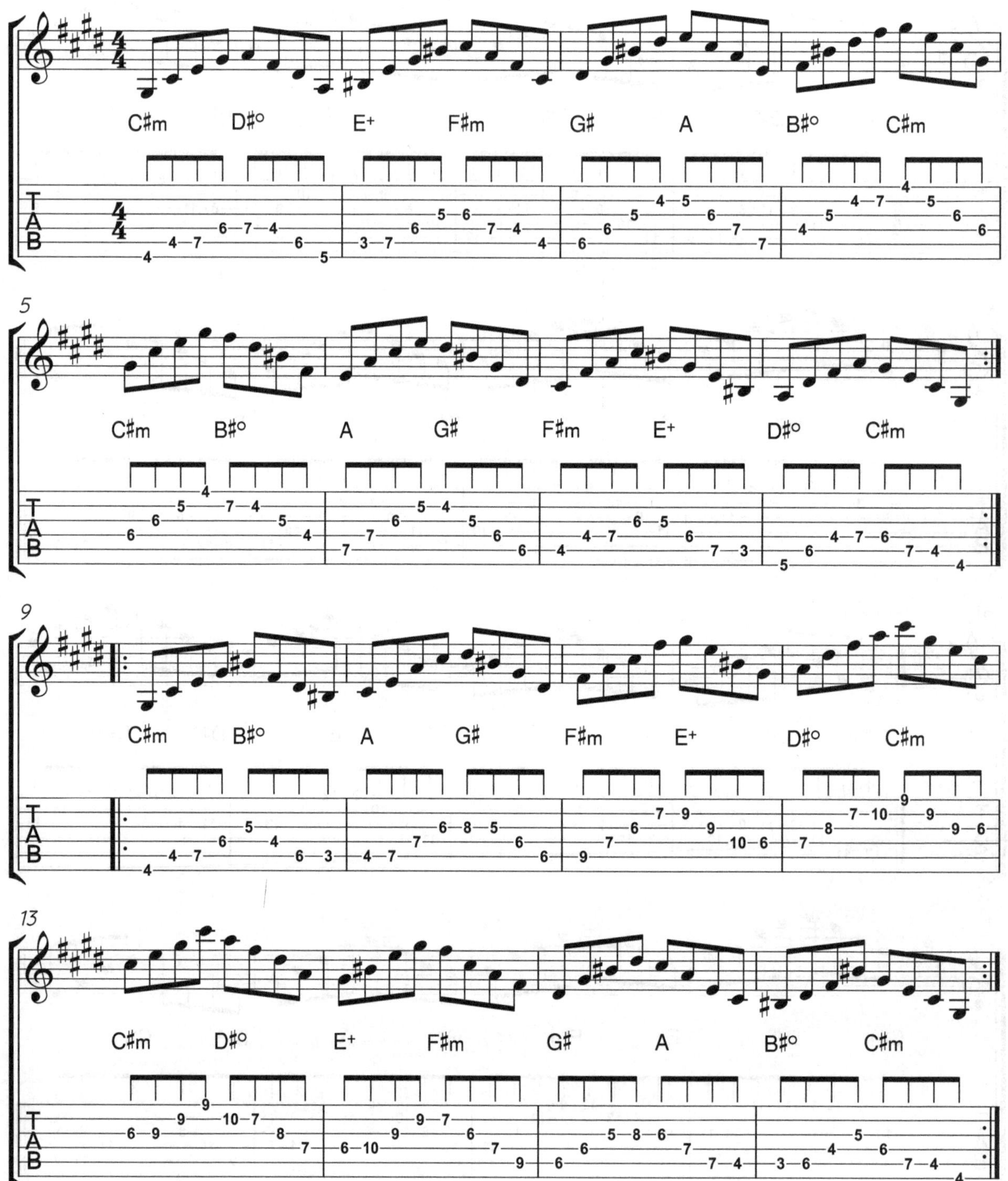

# C♯Harmonic Minor Scale 4/4 Sequence ③
# Second Inversion (Alternative Position)

# F♯Melodic Minor Scale 4/4 Sequence ③
# Root Position

# F♯Melodic Minor Scale 4/4 Sequence ③
# Root Position (Alternative Position)

# F♯Melodic Minor Scale 4/4 Sequence ③
# First Inversion

# F♯Melodic Minor Scale 4/4 Sequence ③
# First Inversion (Alternative Position)

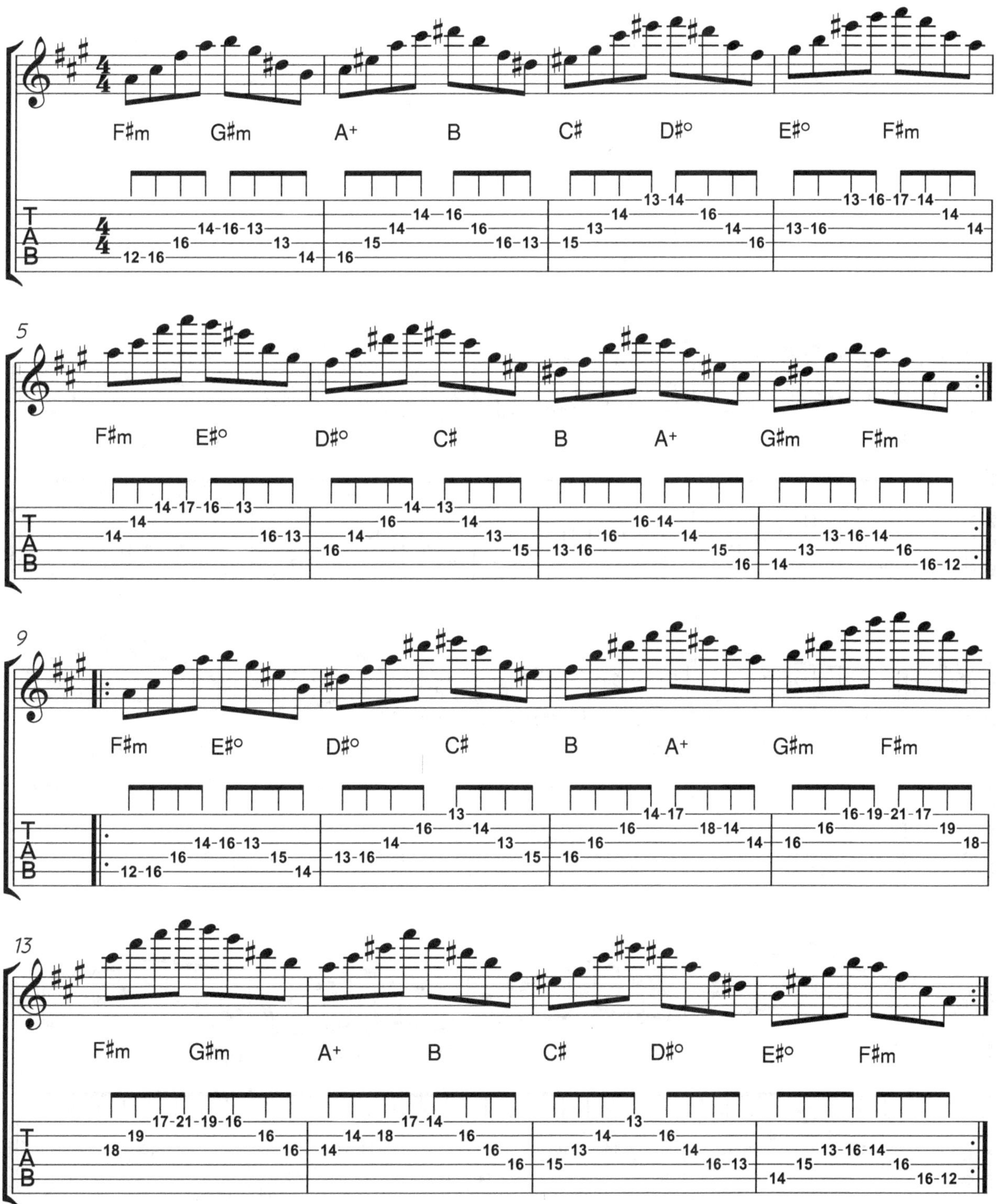

# F♯Melodic Minor Scale 4/4 Sequence ③
## Second Inversion

# F♯ Melodic Minor Scale 4/4 Sequence ③
# Second Inversion (Alternative Position)

# B Harmonic Major Scale 4/4 Sequence ③
# Root Position

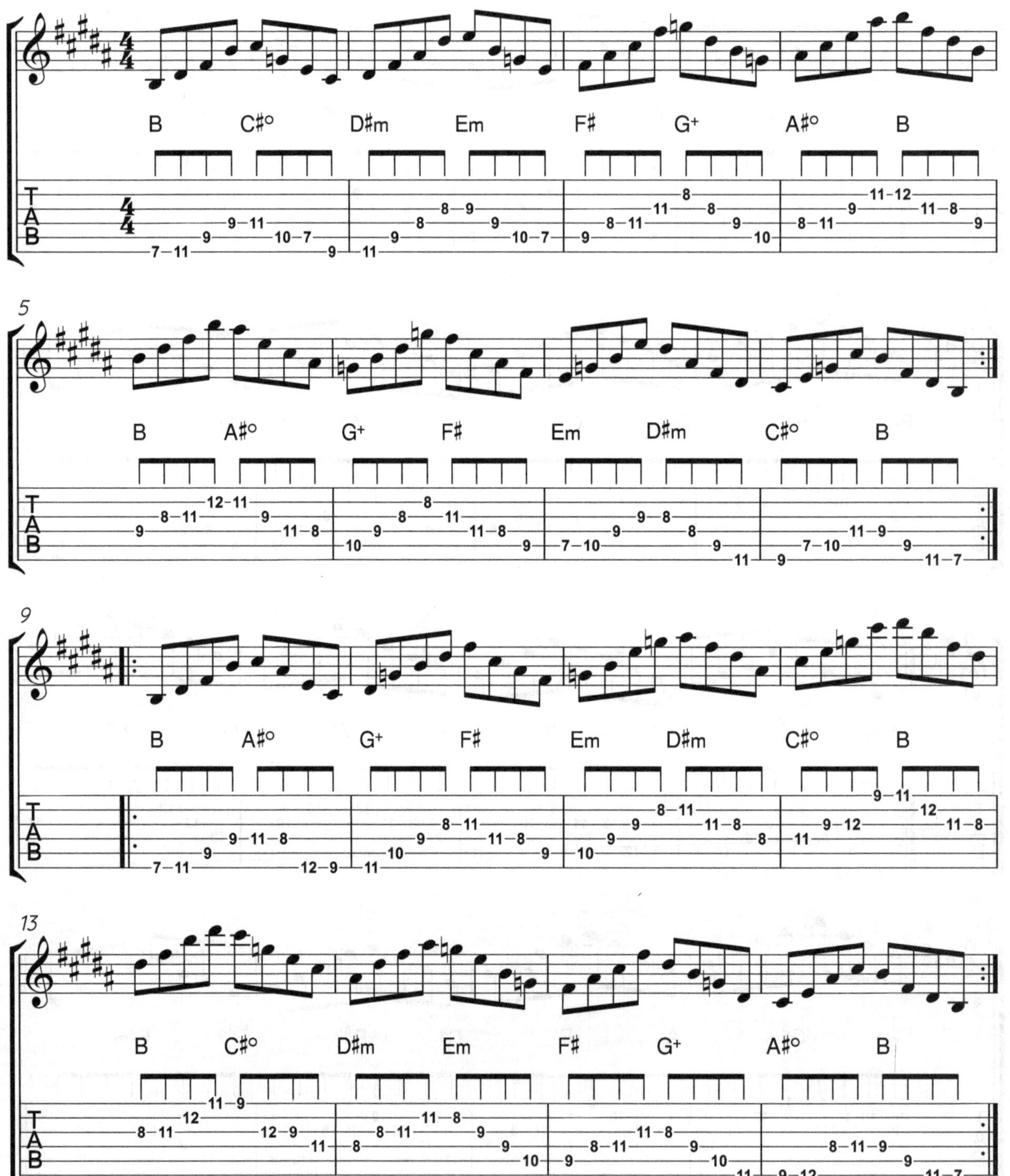

# B Harmonic Major Scale 4/4 Sequence ③
# Root Position (Alternative Position)

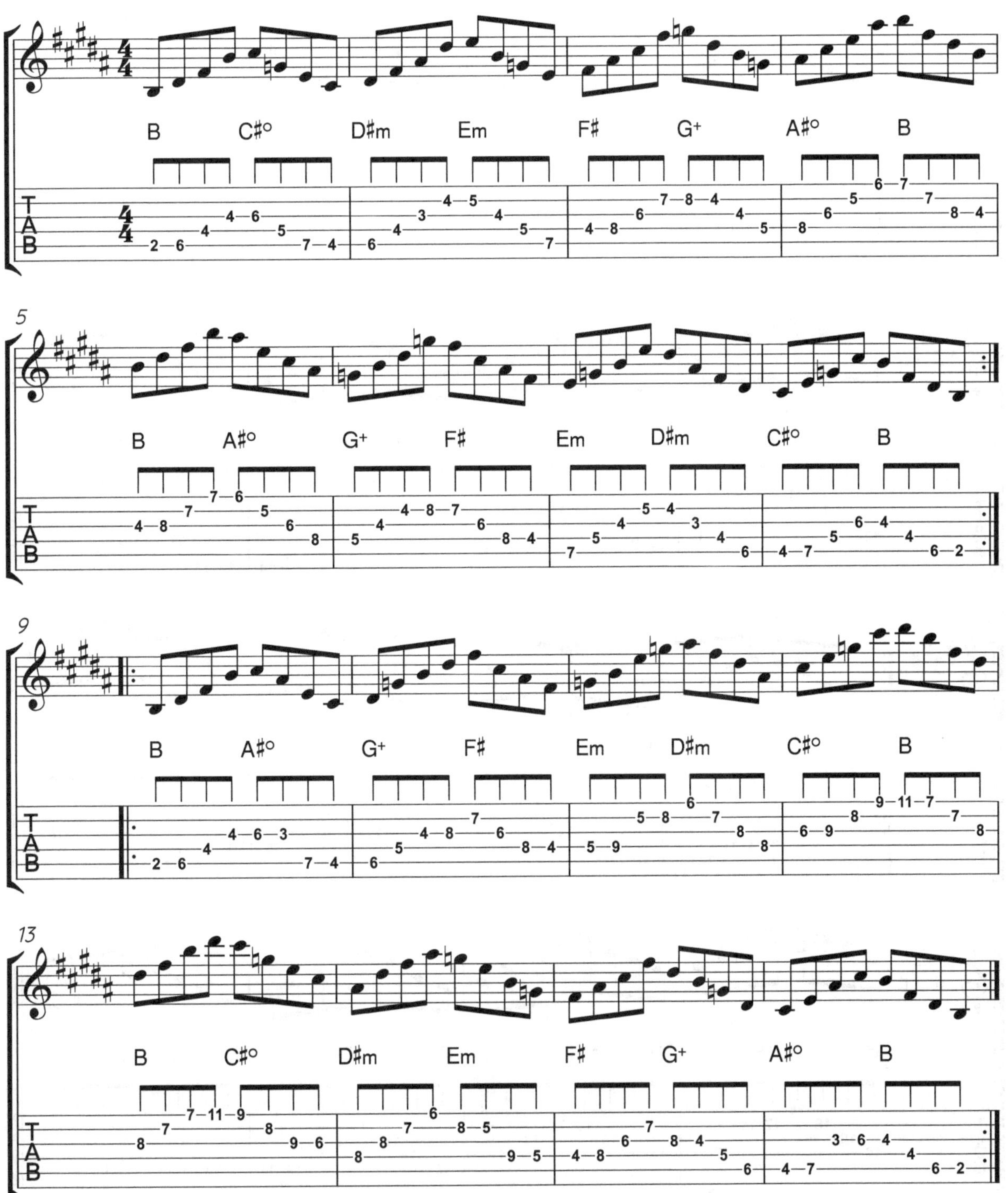

# B Harmonic Major Scale 4/4 Sequence ③
## First Inversion

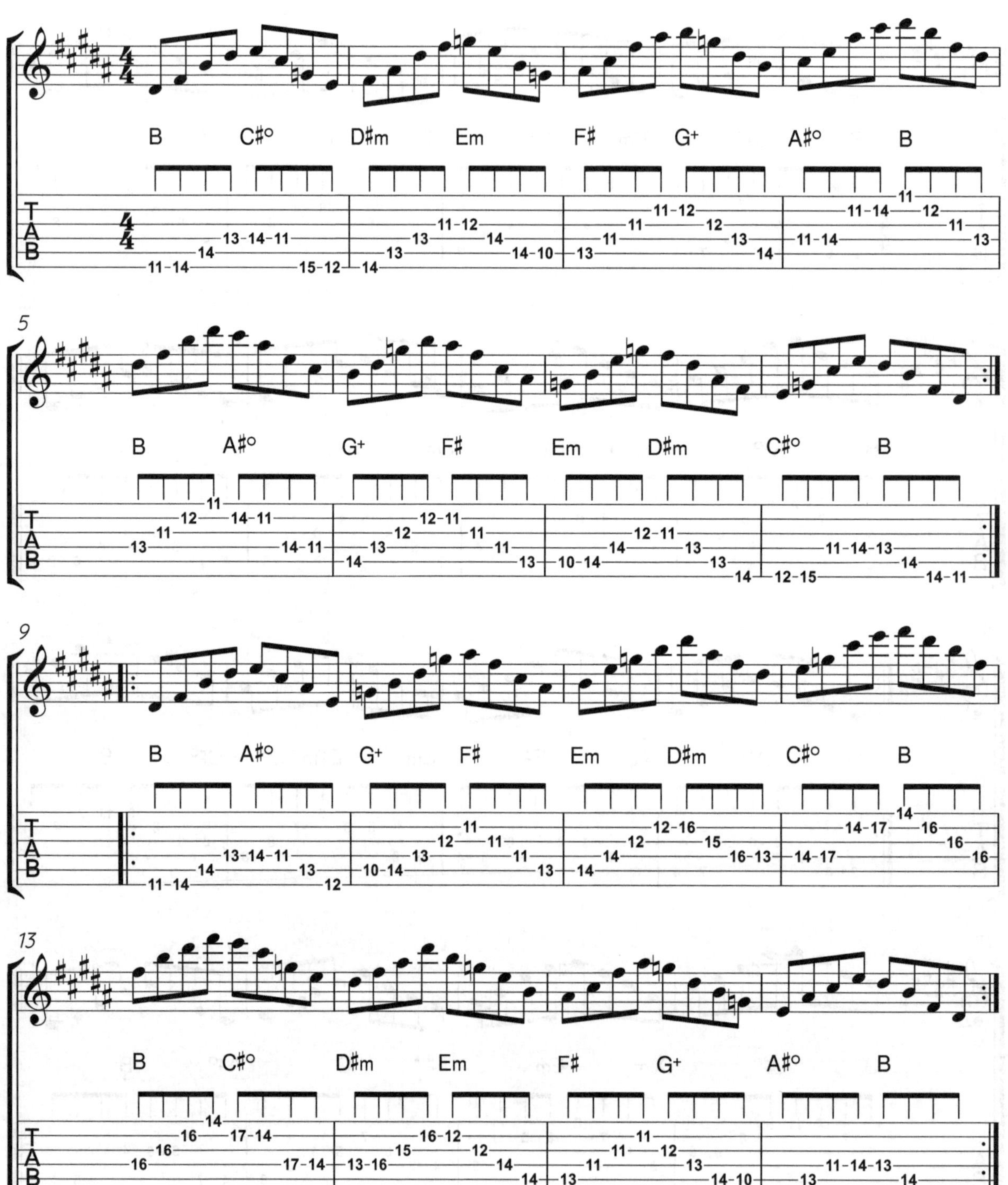

# B Harmonic Major Scale 4/4 Sequence ③
## First Inversion (Alternative Position)

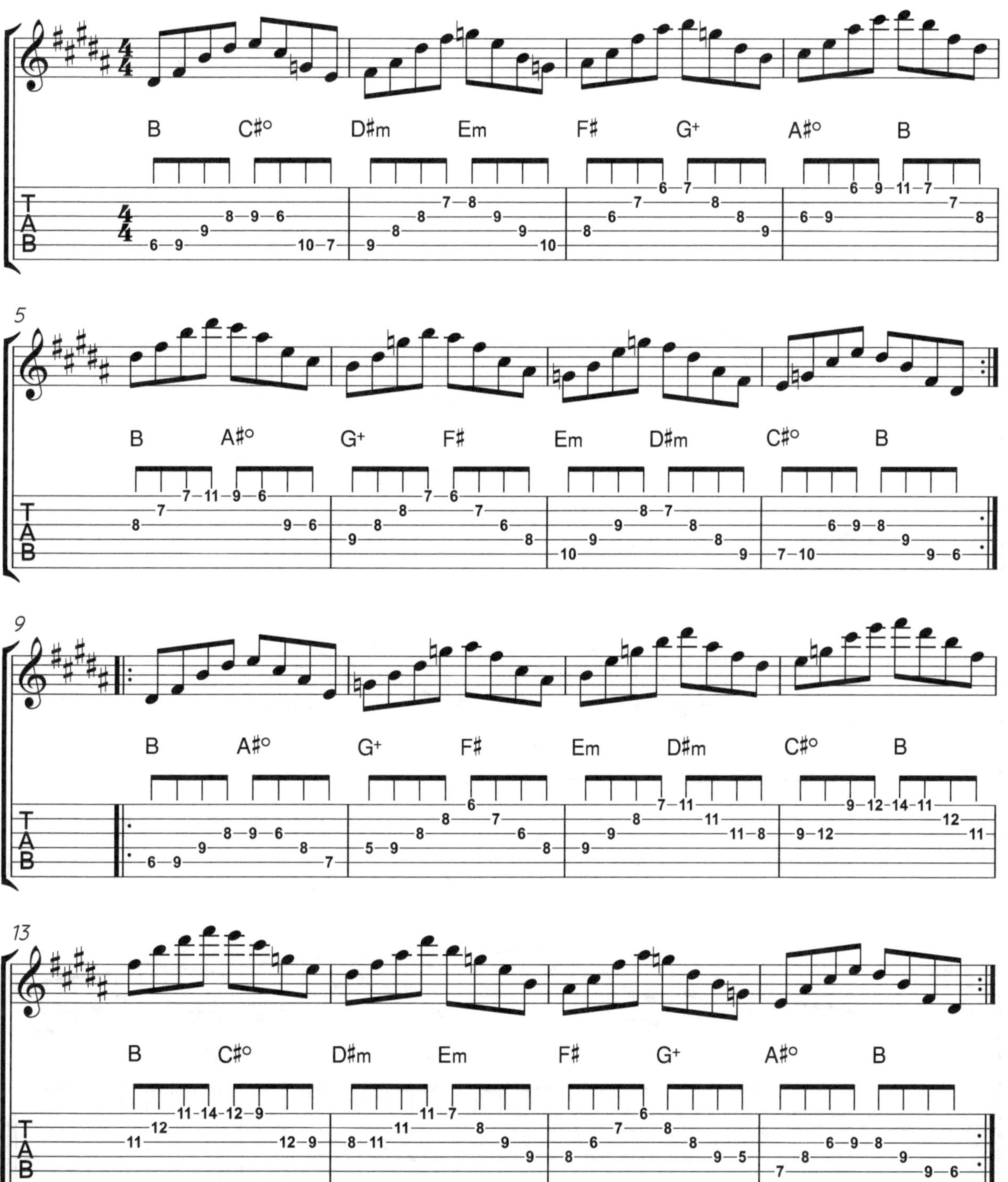

# B Harmonic Major Scale 4/4 Sequence ③
## Second Inversion

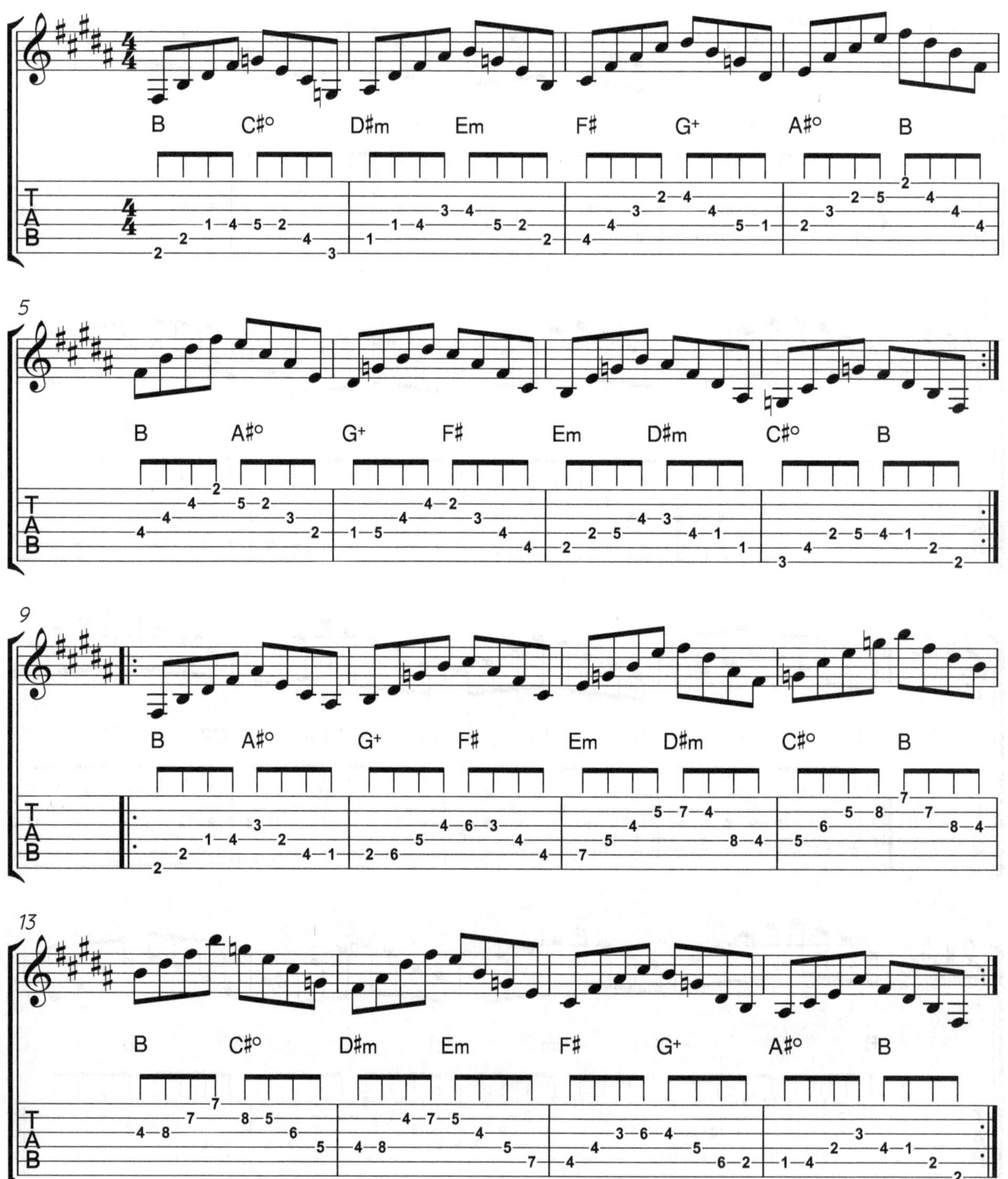

# B Harmonic Major Scale 4/4 Sequence ③
# Second Inversion (Alternative Position)

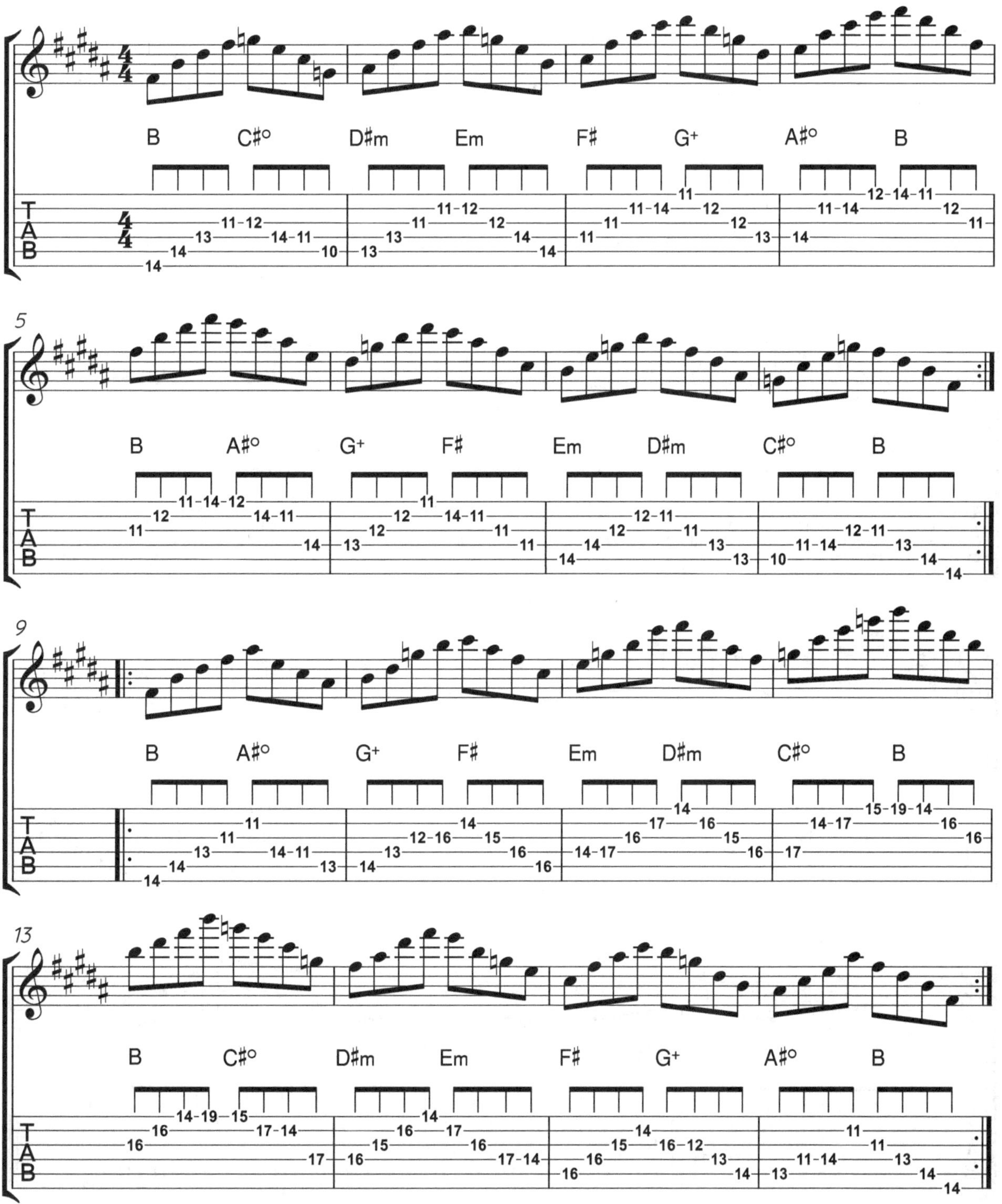

# E Major Scale 6/8 Sequence ①
# Root Position

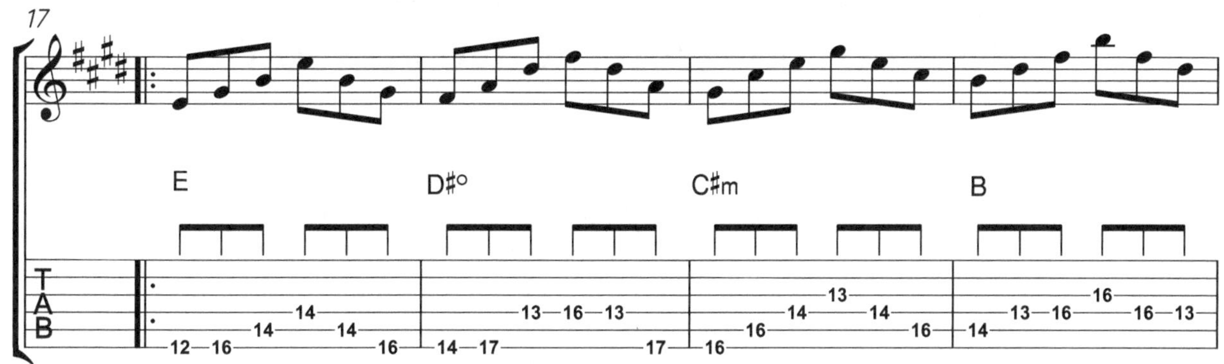
17
E
D#o
C#m
B
TAB

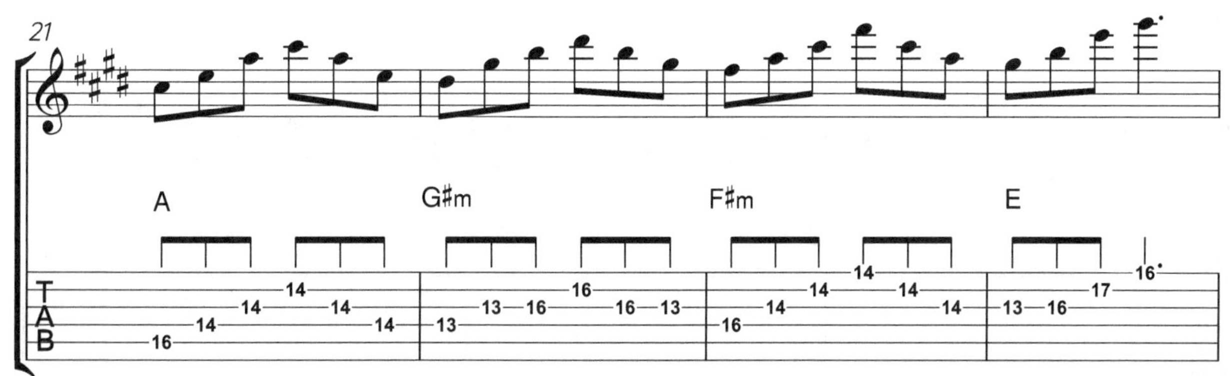
21
A
G#m
F#m
E
TAB

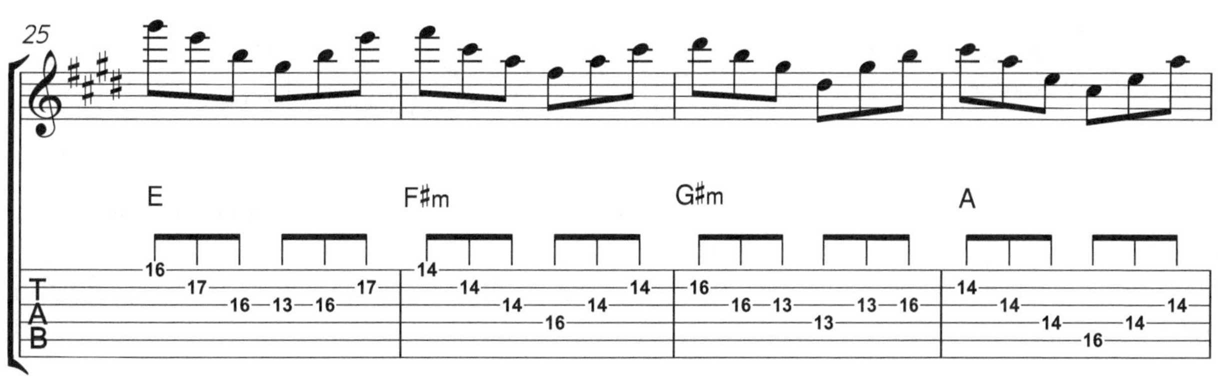
25
E
F#m
G#m
A
TAB

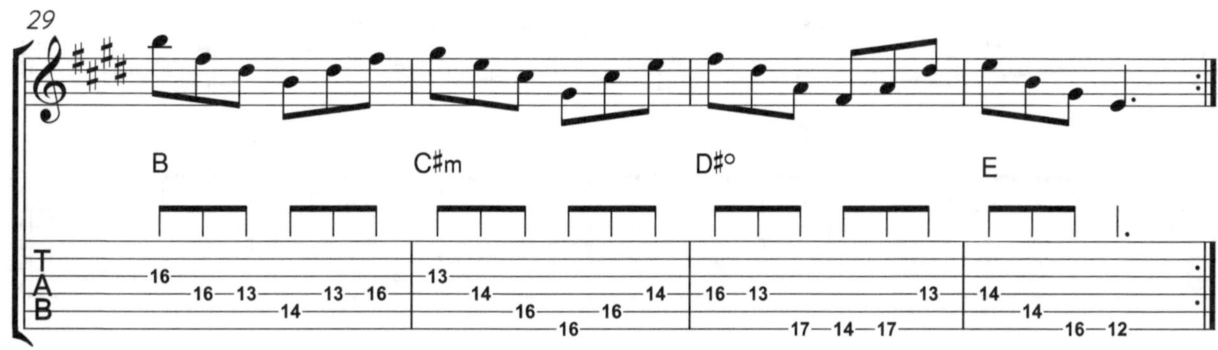
29
B
C#m
D#o
E
TAB

# E Major Scale 6/8 Sequence ①
## Root Position (Alternative Position)

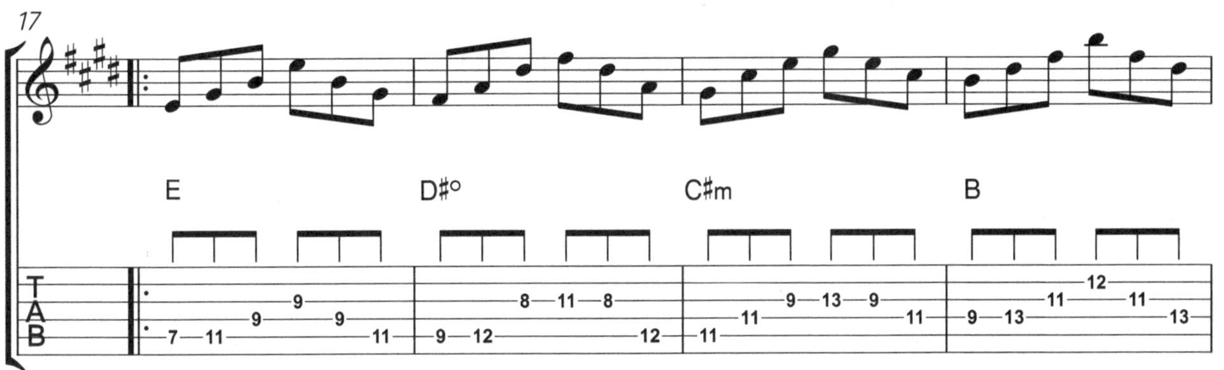
17
E
D♯°
C♯m
B
T
A
B

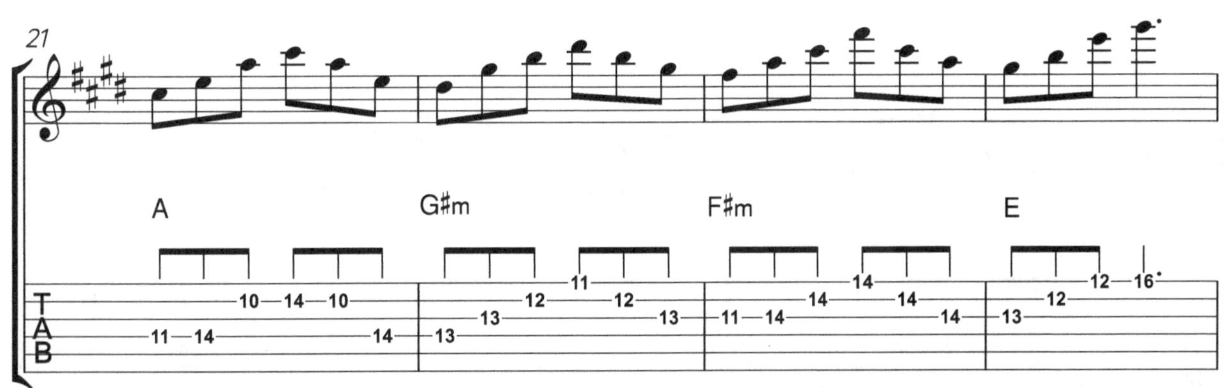
21
A
G♯m
F♯m
E
T
A
B

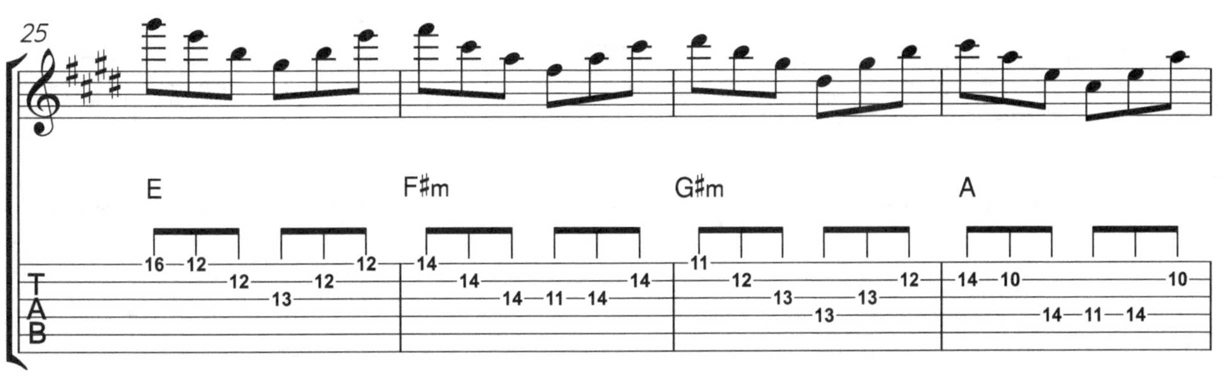
25
E
F♯m
G♯m
A
T
A
B

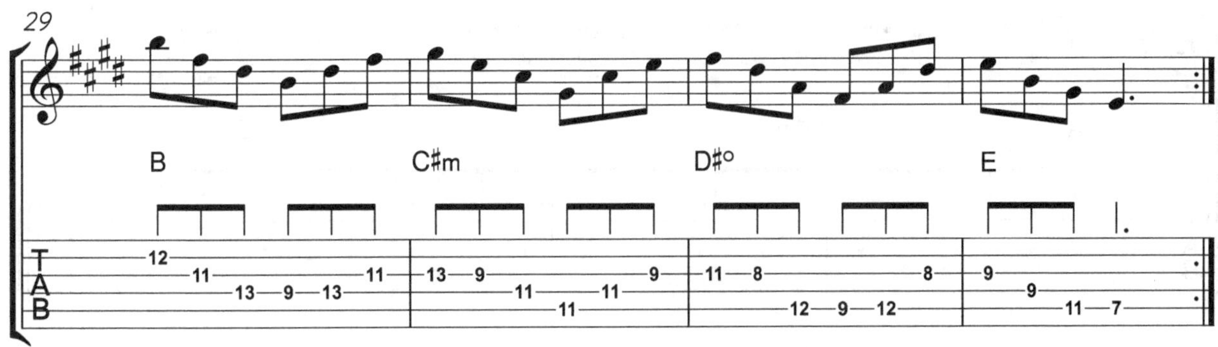
29
B
C♯m
D♯°
E
T
A
B

# E Major Scale 6/8 Sequence ①
## First Inversion

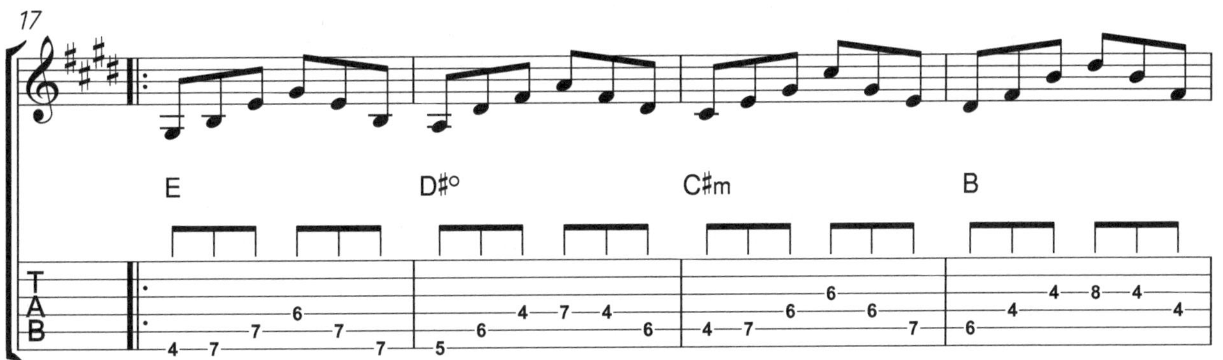
17
E
D♯°
C♯m
B

21
A
G♯m
F♯m
E

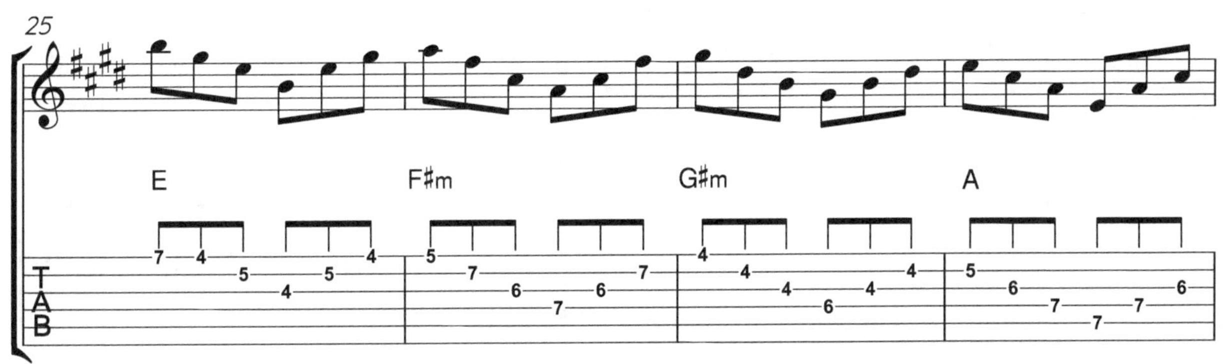
25
E
F♯m
G♯m
A

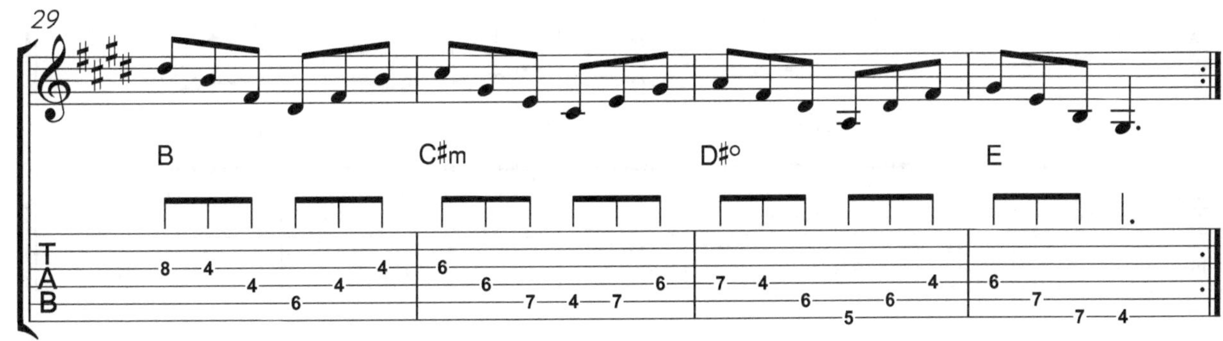
29
B
C♯m
D♯°
E

# E Major Scale 6/8 Sequence ①
# First Inversion (Alternative Position)

17
E
D#o
C#m
B
TAB
21
A
G#m
F#m
E
25
E
F#m
G#m
A
29
B
C#m
D#o
E

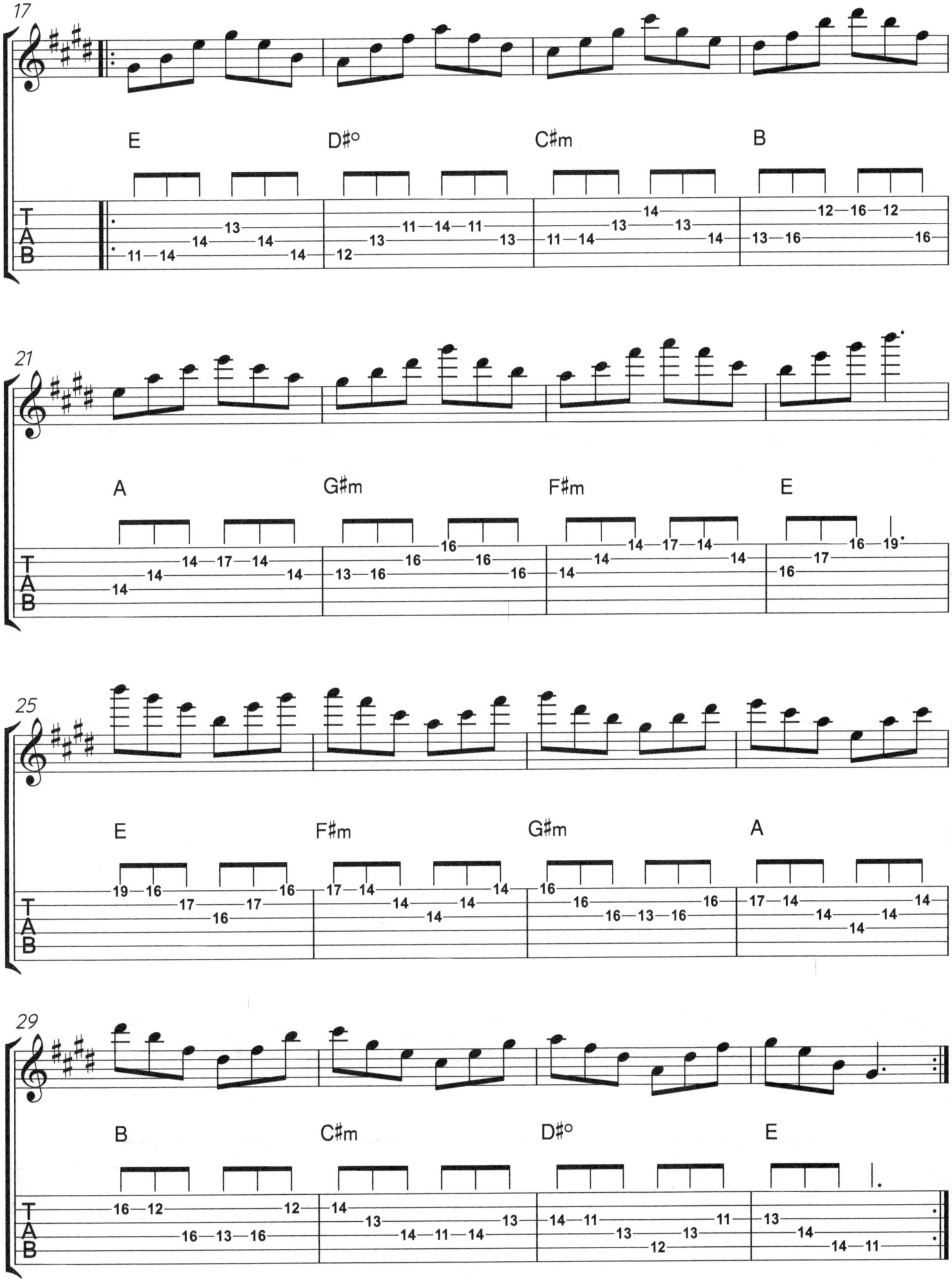

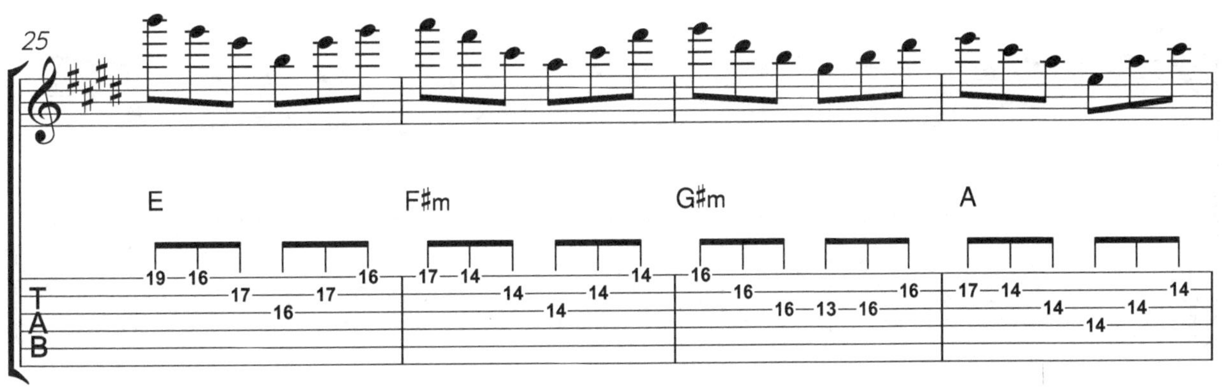

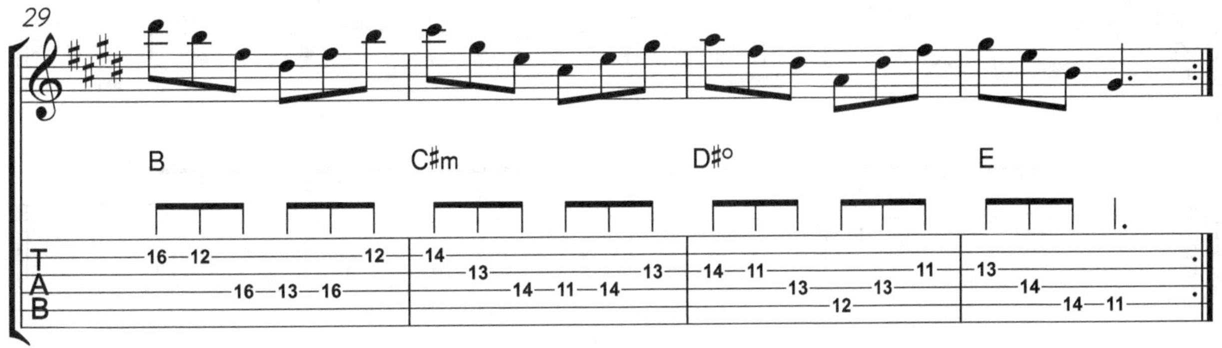

# E Major Scale 6/8 Sequence ①
## Second Inversion

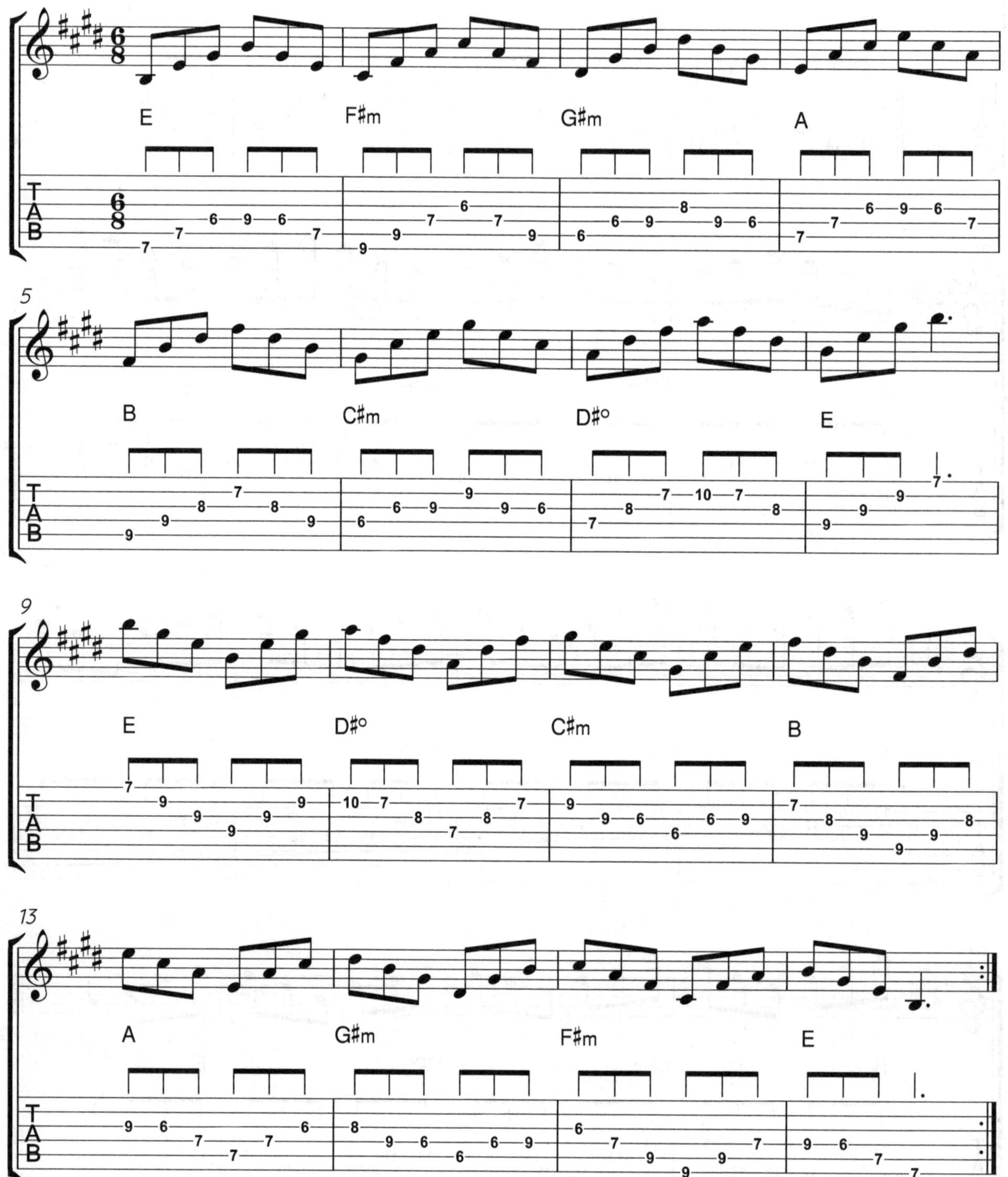

17
E
D♯°
C♯m
B
T
A
B

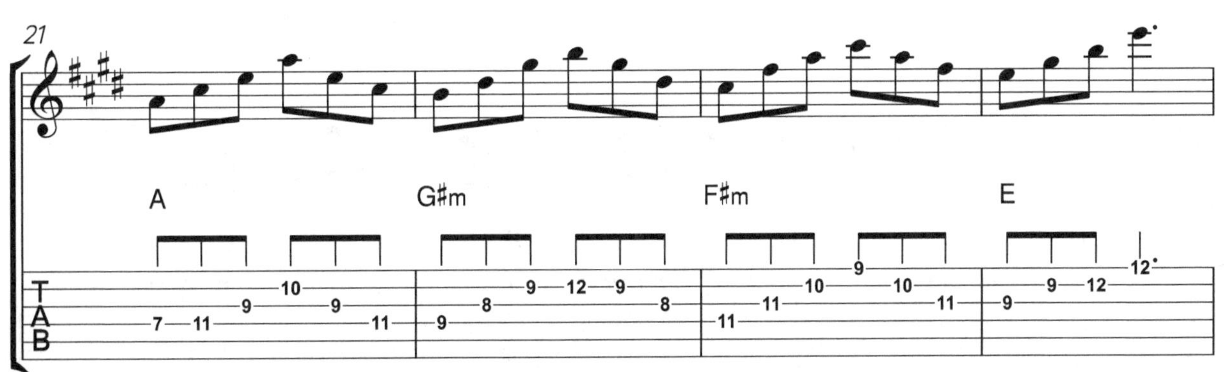
21
A
G♯m
F♯m
E
T
A
B

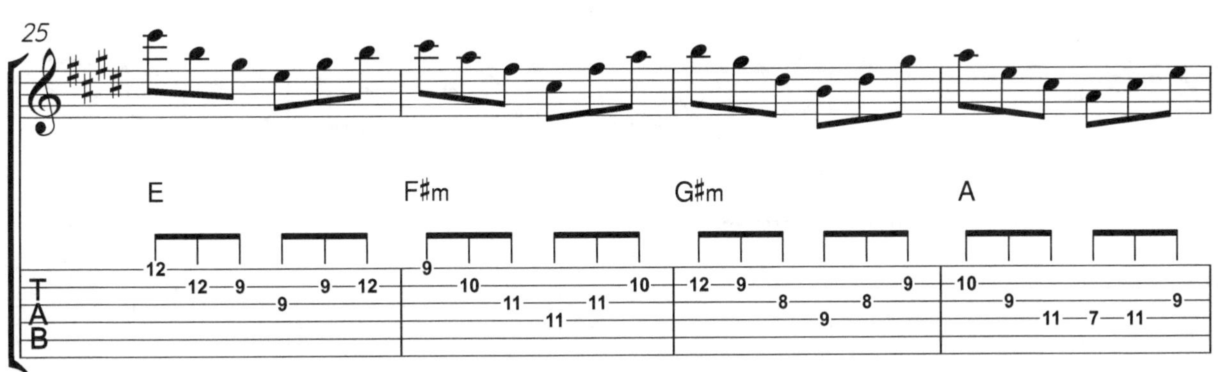
25
E
F♯m
G♯m
A
T
A
B

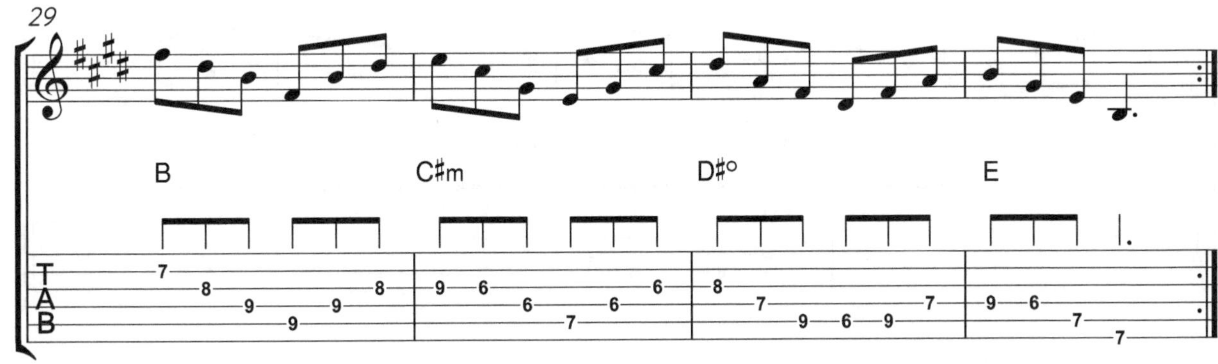
29
B
C♯m
D♯°
E
T
A
B

# E Major Scale 6/8 Sequence ①
# Second Inversion (Alternative Position)

17
E
D#°
C#m
B
TAB

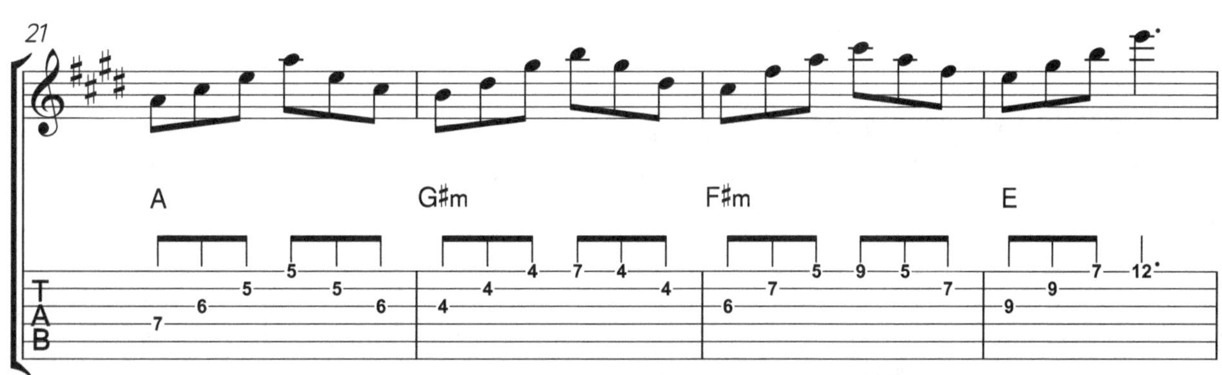
21
A
G#m
F#m
E
TAB

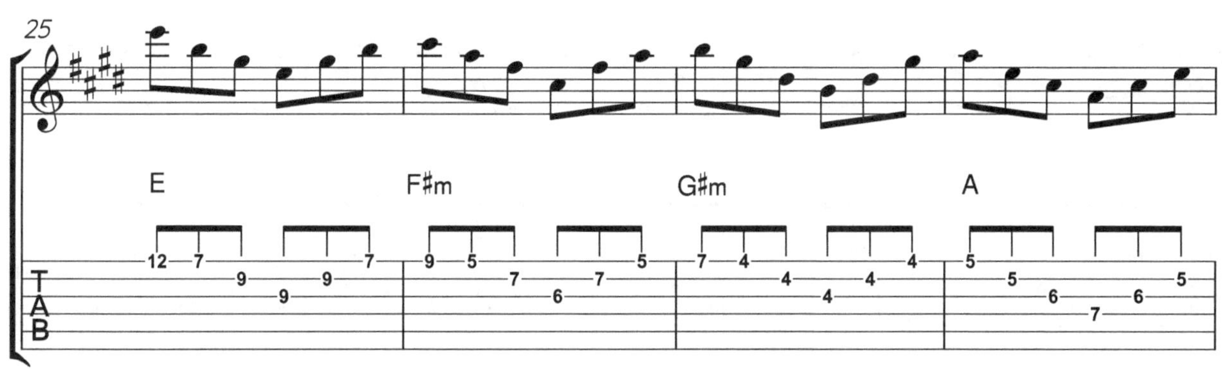
25
E
F#m
G#m
A
TAB

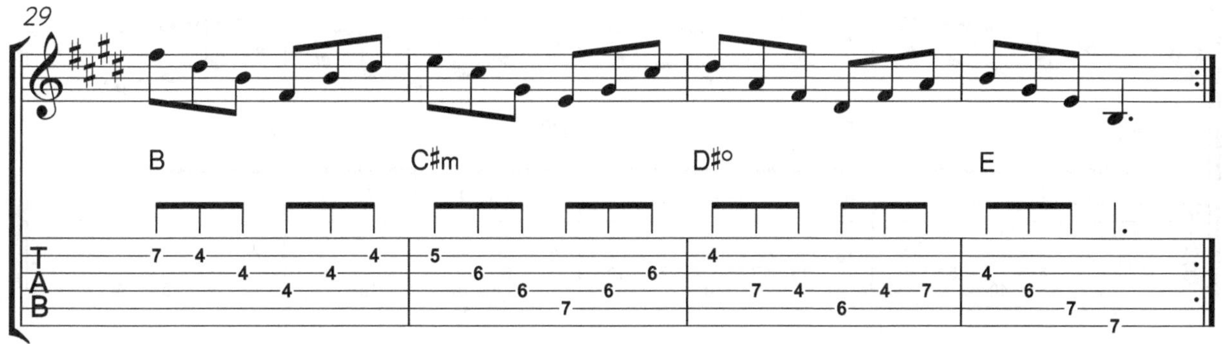
29
B
C#m
D#°
E
TAB

# A Minor Scale 6/8 Sequence ①
## Root Position

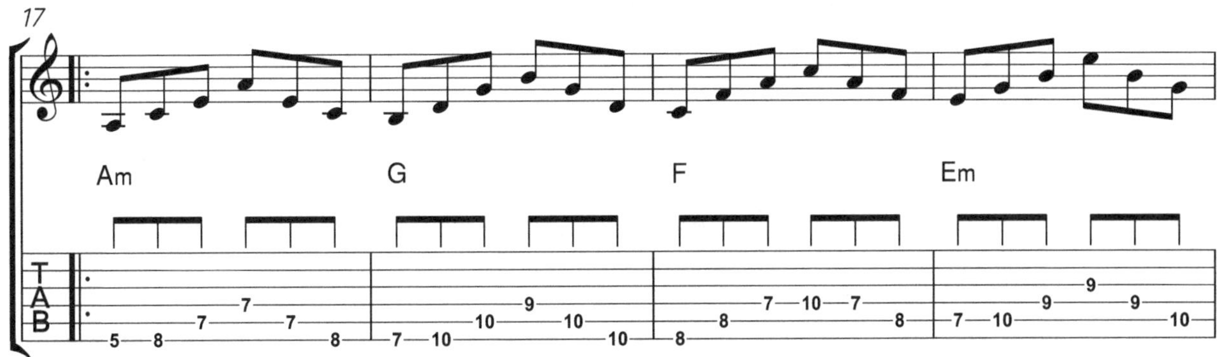
17
Am
G
F
Em
TAB

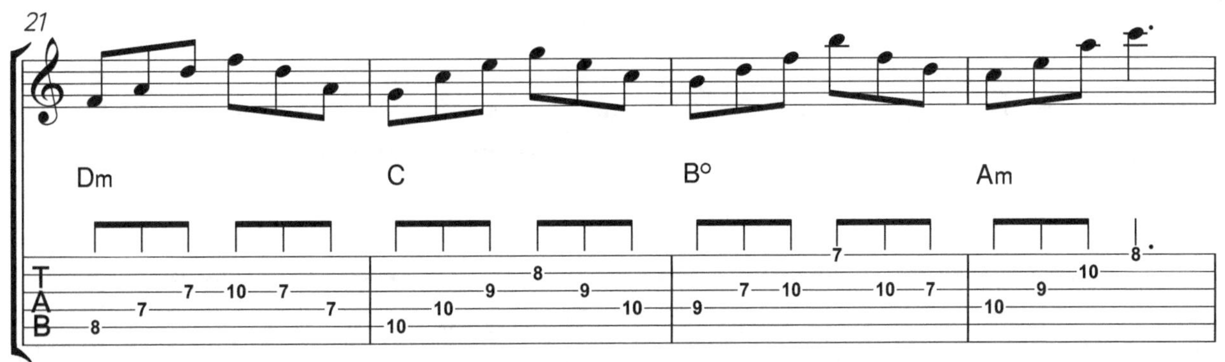
21
Dm
C
B°
Am
TAB

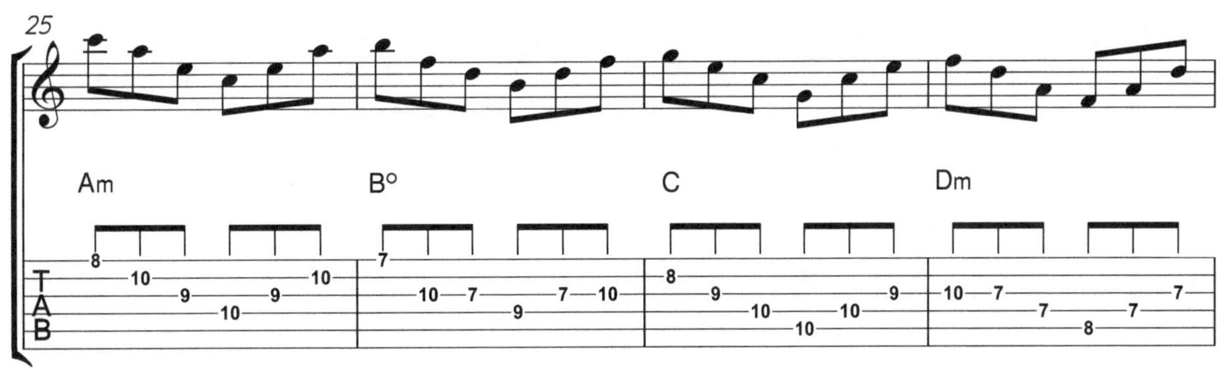
25
Am
B°
C
Dm
TAB

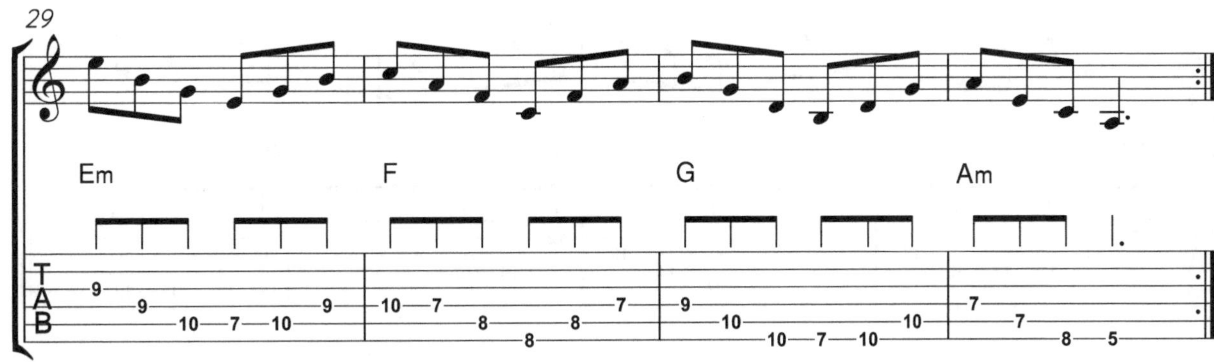
29
Em
F
G
Am
TAB

# A Minor Scale 6/8 Sequence ①
# Root Position (Alternative Position)

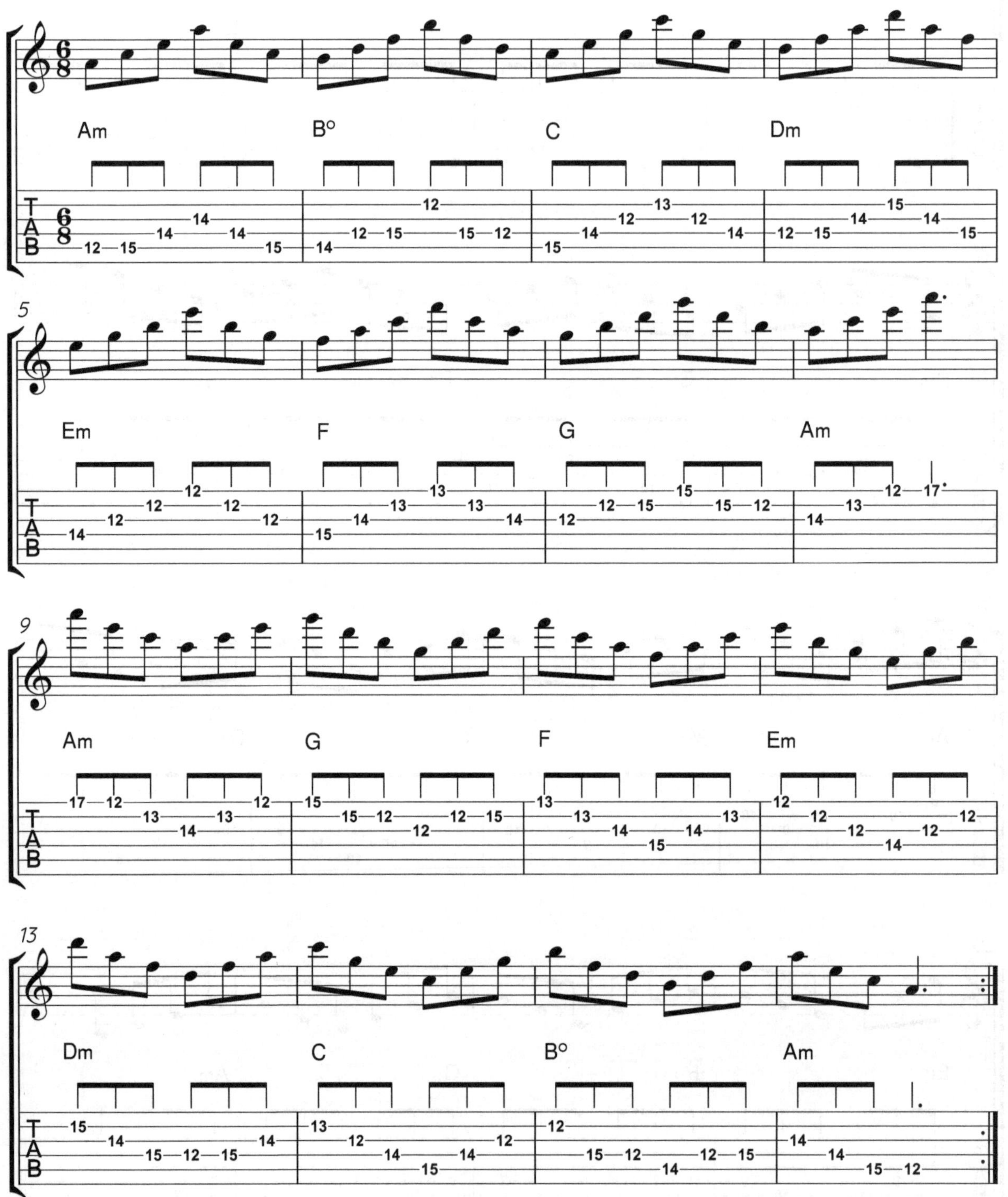

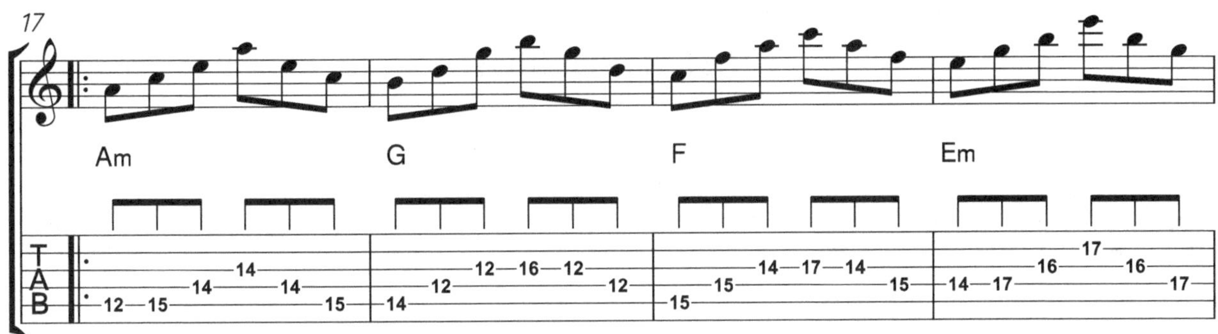
17
Am
G
F
Em

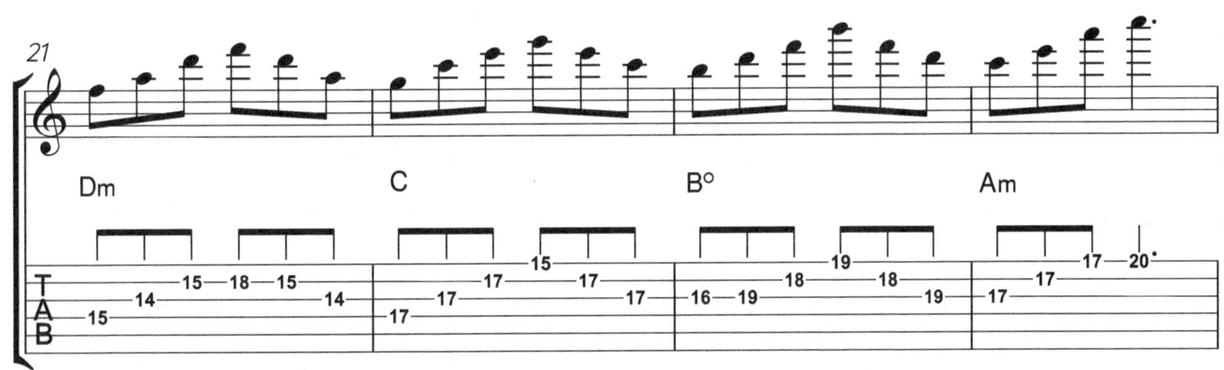
21
Dm
C
B°
Am

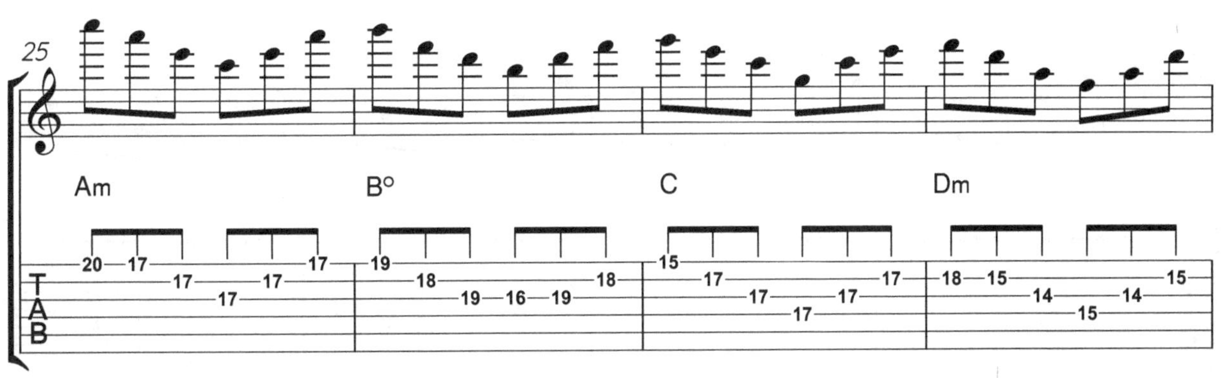
25
Am
B°
C
Dm

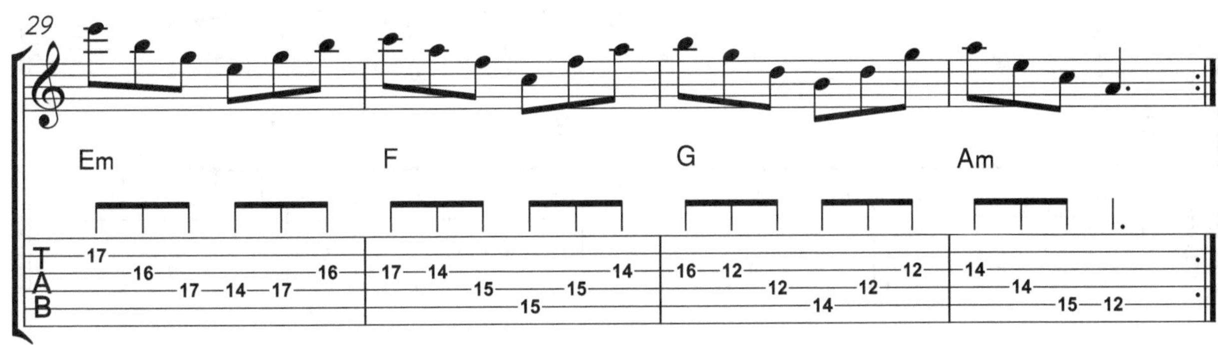
29
Em
F
G
Am

# A Minor Scale 6/8 Sequence ①
## First Inversion

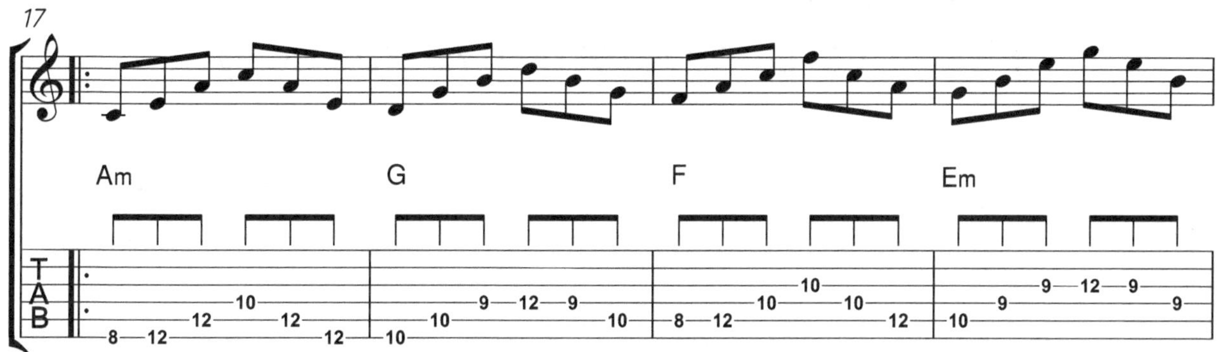
17
Am
G
F
Em

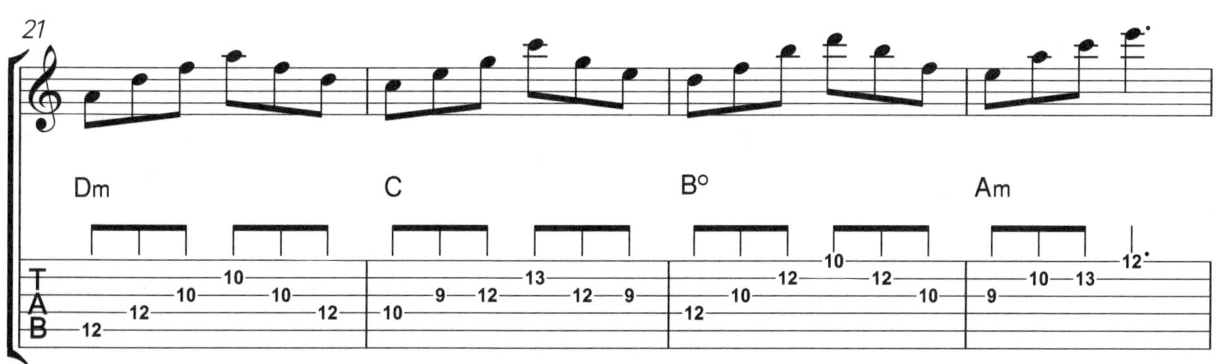
21
Dm
C
B°
Am

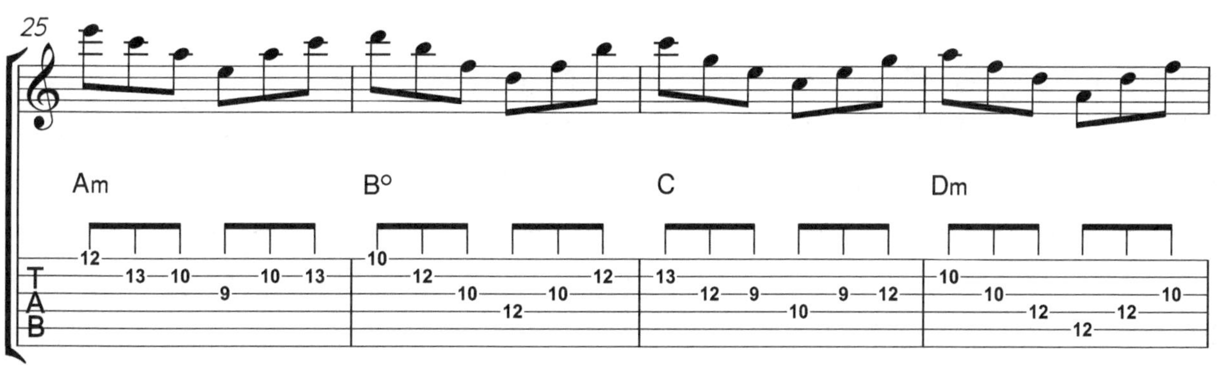
25
Am
B°
C
Dm

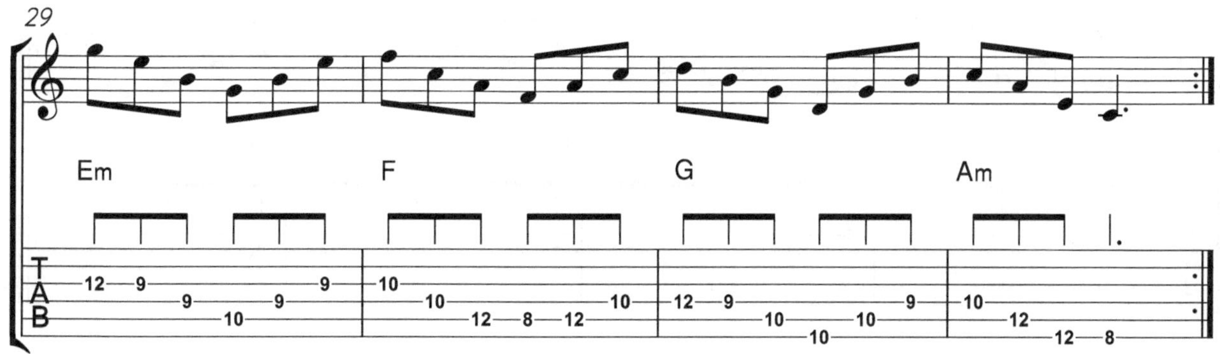
29
Em
F
G
Am

# A Minor Scale 6/8 Sequence ①
# First Inversion (Alternative Position)

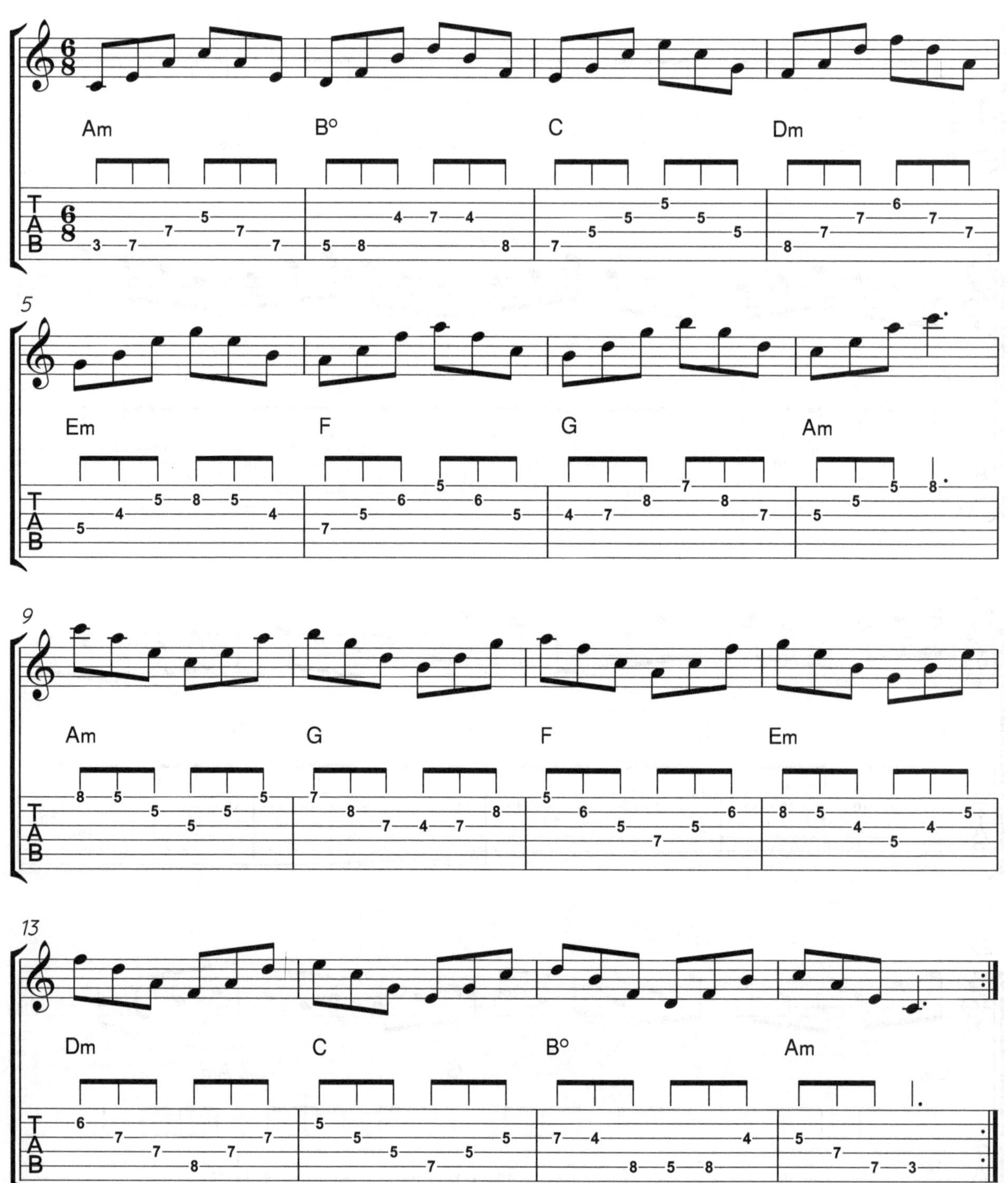

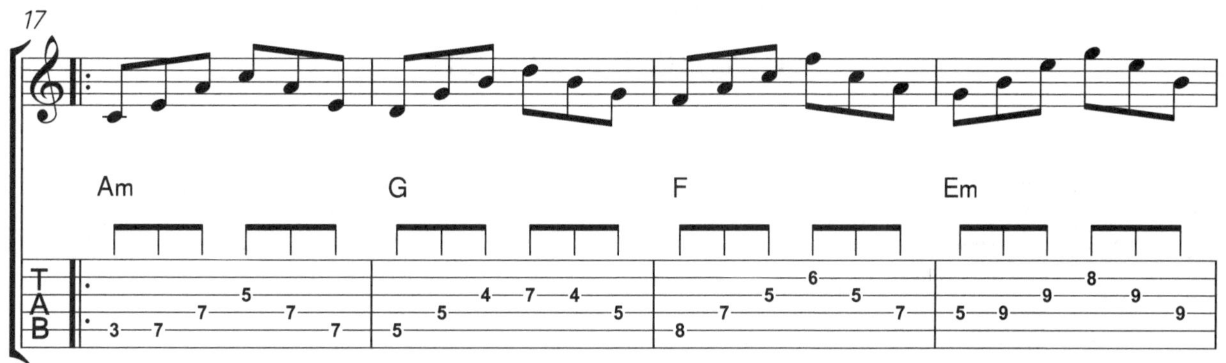
17
Am
G
F
Em
T
A
B
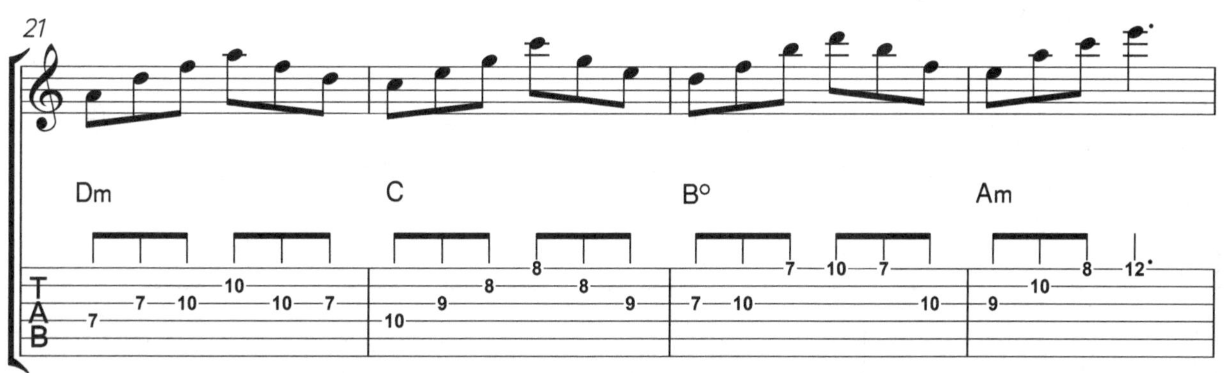
21
Dm
C
B°
Am
T
A
B
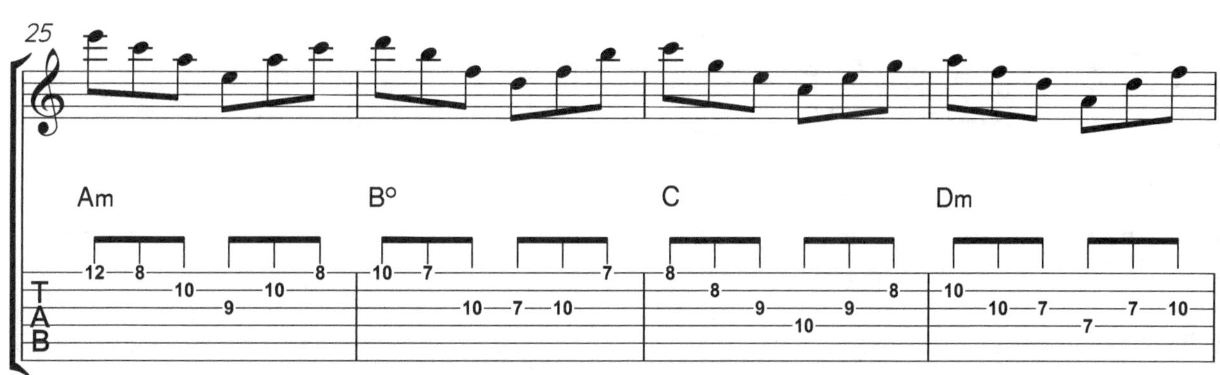
25
Am
B°
C
Dm
T
A
B
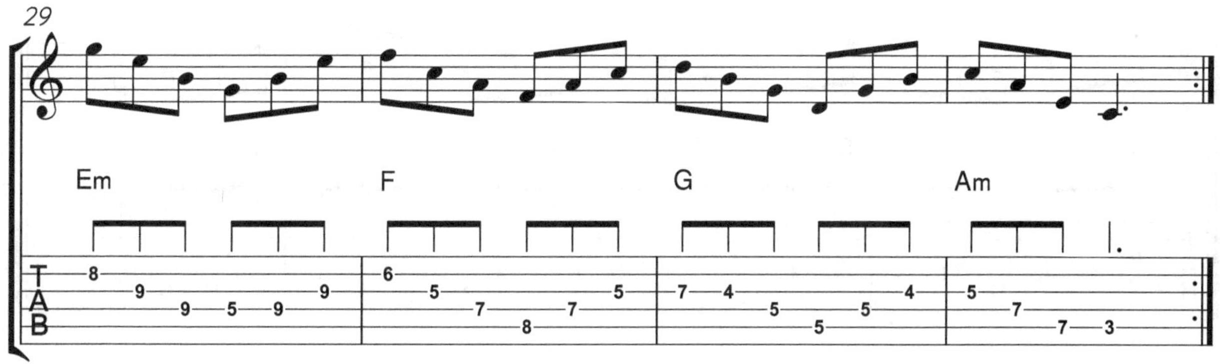
29
Em
F
G
Am
T
A
B

# A Minor Scale 6/8 Sequence ①
# Second Inversion

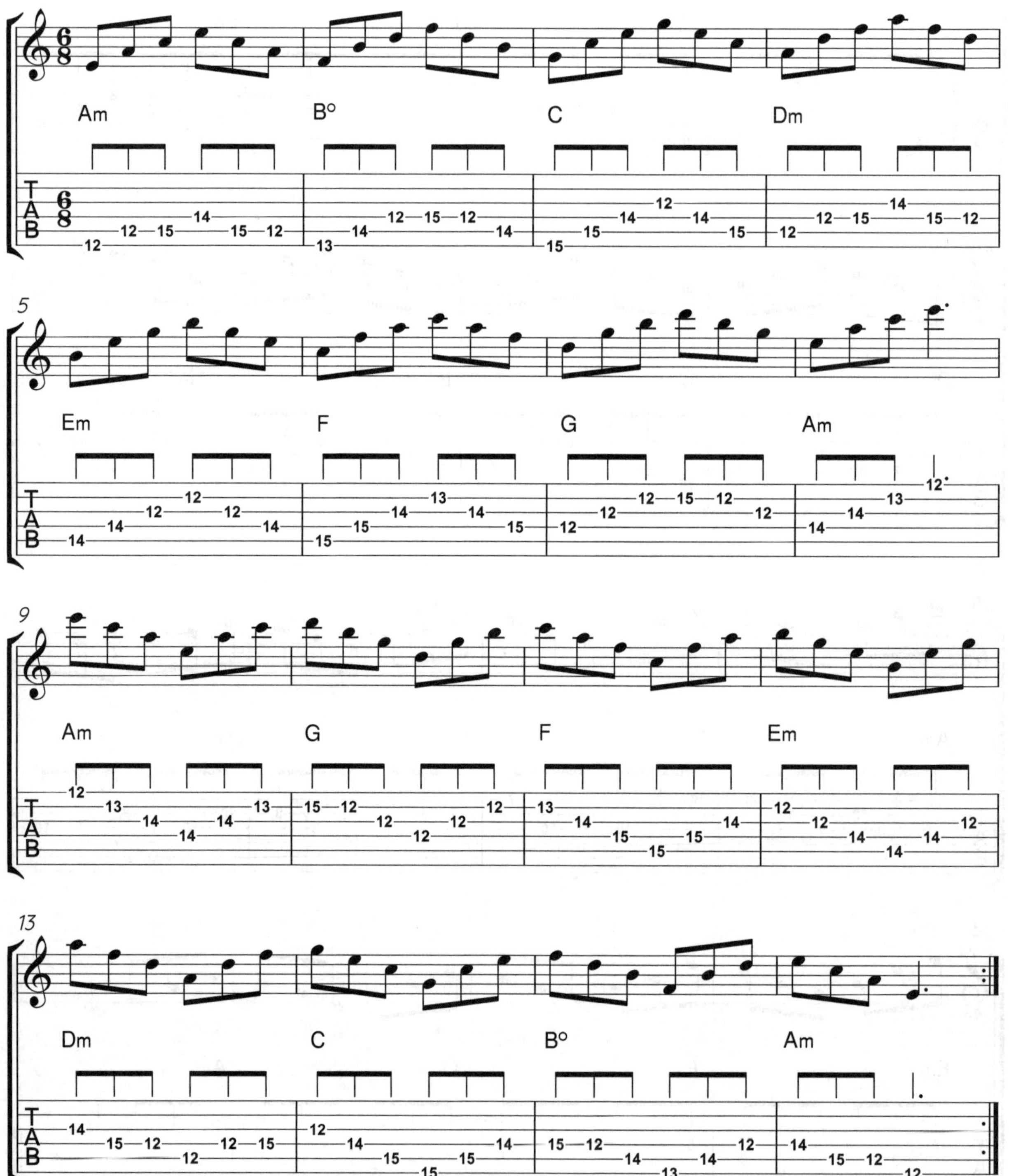

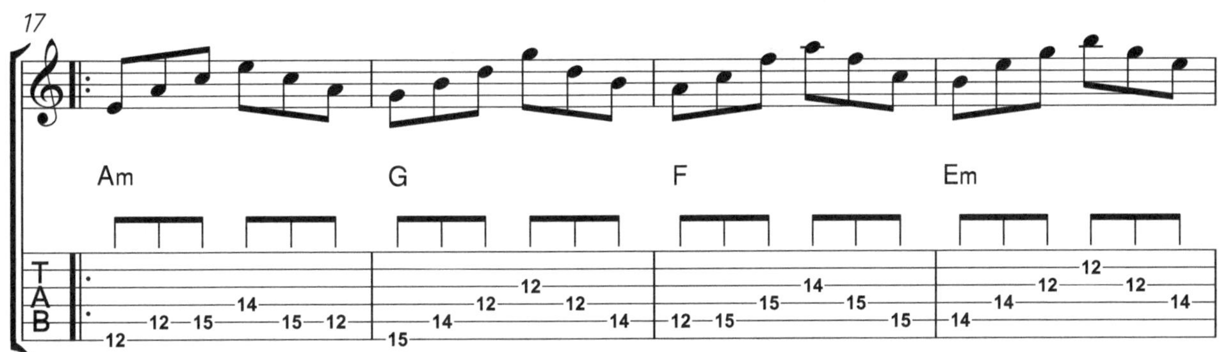
17
Am
G
F
Em
TAB

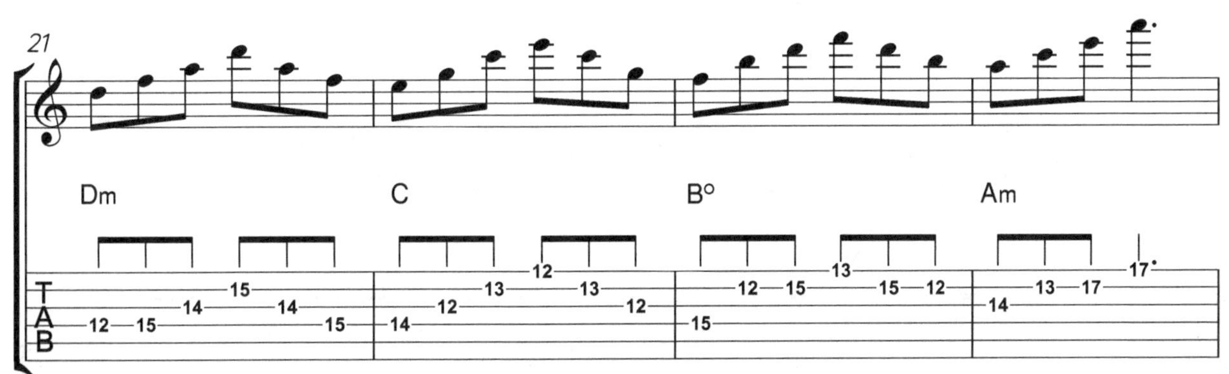
21
Dm
C
B°
Am
TAB

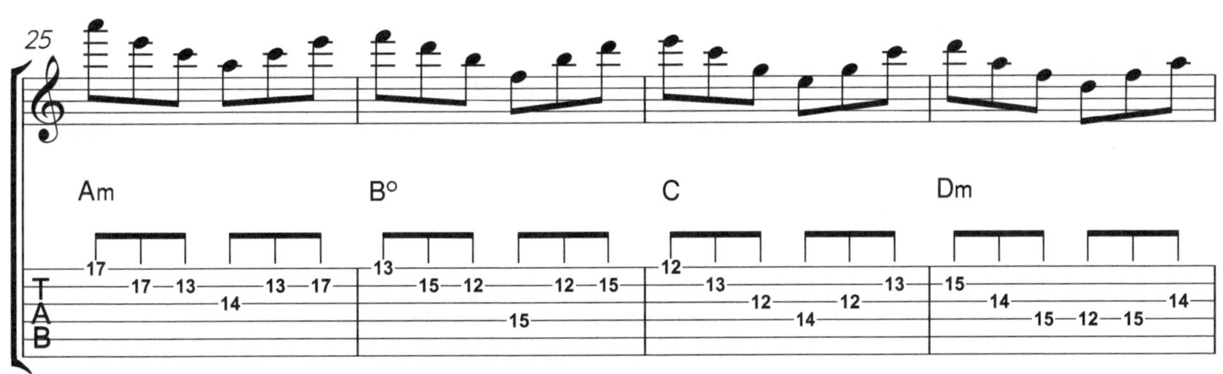
25
Am
B°
C
Dm
TAB

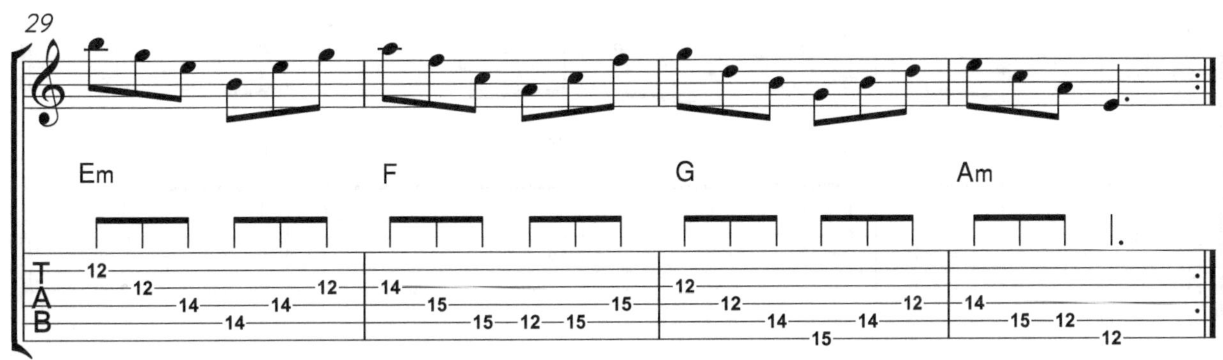
29
Em
F
G
Am
TAB

# A Minor Scale 6/8 Sequence ①
# Second Inversion (Alternative Position)

17
Am
G
F
Em
TAB

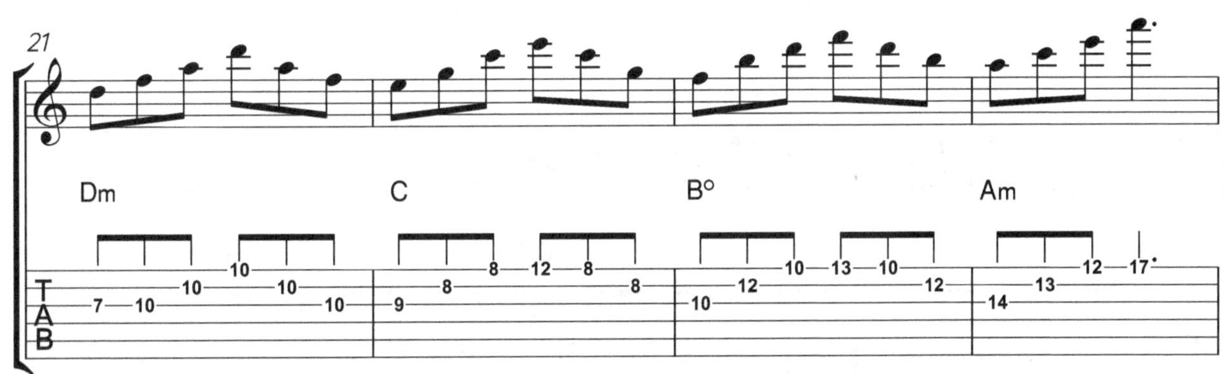
21
Dm
C
B°
Am
TAB

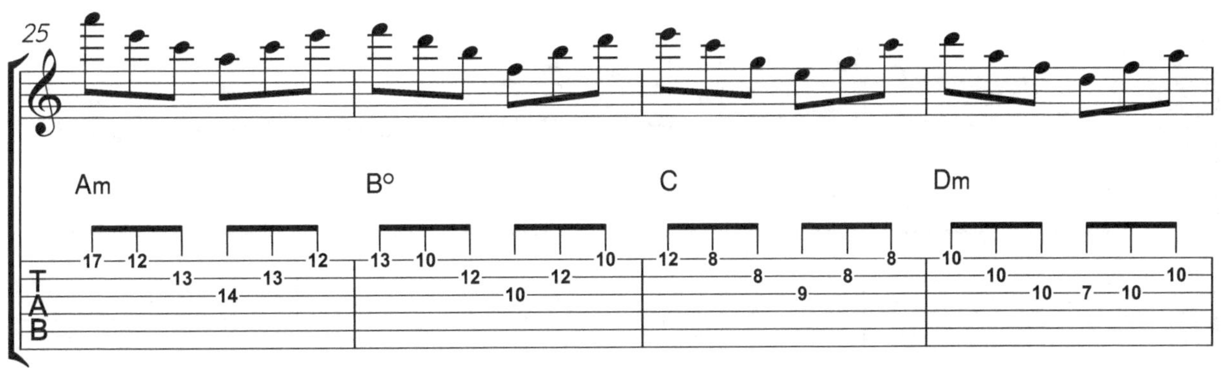
25
Am
B°
C
Dm
TAB

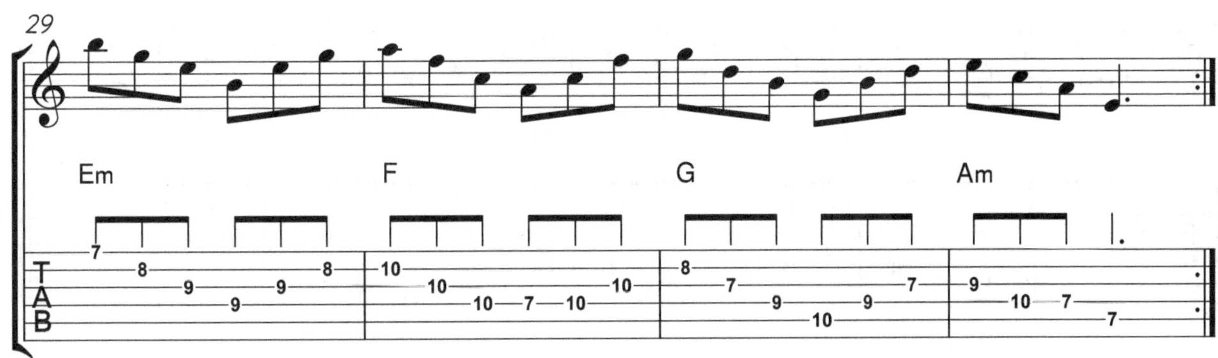
29
Em
F
G
Am
TAB

# D Harmonic Minor Scale 6/8 Sequence ①
# Root Position

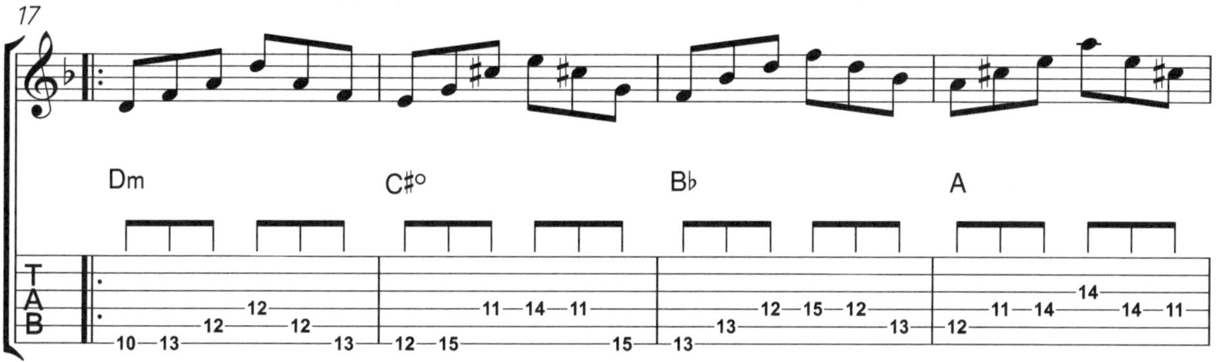
17
Dm
C♯°
B♭
A

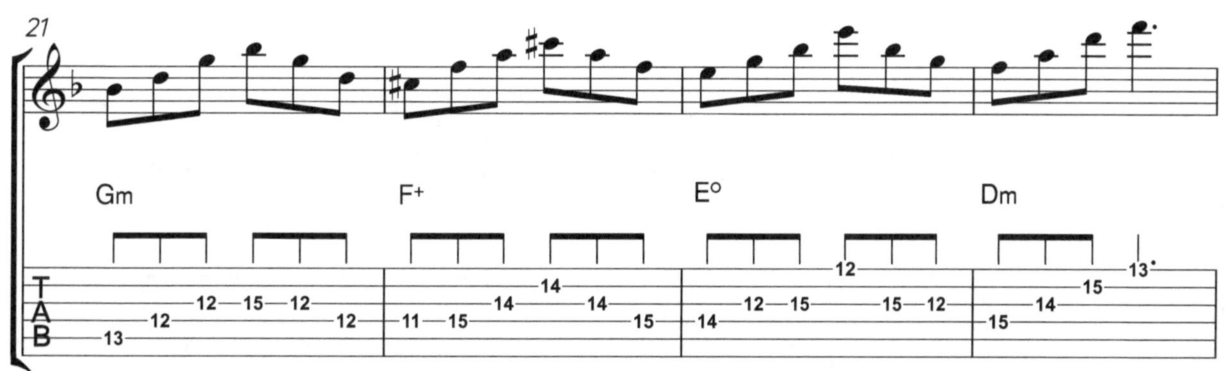
21
Gm
F+
E°
Dm

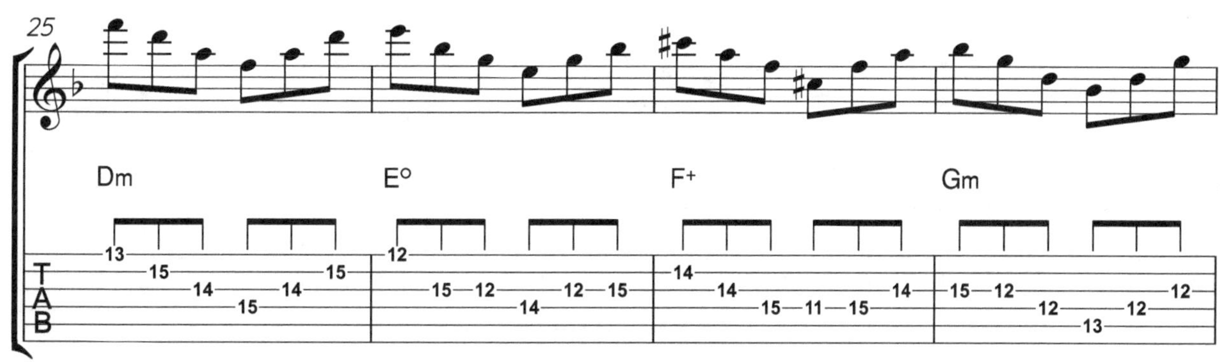
25
Dm
E°
F+
Gm

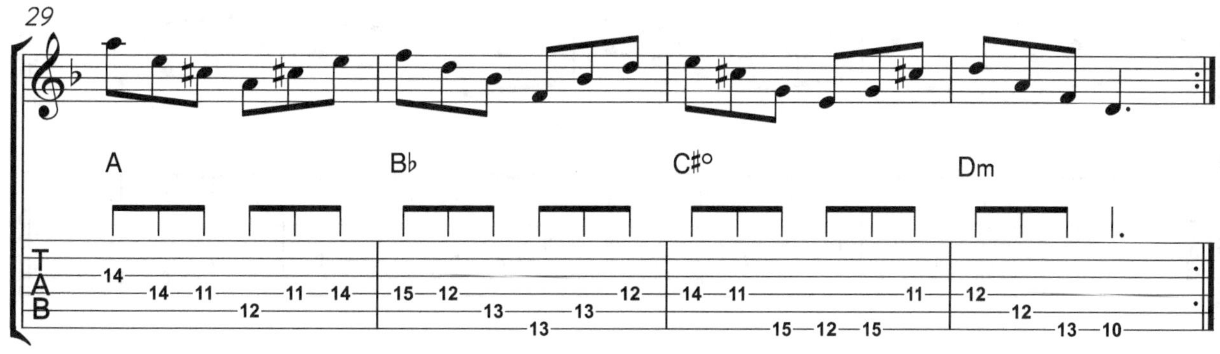
29
A
B♭
C♯°
Dm

# D Harmonic Minor Scale 6/8 Sequence ①
## Root Position (Alternative Position)

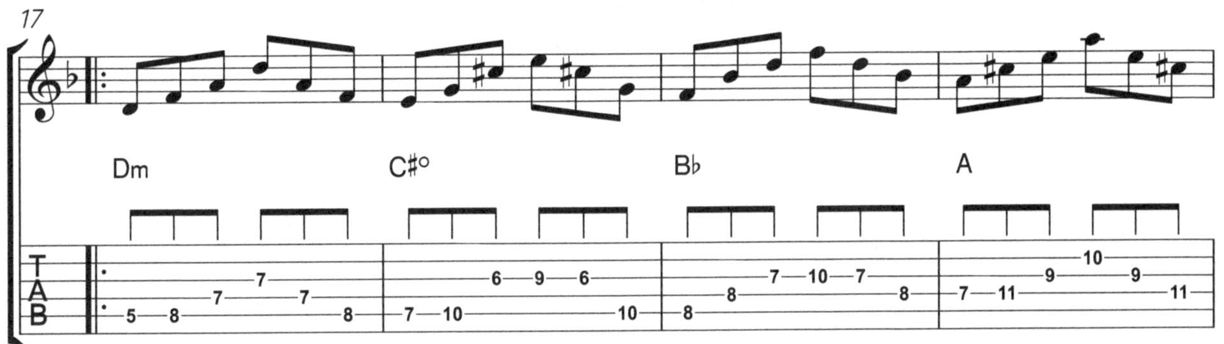
17
Dm
C♯°
B♭
A
TAB

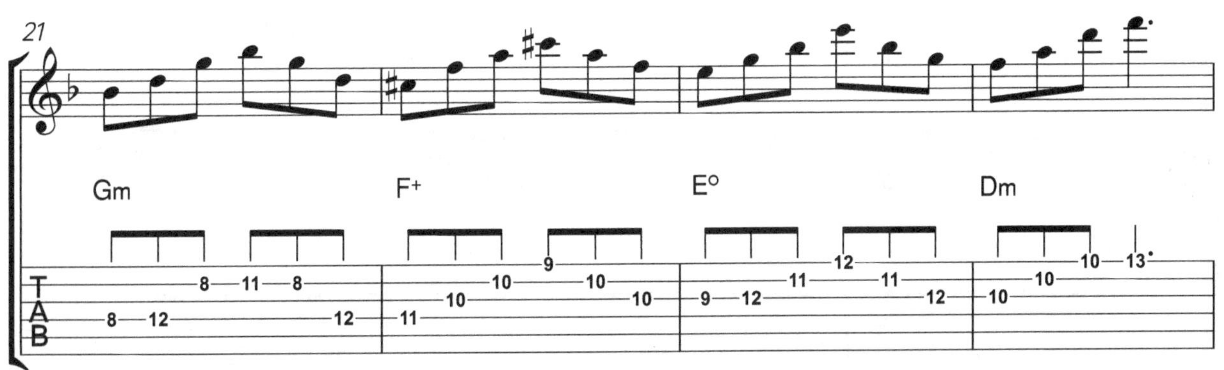
21
Gm
F+
E°
Dm
TAB

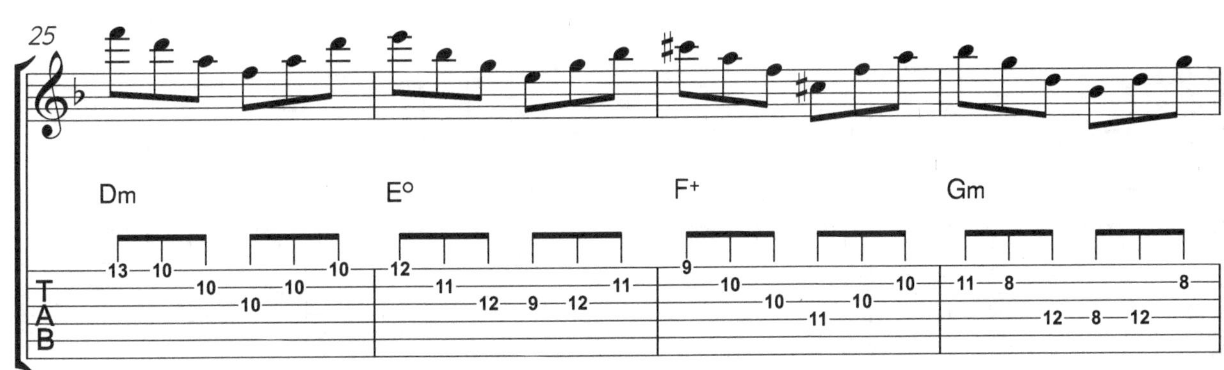
25
Dm
E°
F+
Gm
TAB

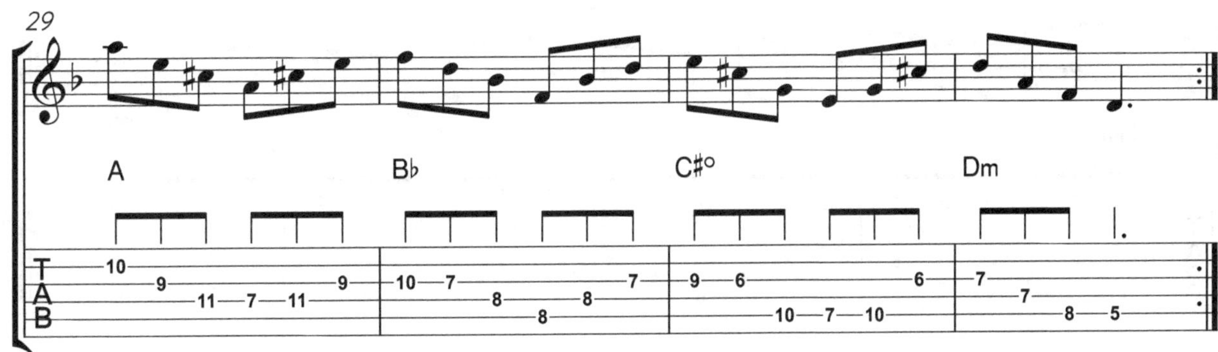
29
A
B♭
C♯°
Dm
TAB

# D Harmonic Minor Scale 6/8 Sequence ①
# First Inversion

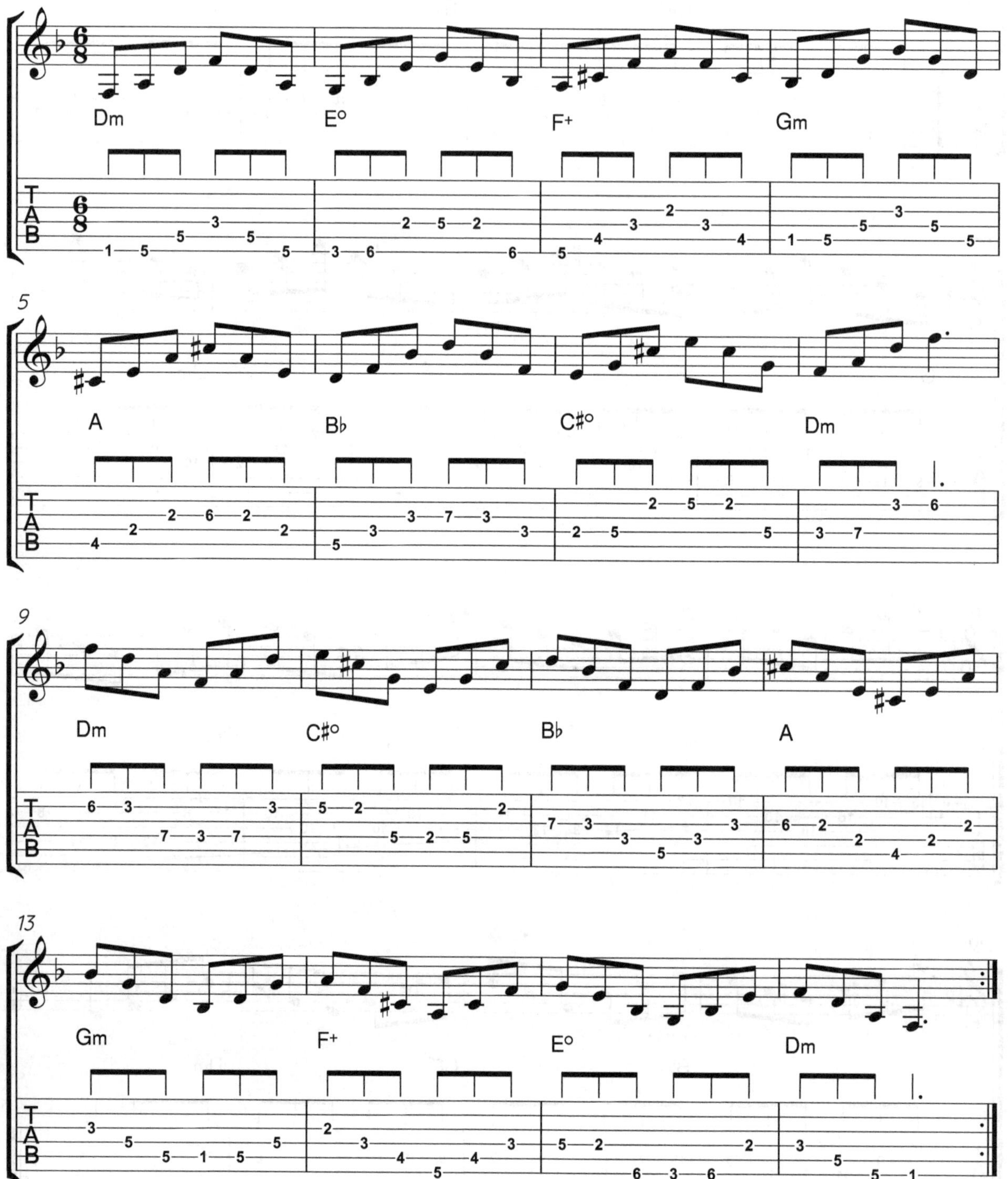

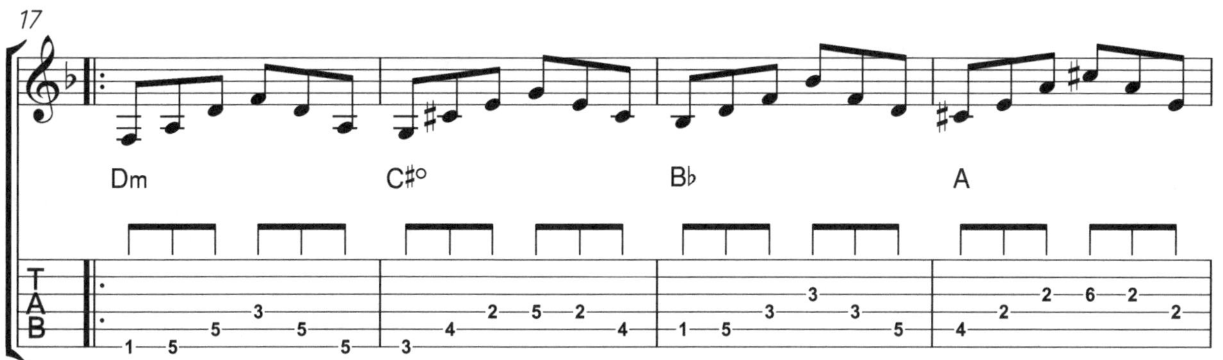
17
Dm
C♯°
B♭
A
TAB

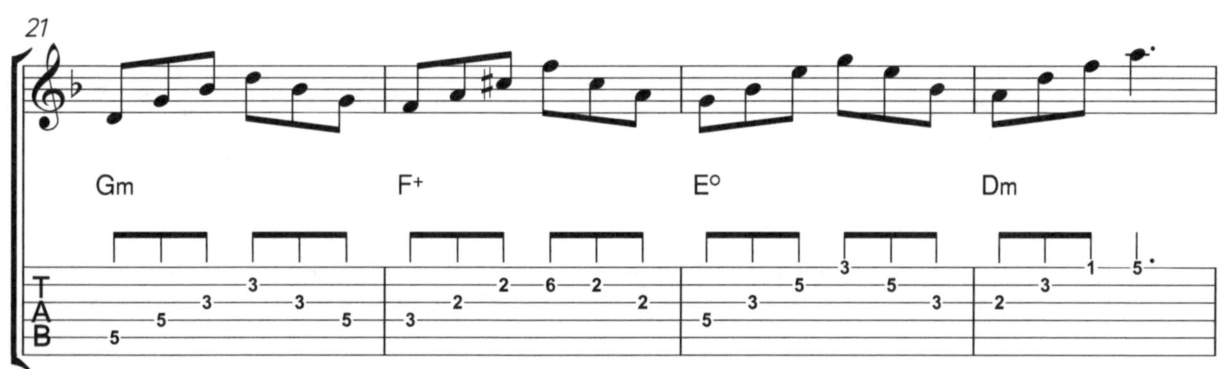
21
Gm
F+
E°
Dm
TAB

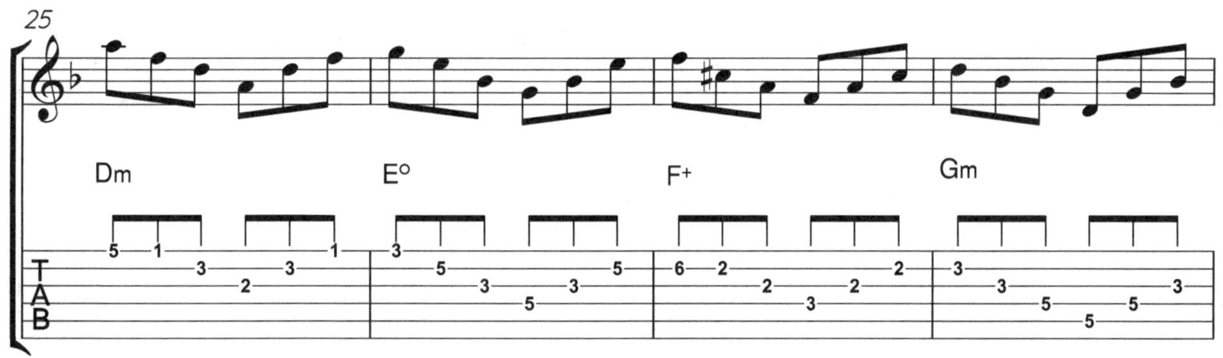
25
Dm
E°
F+
Gm
TAB

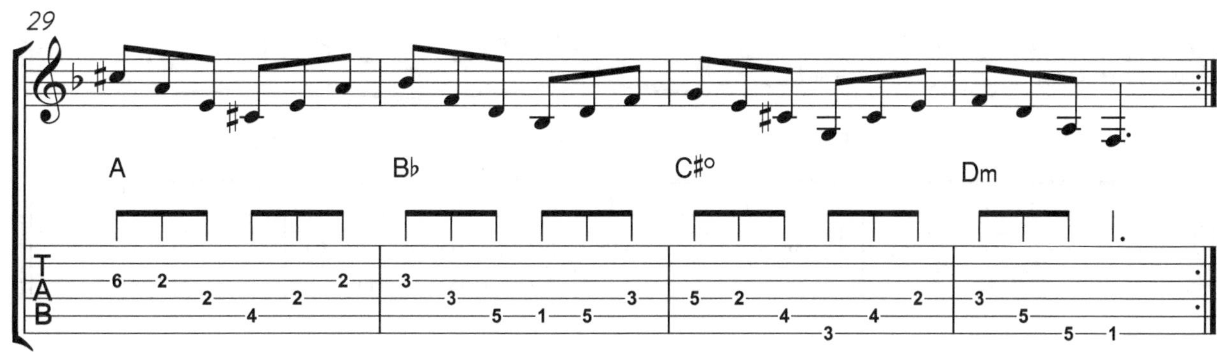
29
A
B♭
C♯°
Dm
TAB

# D Harmonic Minor Scale 6/8 Sequence ①
# First Inversion (Alternative Position)

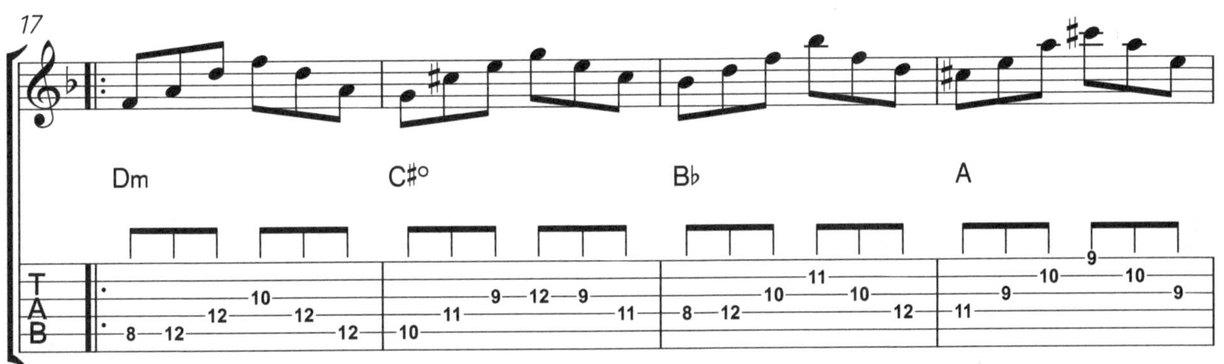
17
Dm
C♯o
B♭
A
TAB

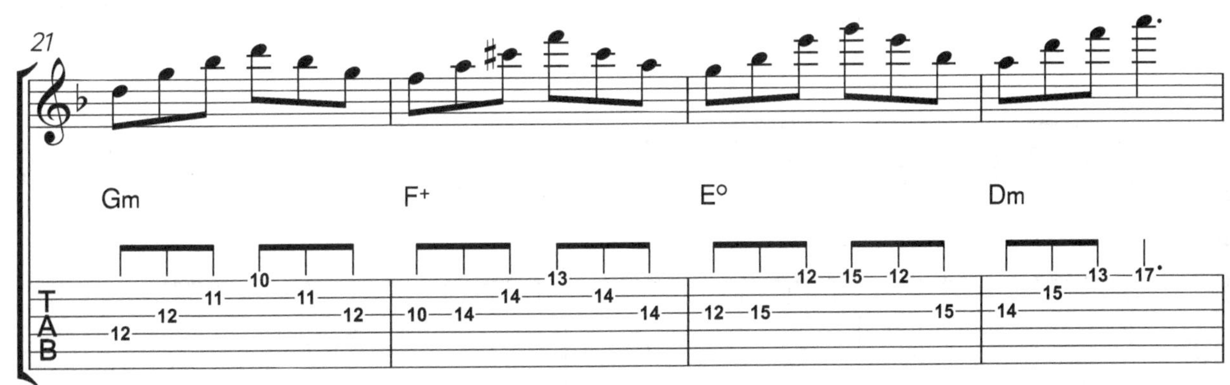
21
Gm
F+
Eo
Dm
TAB

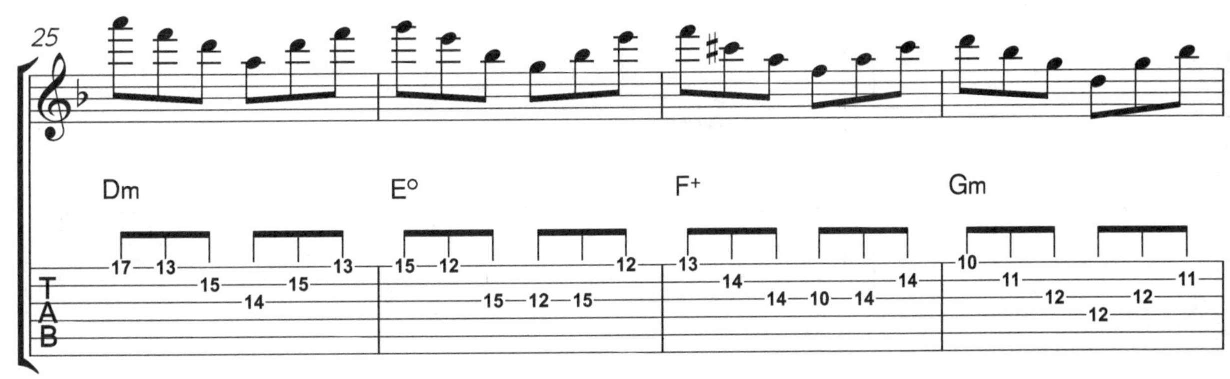
25
Dm
Eo
F+
Gm
TAB

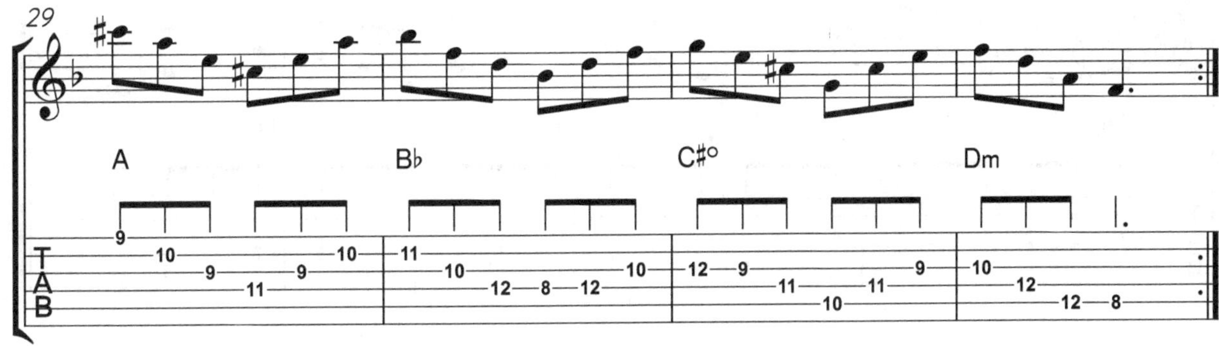
29
A
B♭
C♯o
Dm
TAB

# D Harmonic Minor Scale 6/8 Sequence ①
## Second Inversion

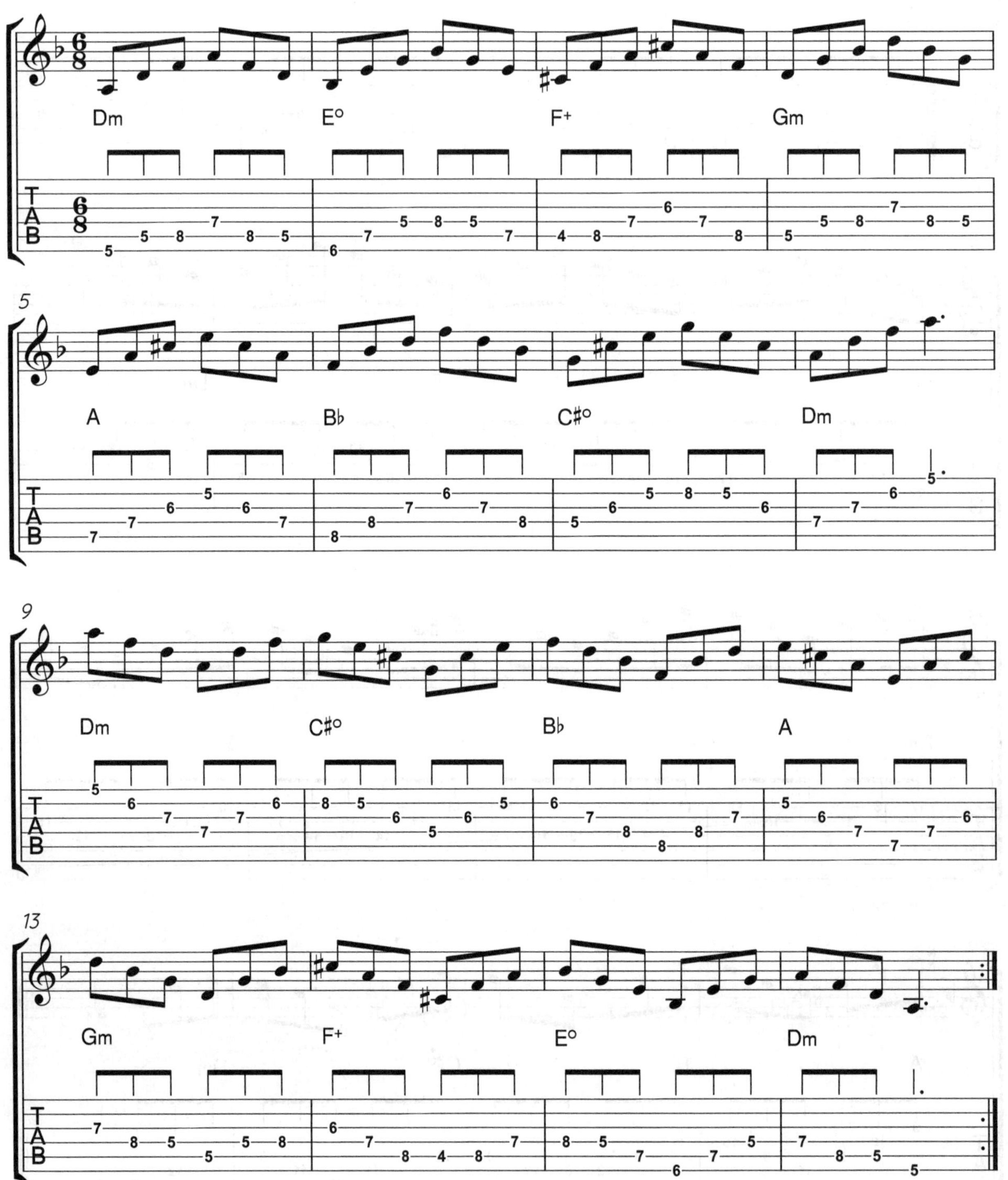

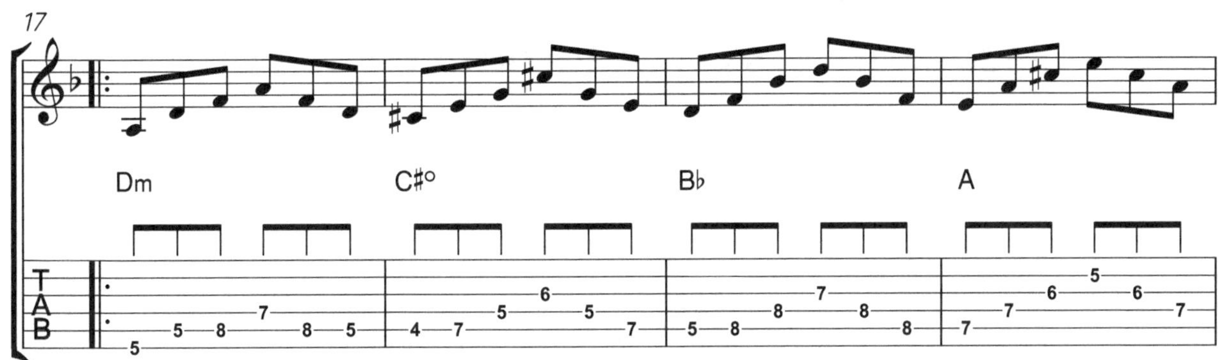
17
Dm
C♯o
B♭
A

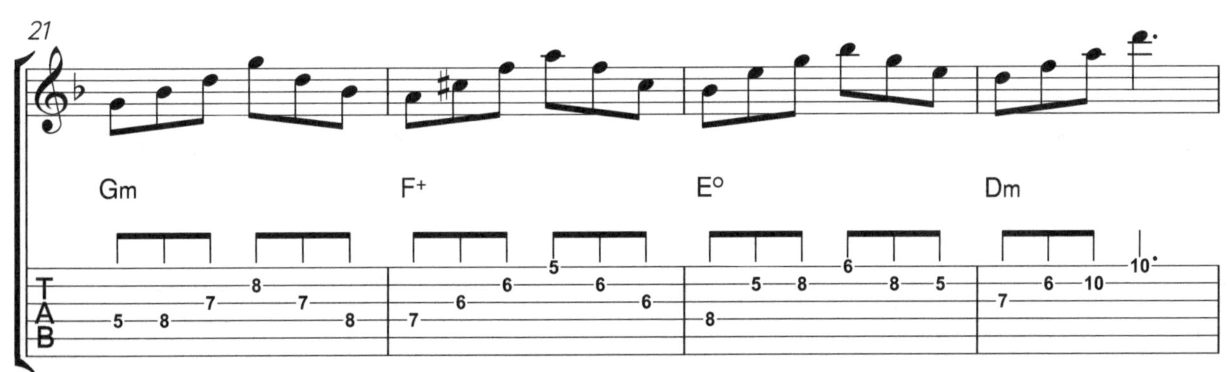
21
Gm
F+
Eo
Dm

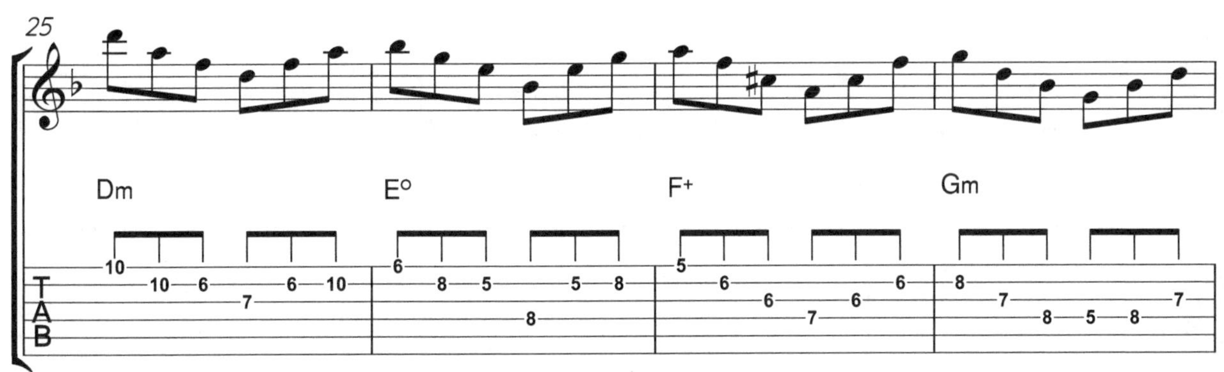
25
Dm
Eo
F+
Gm

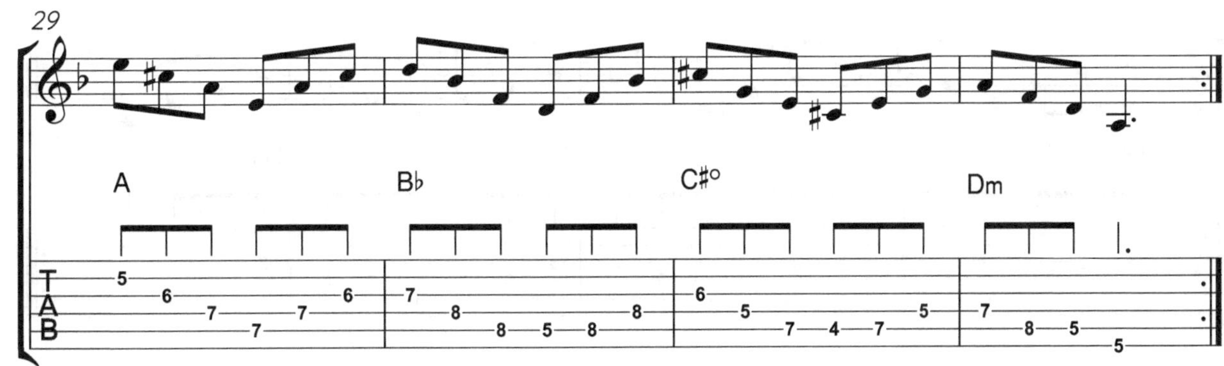
29
A
B♭
C♯o
Dm

# D Harmonic Minor Scale 6/8 Sequence ①
# Second Inversion (Alternative Position)

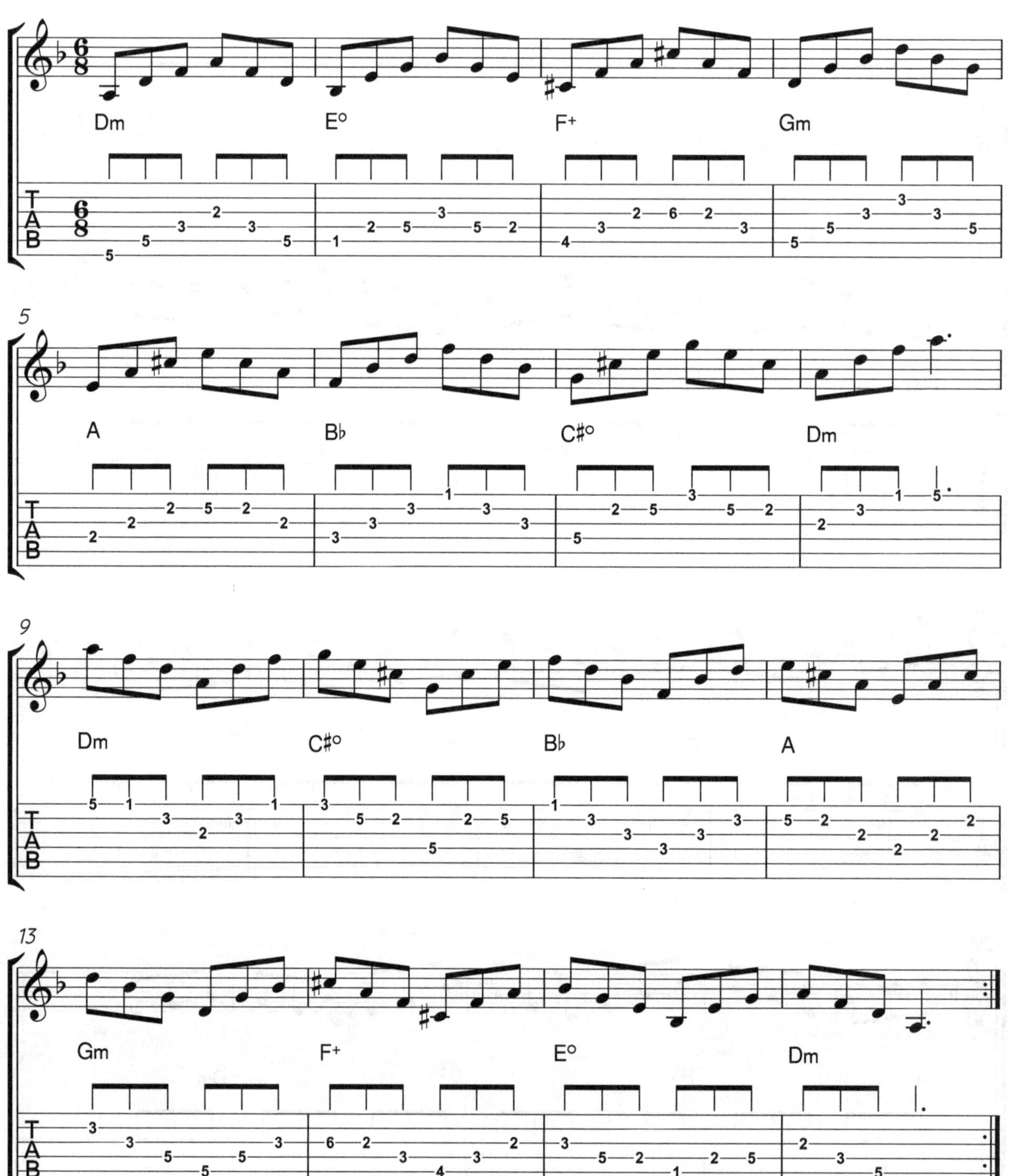

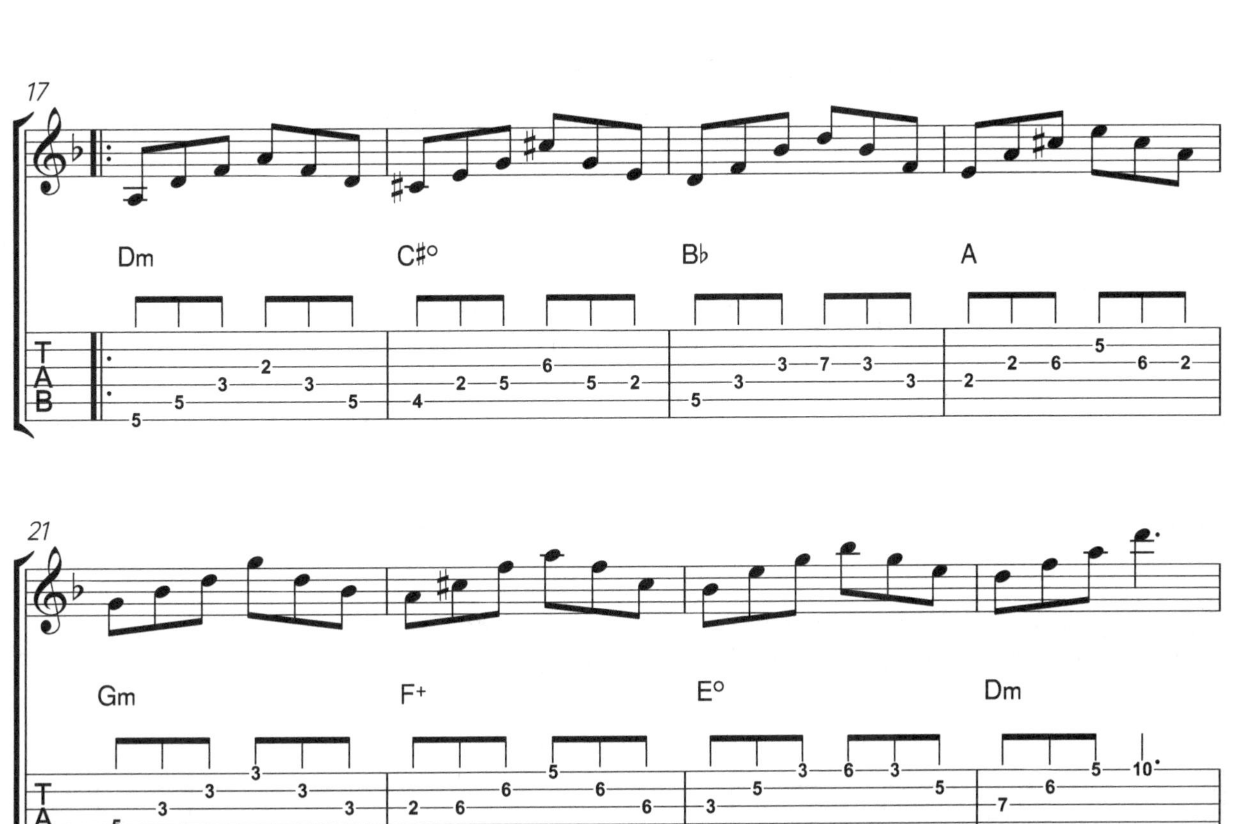
17
Dm
C♯°
B♭
A
T
A
B
21
Gm
F+
E°
Dm

25
Dm
E°
F+
Gm
T
A
B

29
A
B♭
C♯°
Dm
T
A
B

# G Melodic Minor Scale 6/8 Sequence ①
# Root Position

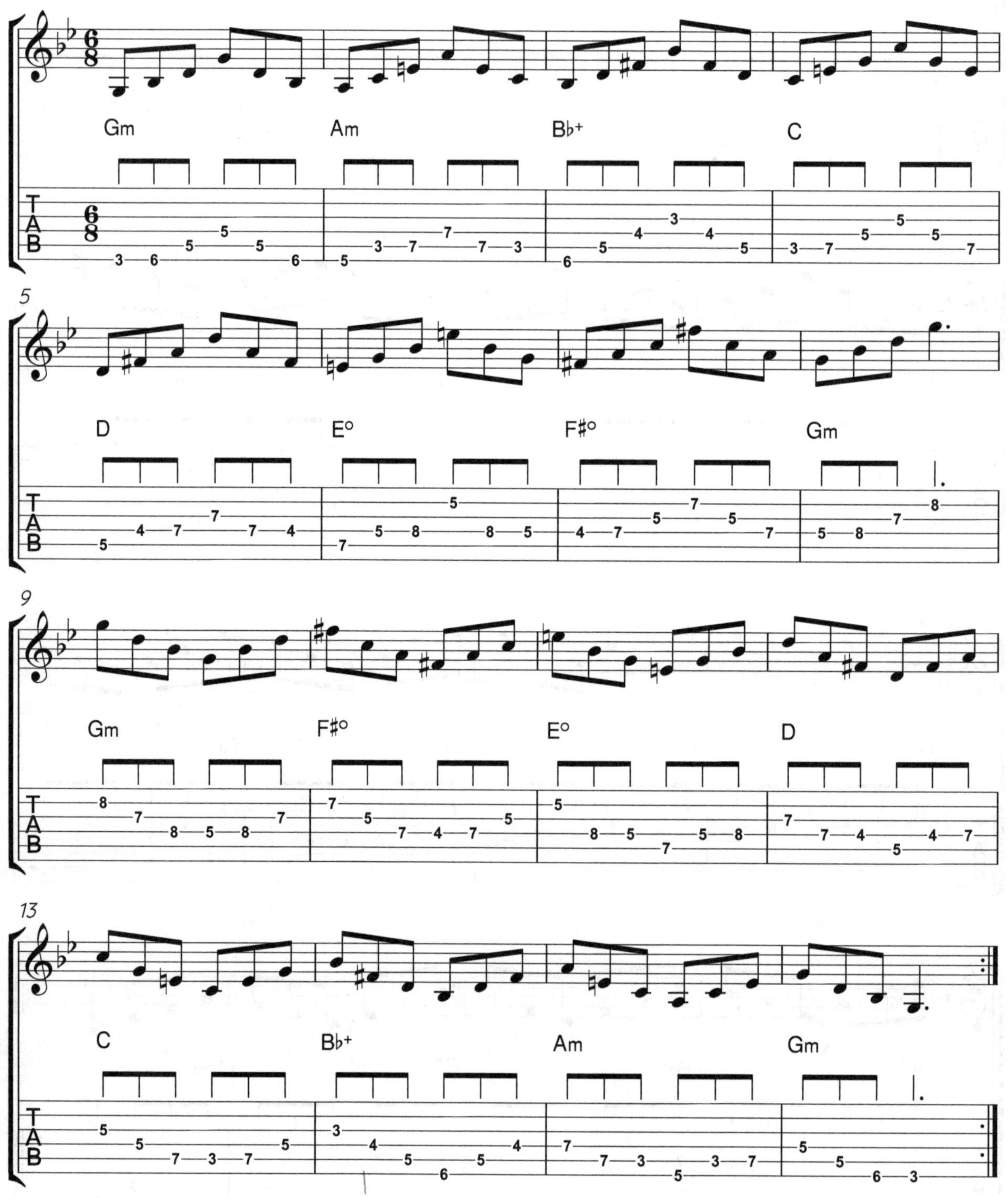

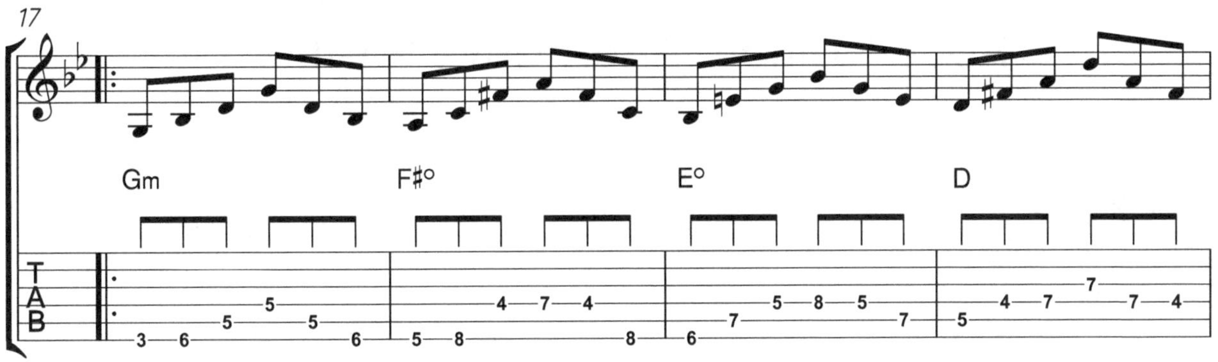
17
Gm
F♯o
Eo
D
T
A
B

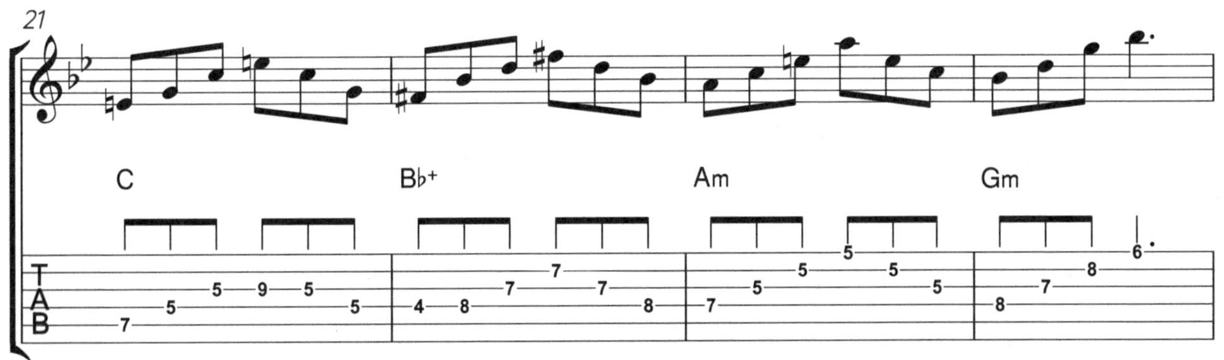
21
C
B♭+
Am
Gm

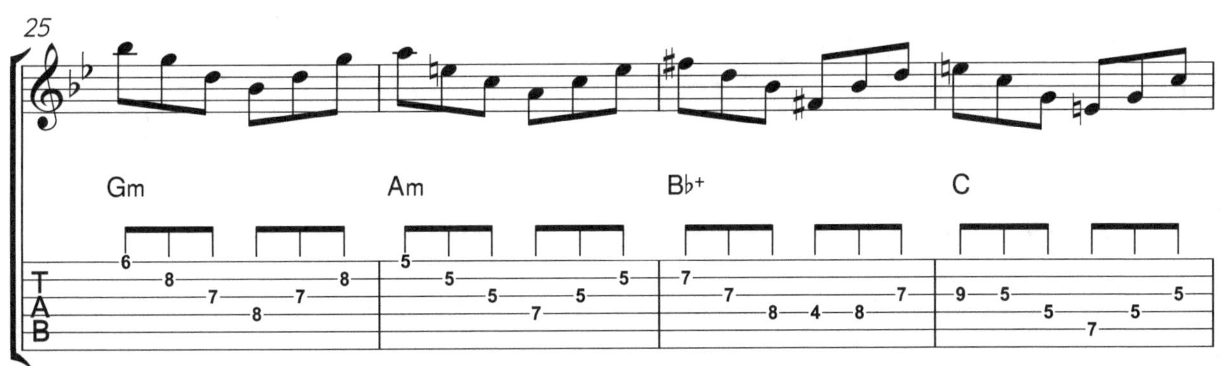
25
Gm
Am
B♭+
C

29
D
Eo
F♯o
Gm

# G Melodic Minor Scale 6/8 Sequence ①
# Root Position (Alternative Position)

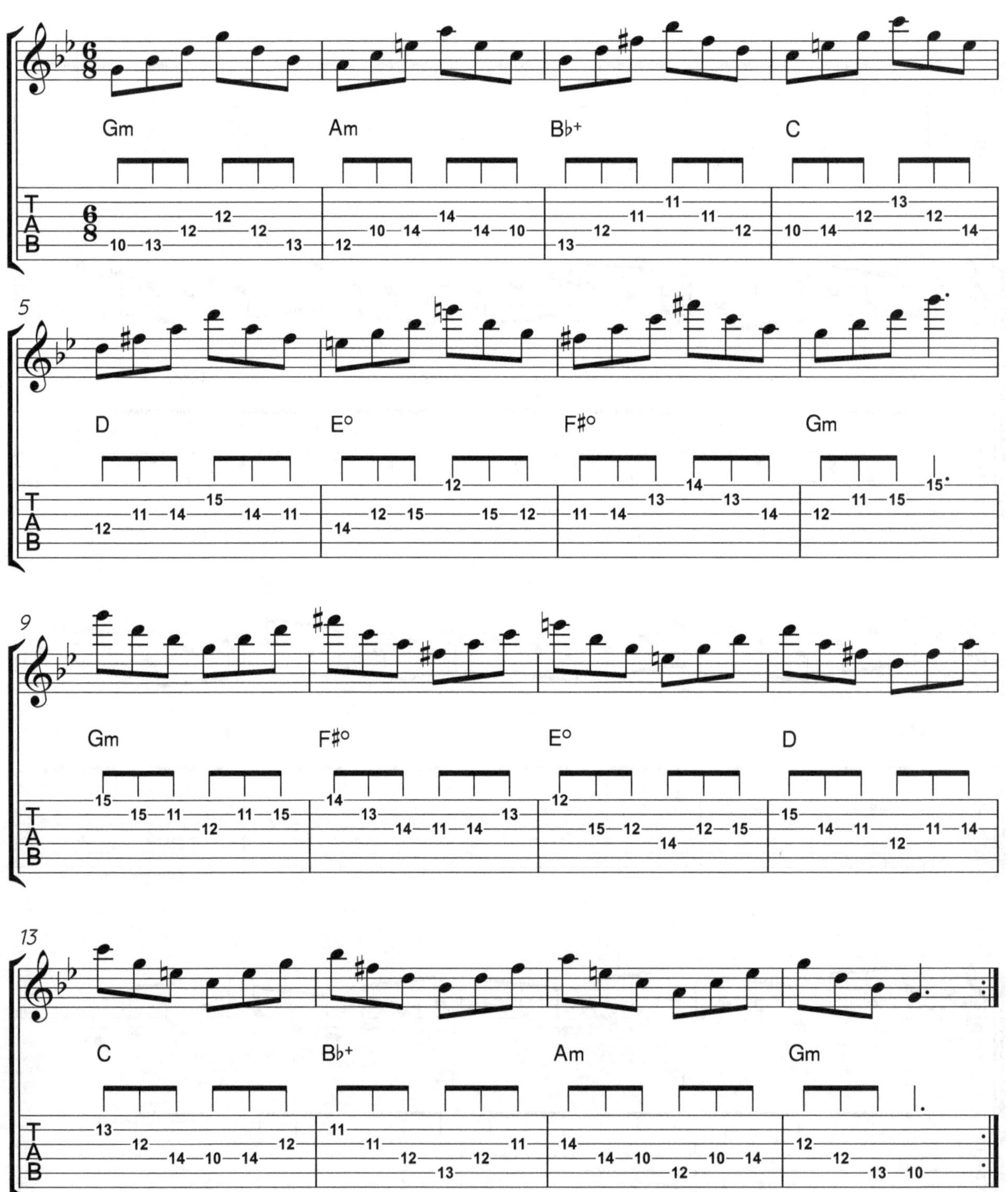

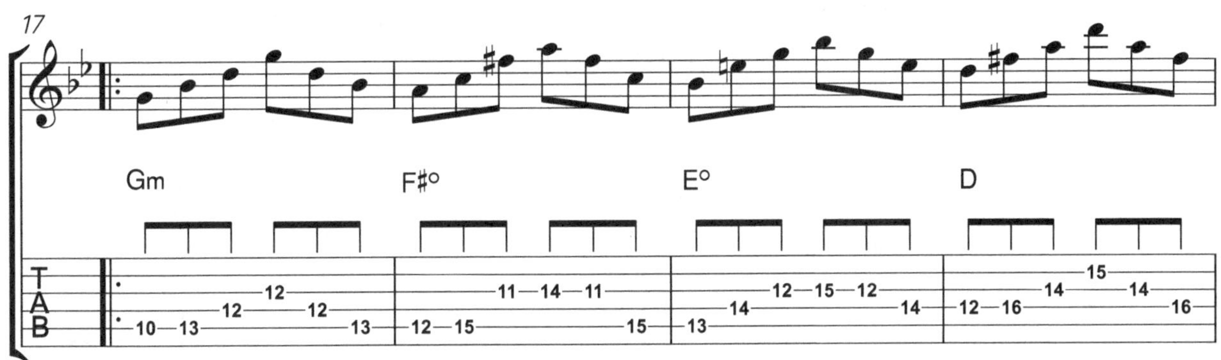
17
Gm
F♯°
E°
D

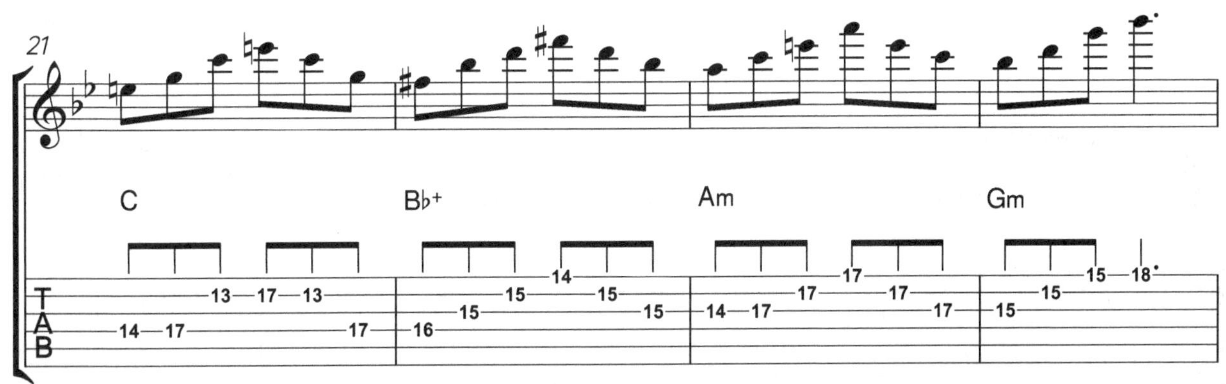
21
C
B♭+
Am
Gm

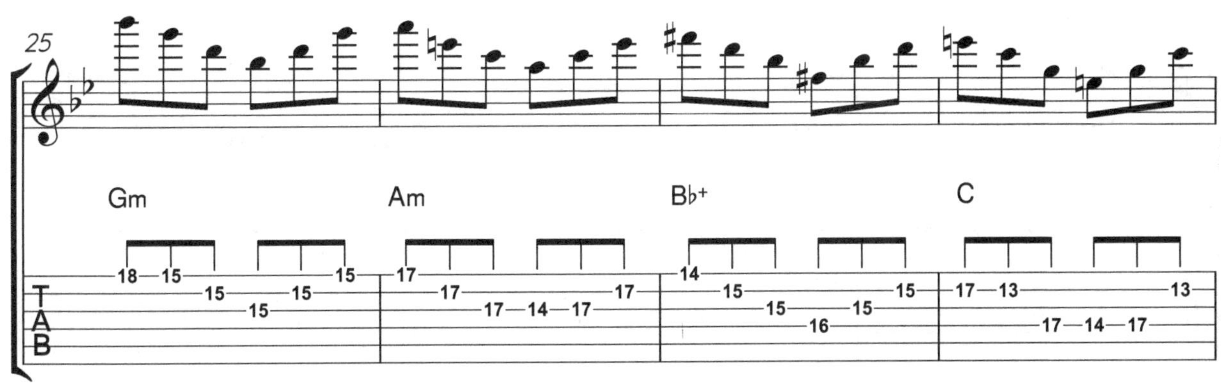
25
Gm
Am
B♭+
C

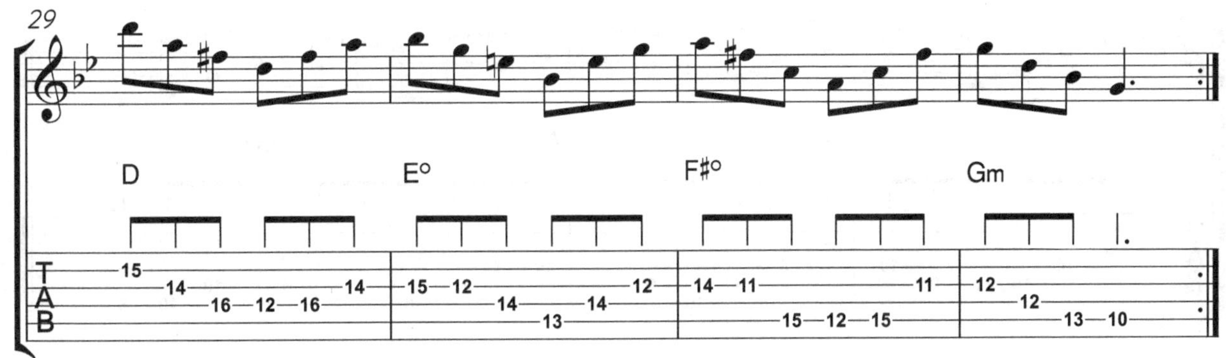
29
D
E°
F♯°
Gm

# G Melodic Minor Scale 6/8 Sequence ①
# First Inversion

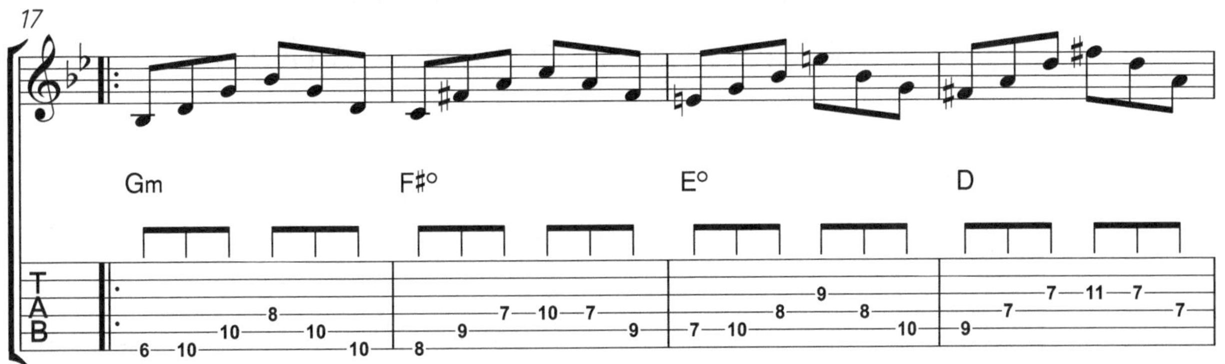
17
Gm
F♯o
Eo
D
TAB

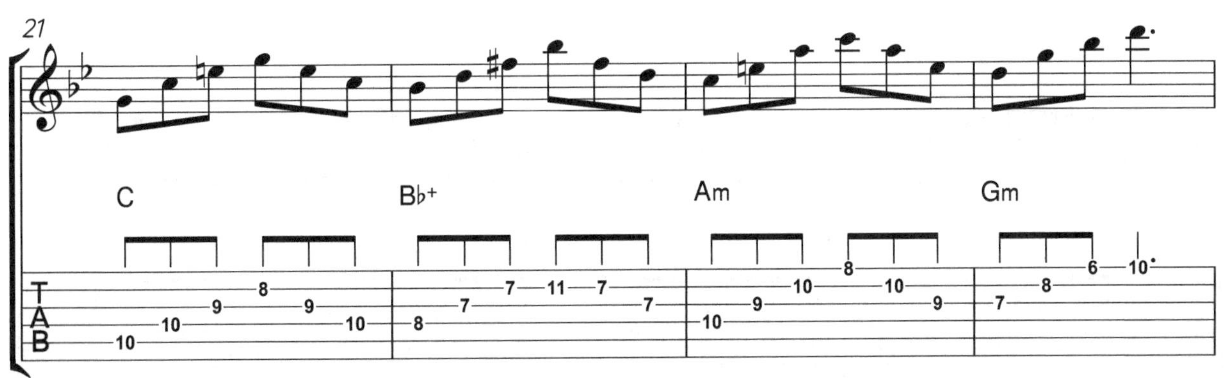
21
C
B♭+
Am
Gm
TAB

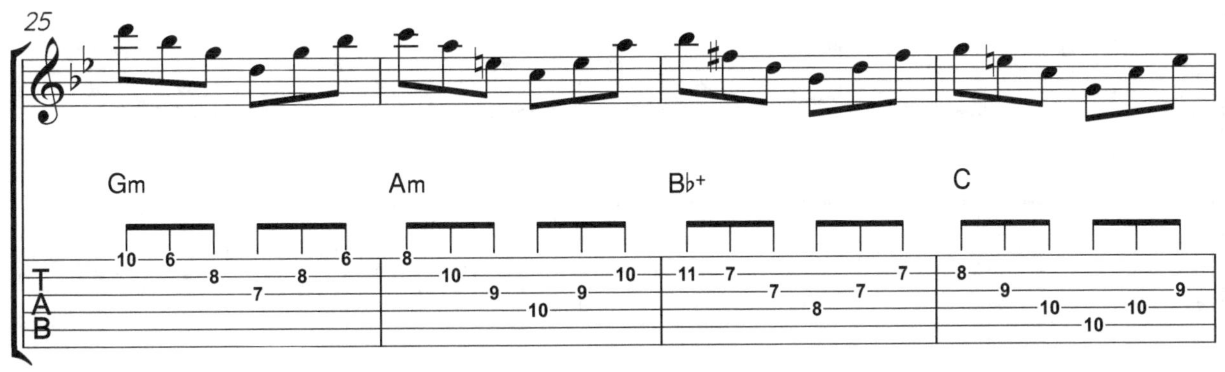
25
Gm
Am
B♭+
C
TAB

29
D
Eo
F♯o
Gm
TAB

# G Melodic Minor Scale 6/8 Sequence ①
# First Inversion (Alternative Position)

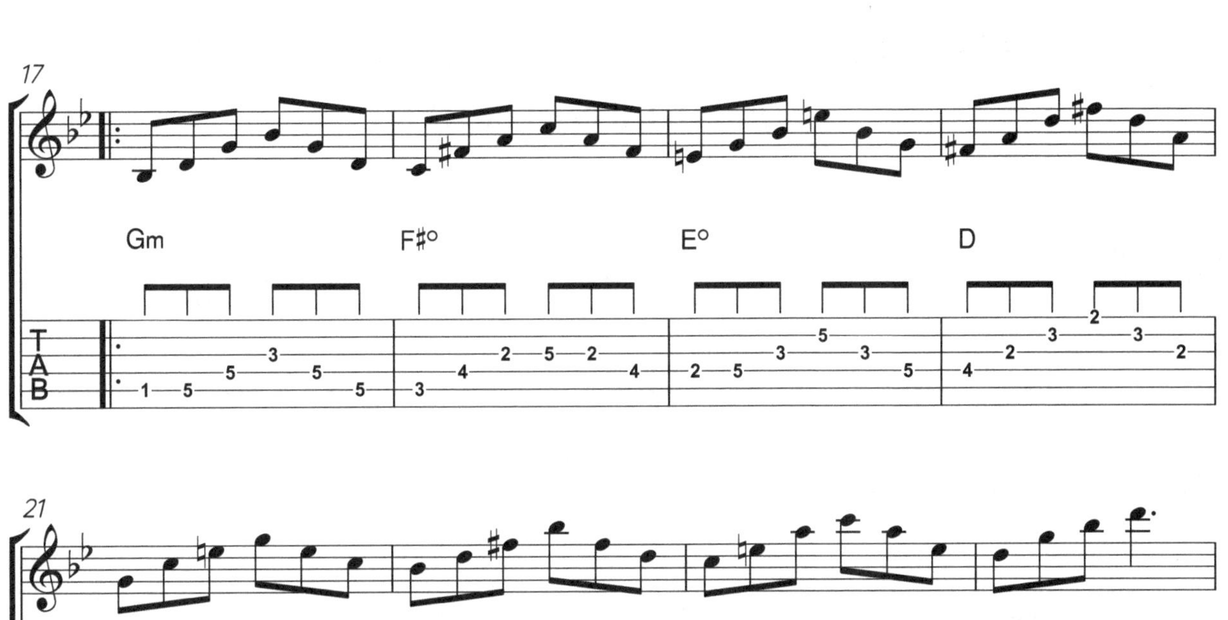
17
Gm
F♯°
E°
D
T
A
B

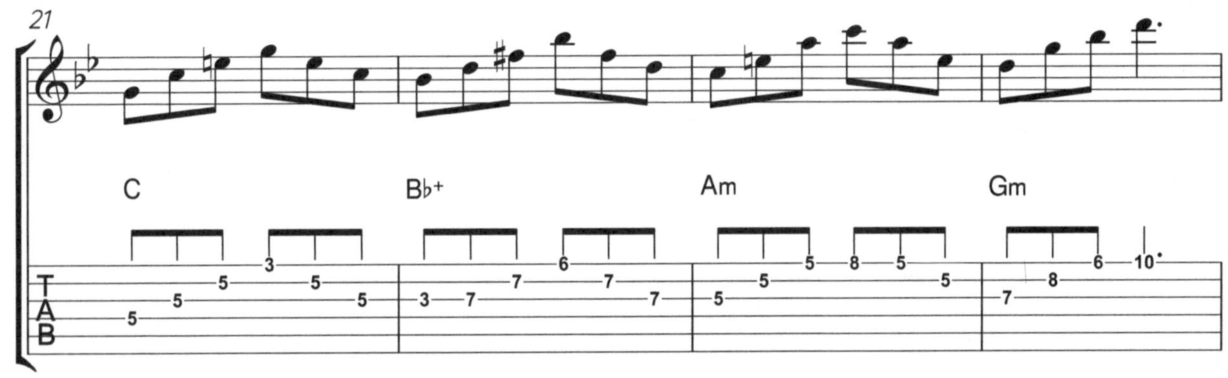
21
C
B♭+
Am
Gm
T
A
B

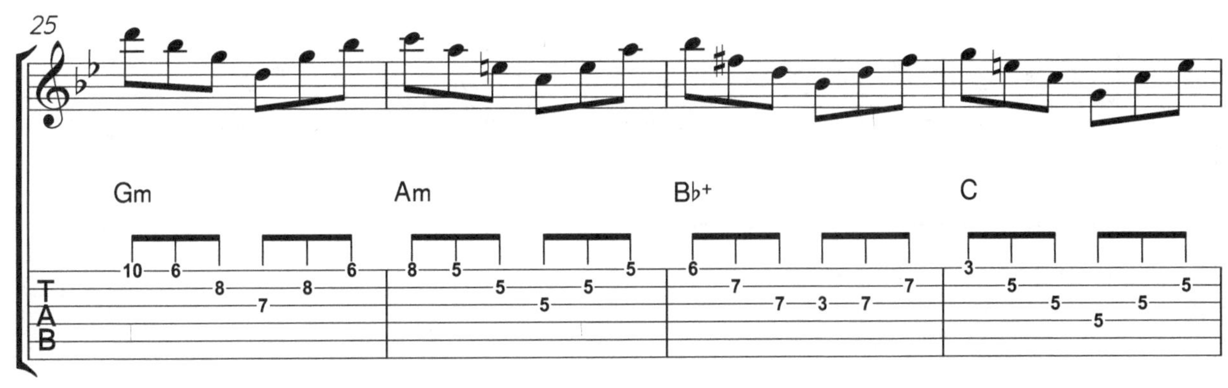
25
Gm
Am
B♭+
C
T
A
B

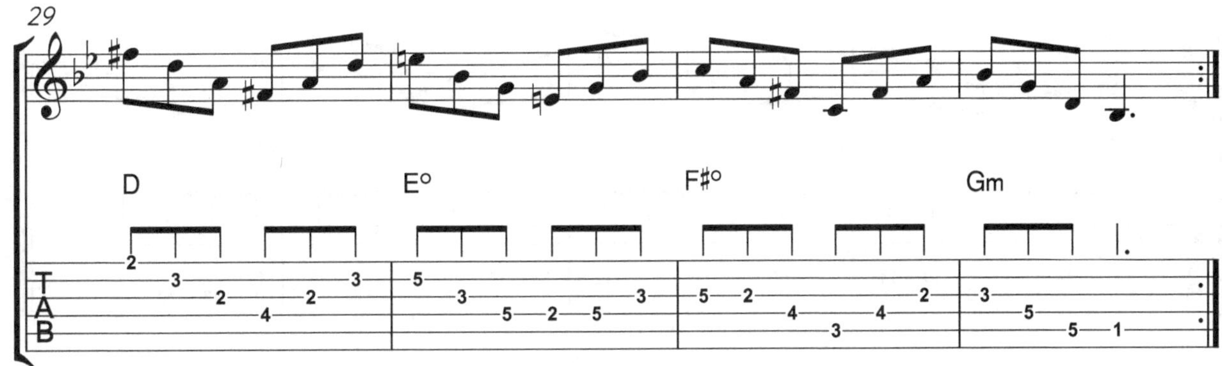
29
D
E°
F♯°
Gm
T
A
B

# G Melodic Minor Scale 6/8 Sequence ①
## Second Inversion

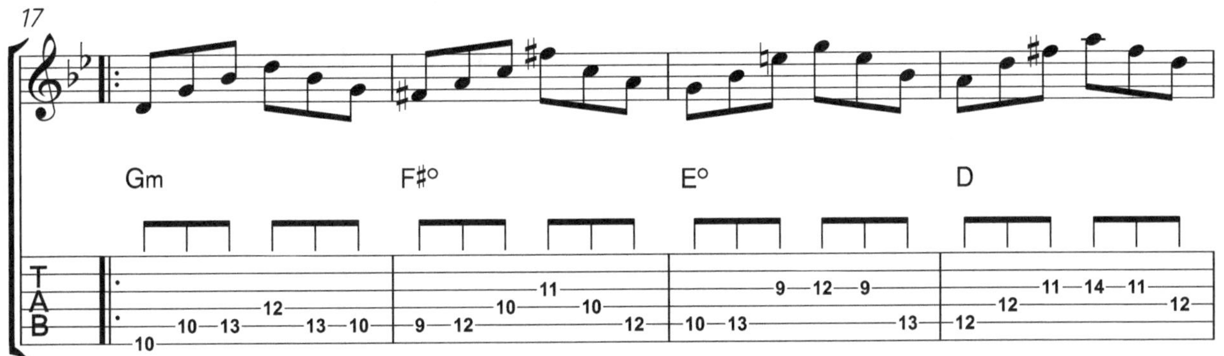
17
Gm
F♯o
Eo
D

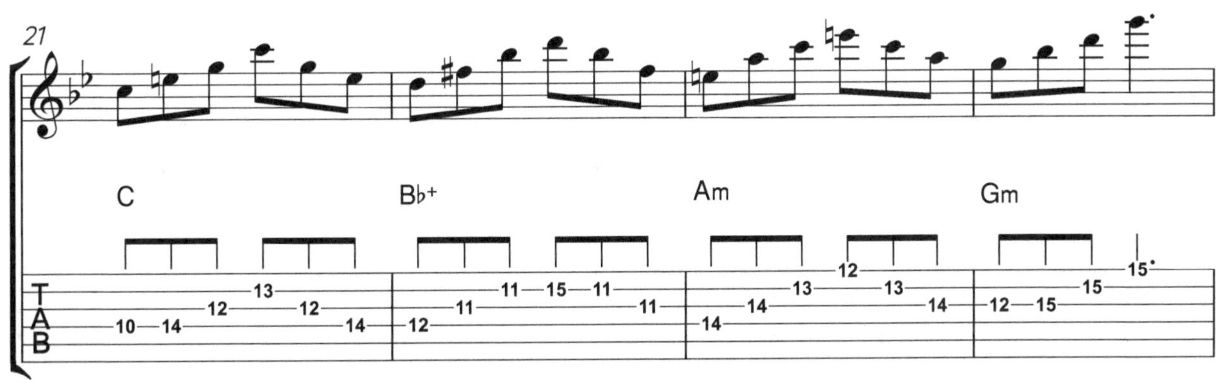
21
C
B♭+
Am
Gm

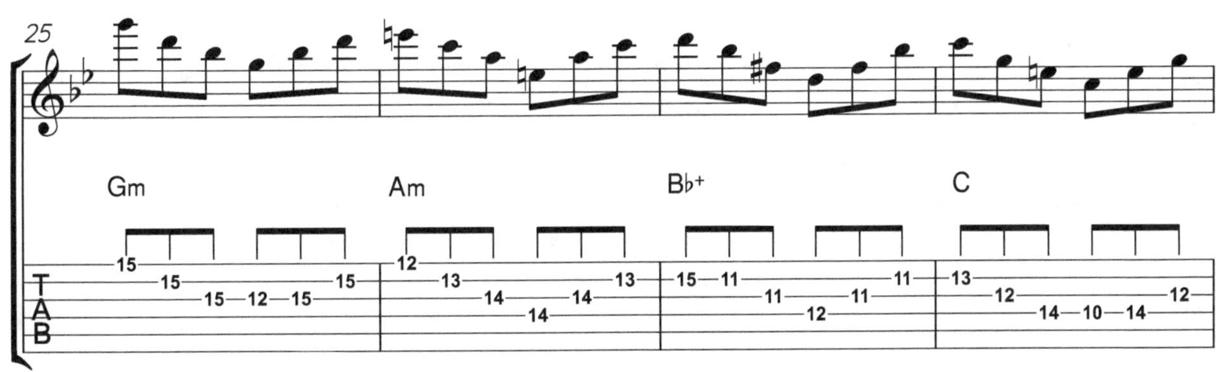
25
Gm
Am
B♭+
C

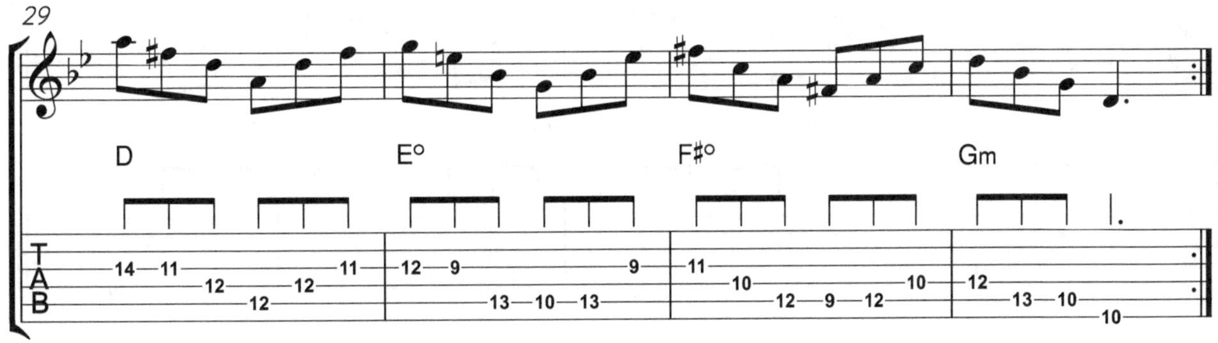
29
D
Eo
F♯o
Gm

# G Melodic Minor Scale 6/8 Sequence ①
# Second Inversion (Alternative Position)

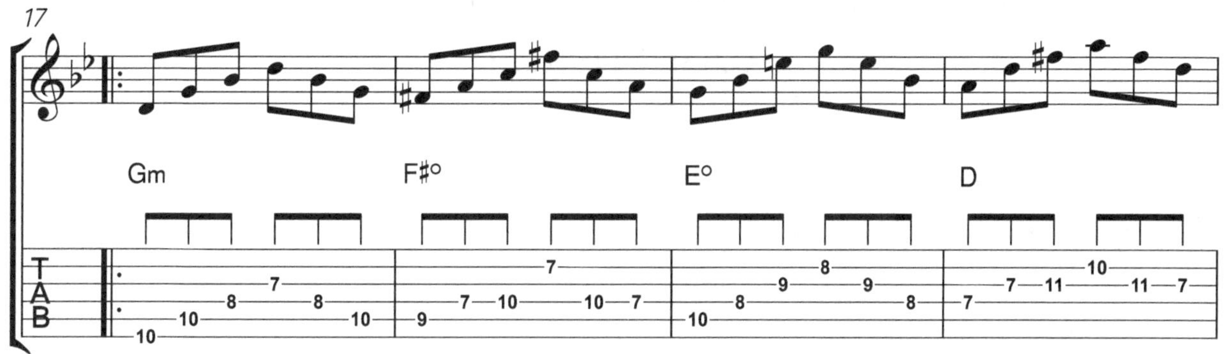
17
Gm
F♯o
Eo
D
TAB

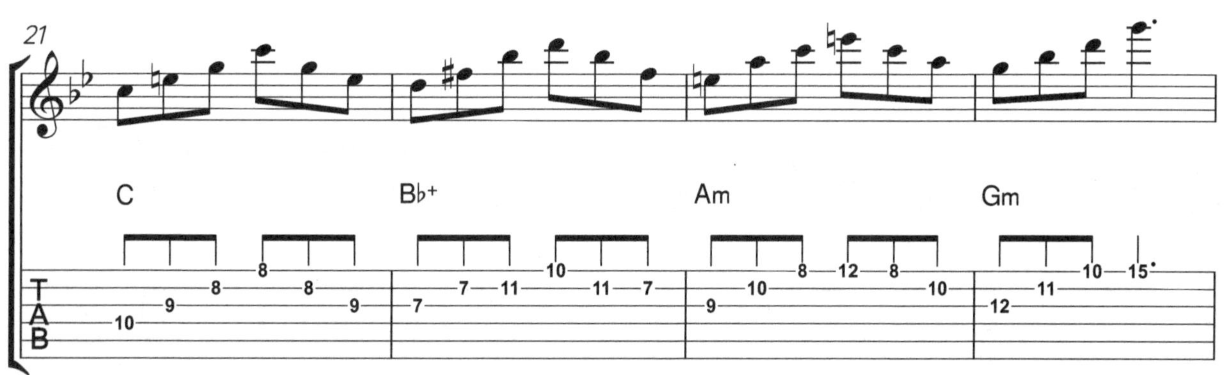
21
C
B♭+
Am
Gm
TAB

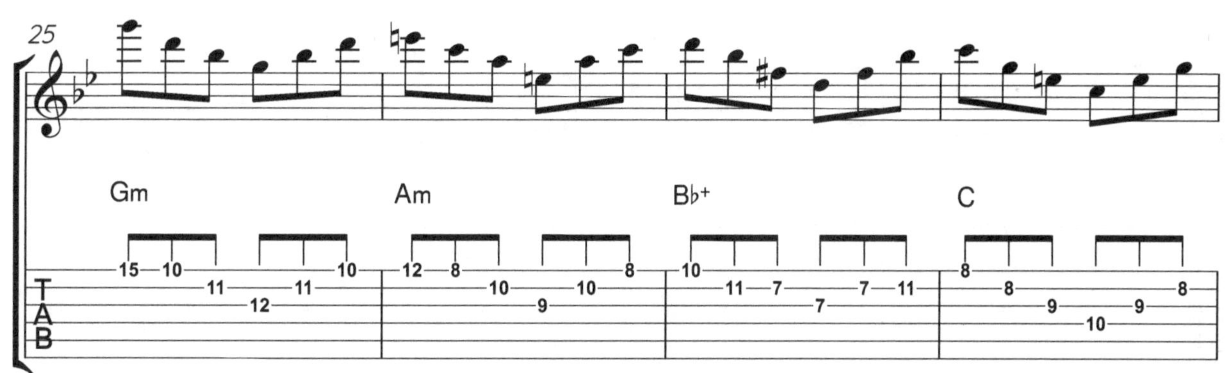
25
Gm
Am
B♭+
C
TAB

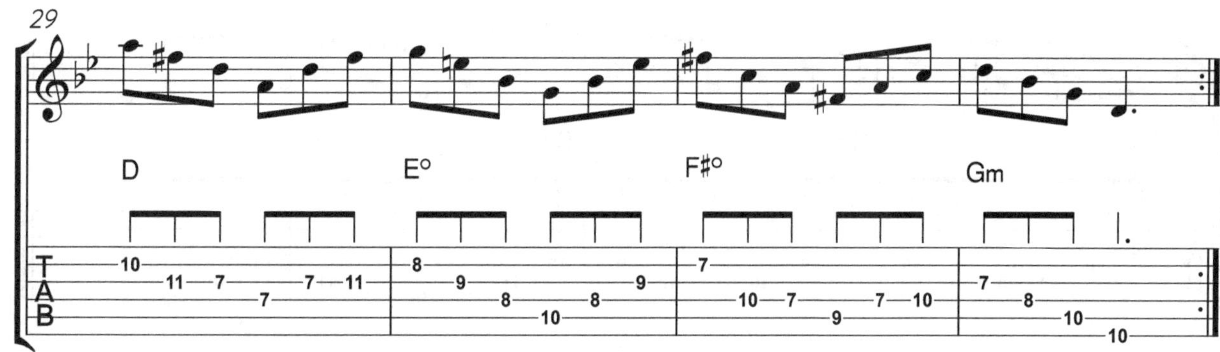
29
D
Eo
F♯o
Gm
TAB

# C Harmonic Major Scale 6/8 Sequence ①
# Root Position

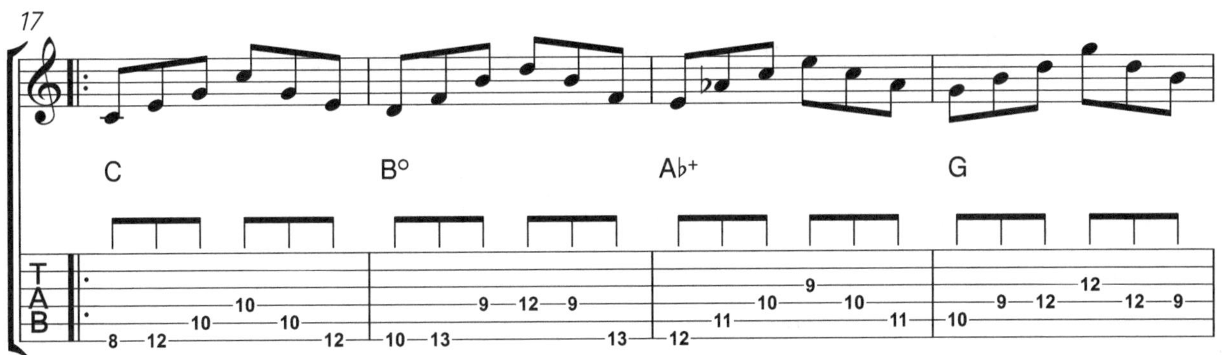
17
C
B°
A♭+
G

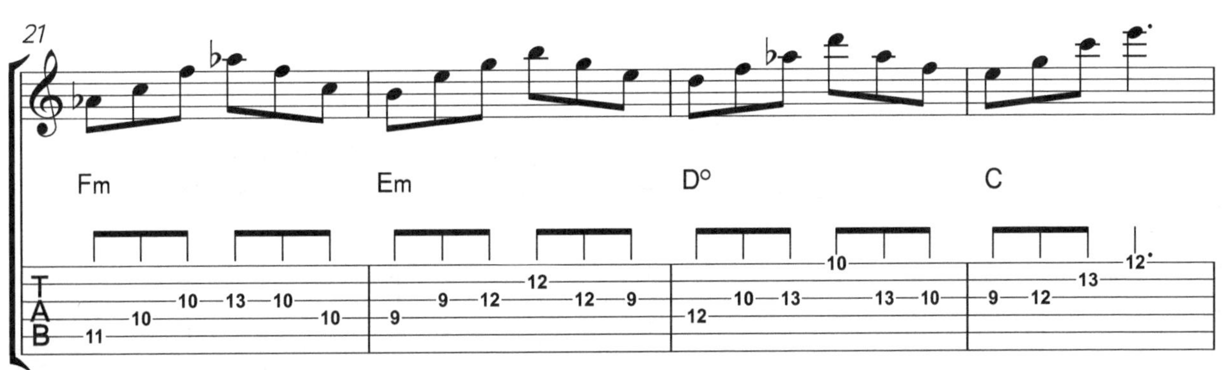
21
Fm
Em
D°
C

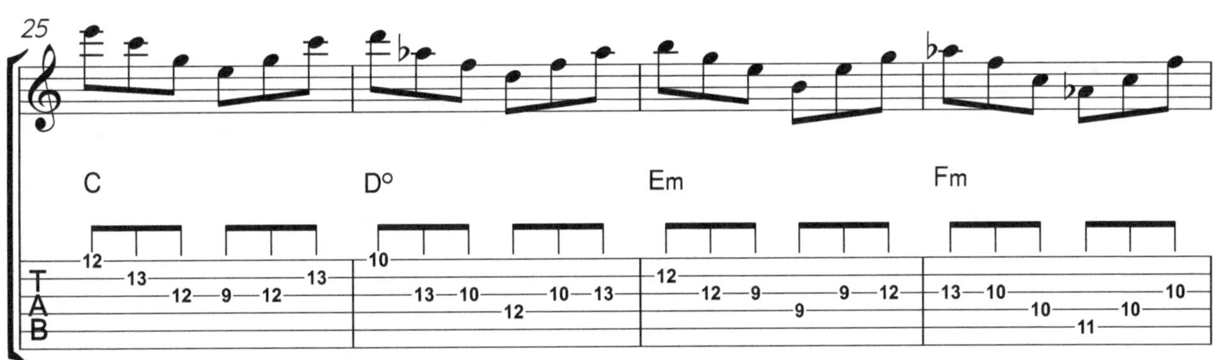
25
C
D°
Em
Fm

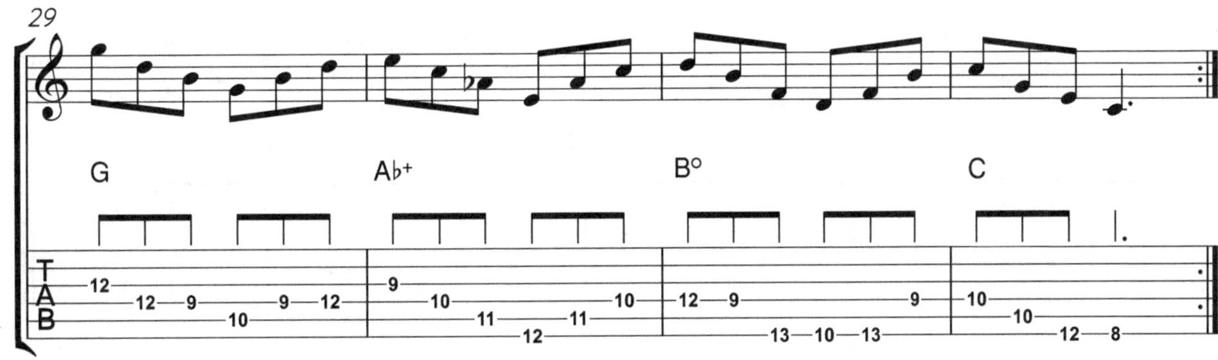
29
G
A♭+
B°
C

# C Harmonic Major Scale 6/8 Sequence ①
# Root Position (Alternative Position)

17
C
B°
A♭+
G
TAB

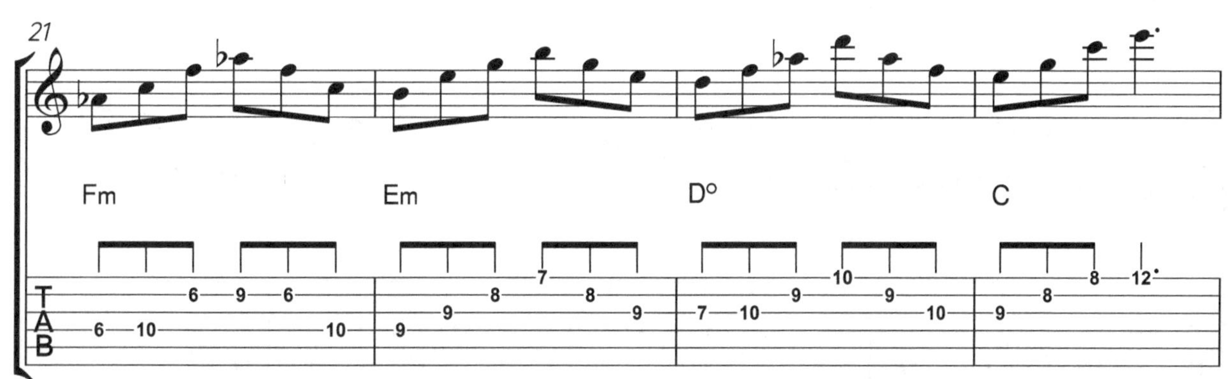
21
Fm
Em
D°
C
TAB

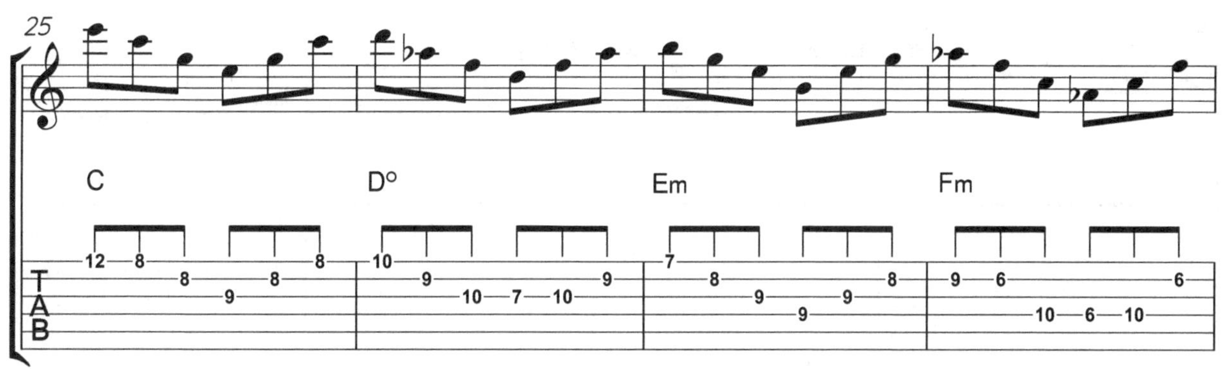
25
C
D°
Em
Fm
TAB

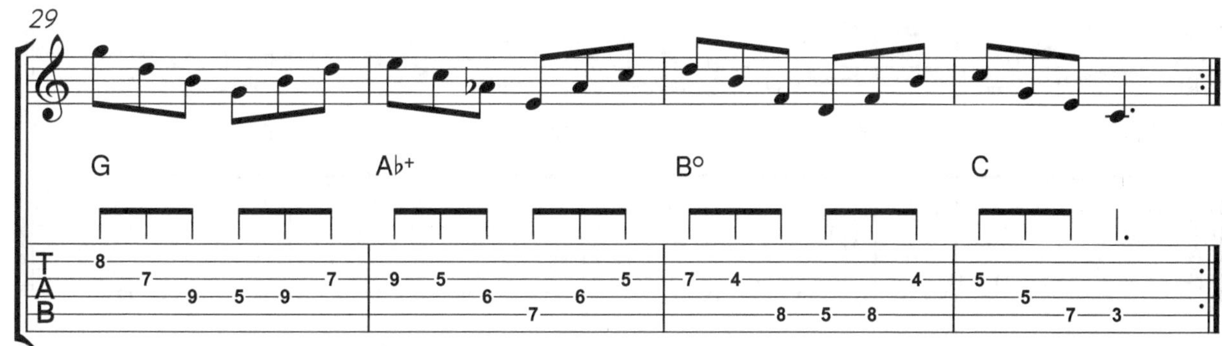
29
G
A♭+
B°
C
TAB

# C Harmonic Major Scale 6/8 Sequence ①
# First Inversion

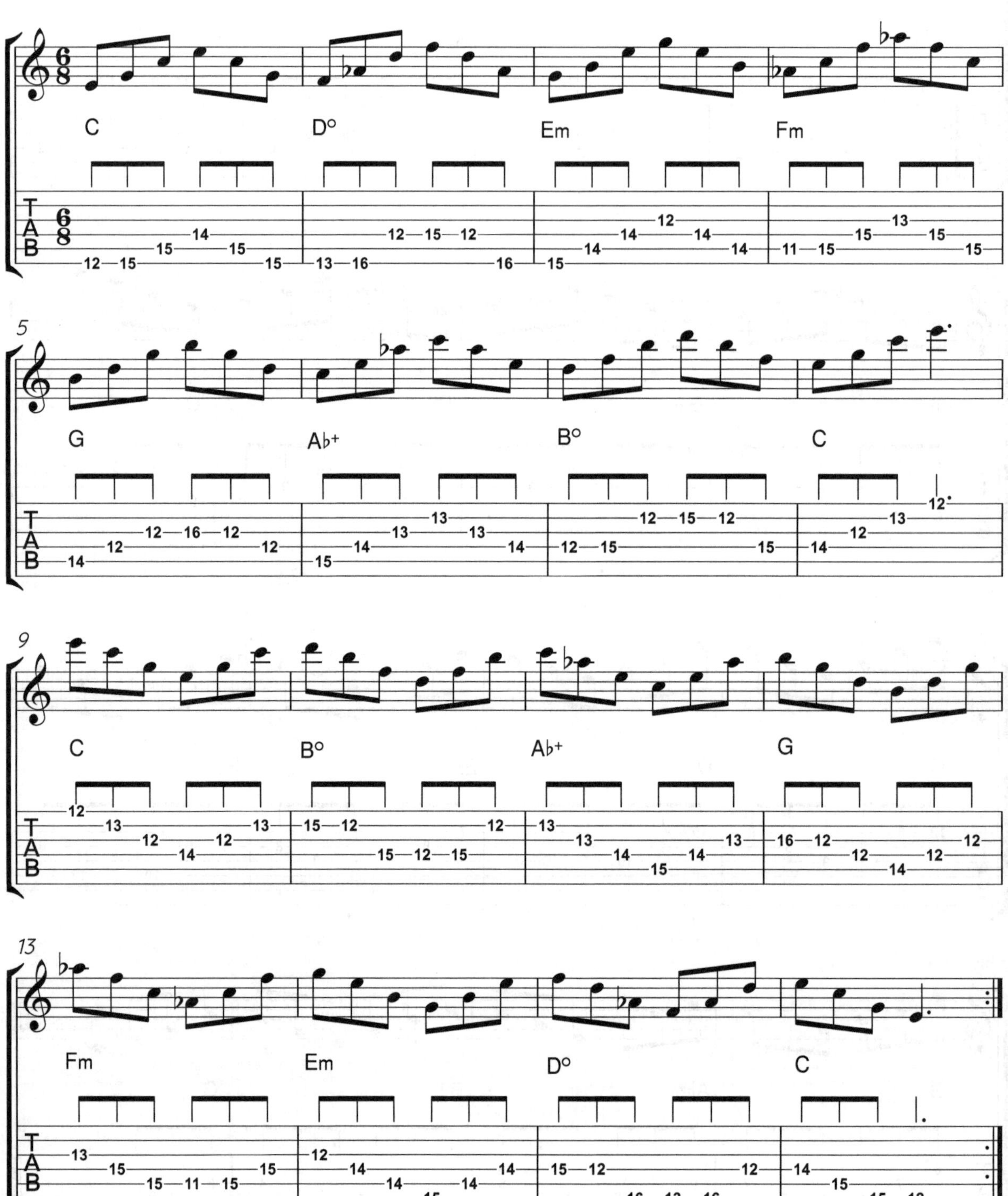

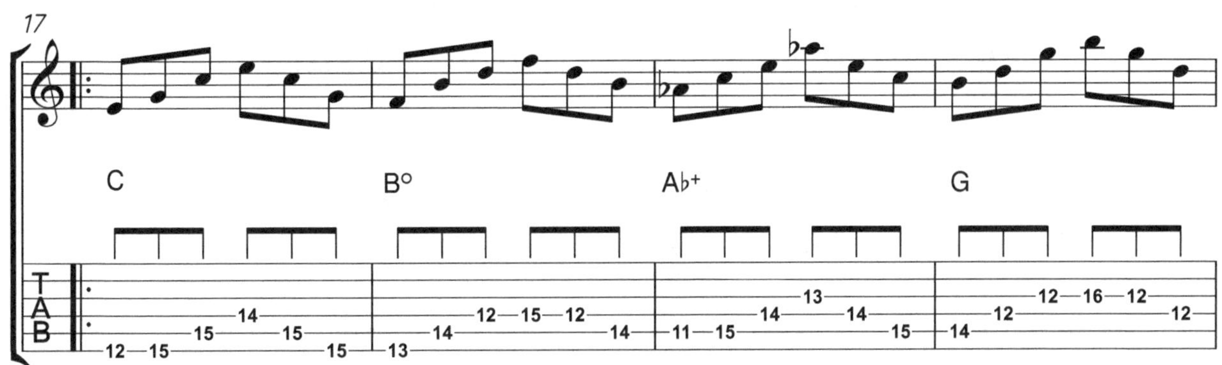
17
C
B°
A♭+
G
TAB

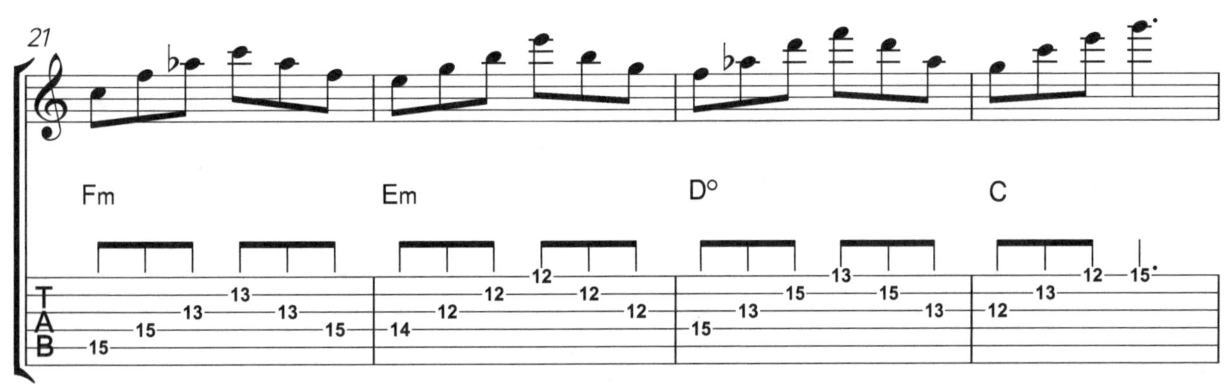
21
Fm
Em
D°
C
TAB

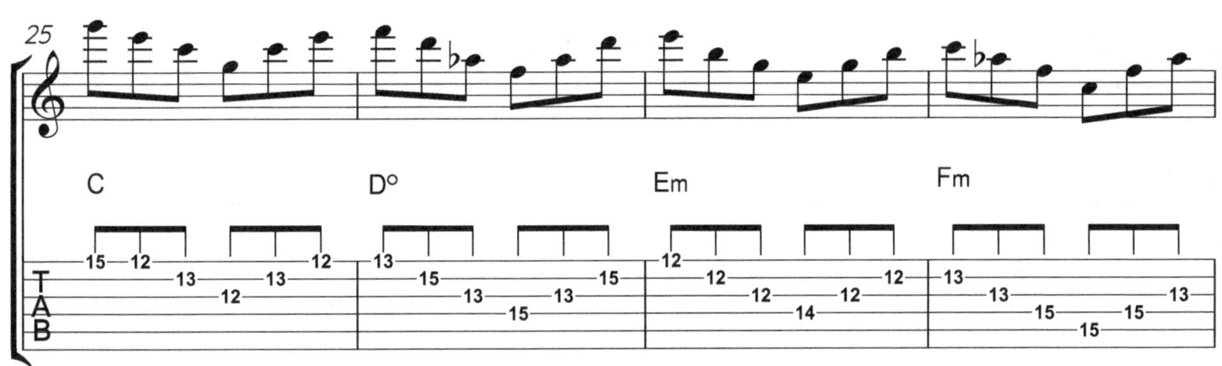
25
C
D°
Em
Fm
TAB

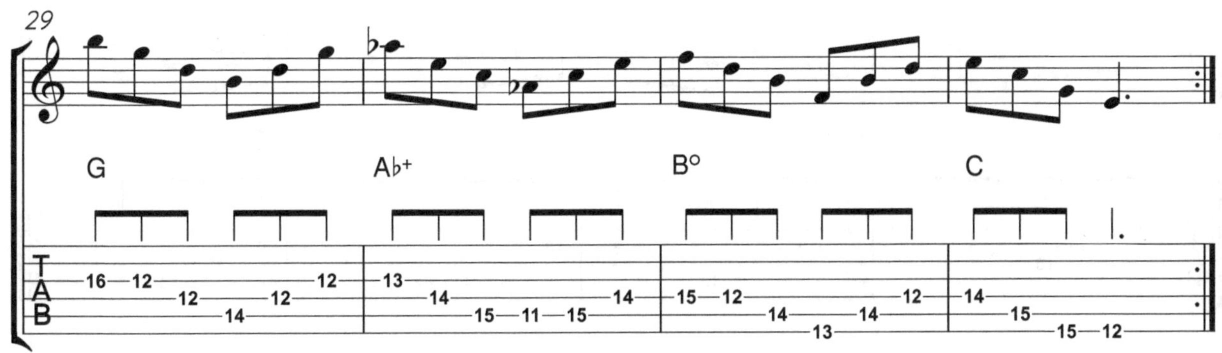
29
G
A♭+
B°
C
TAB

# C Harmonic Major Scale 6/8 Sequence ①
# First Inversion (Alternative Position)

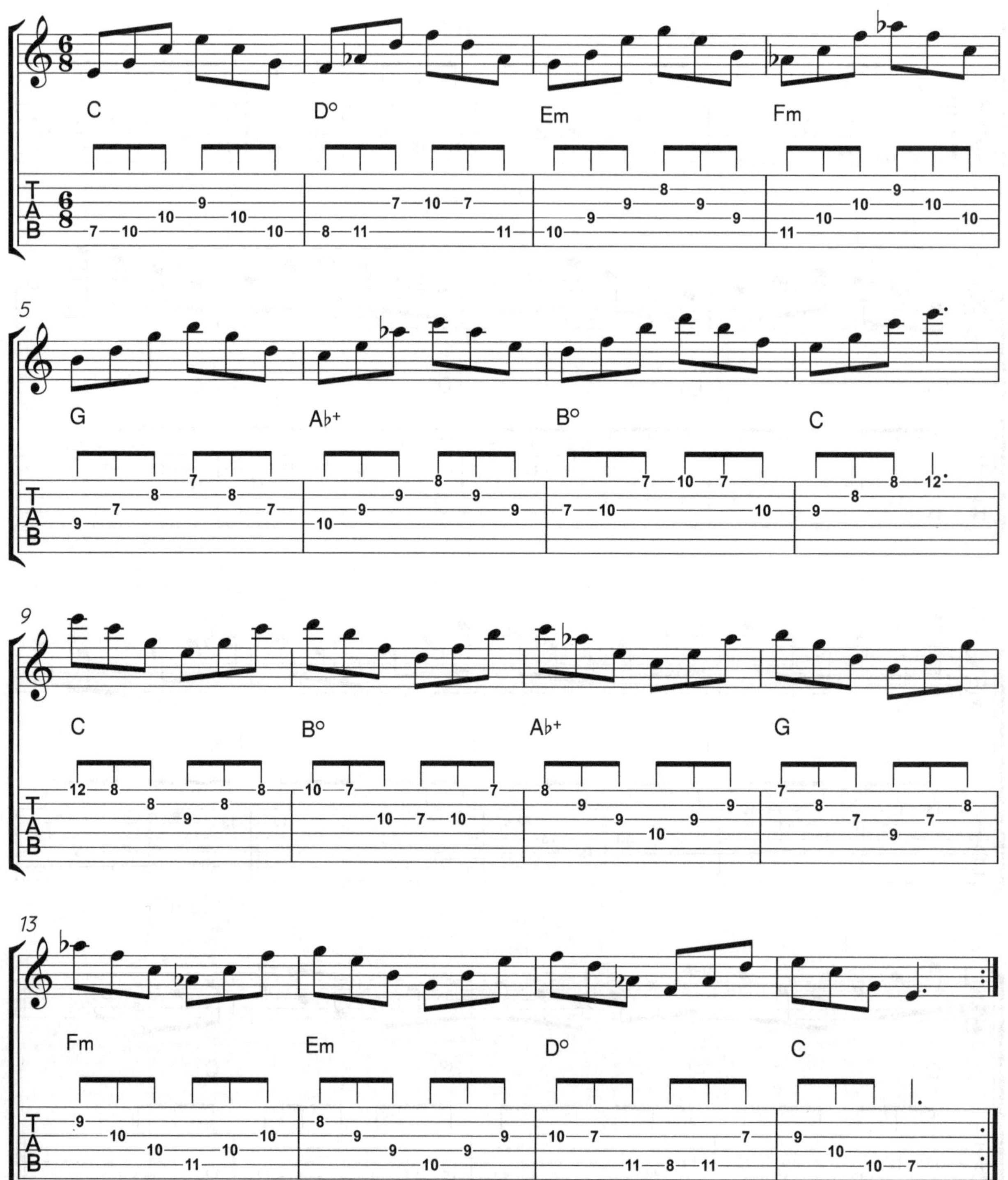

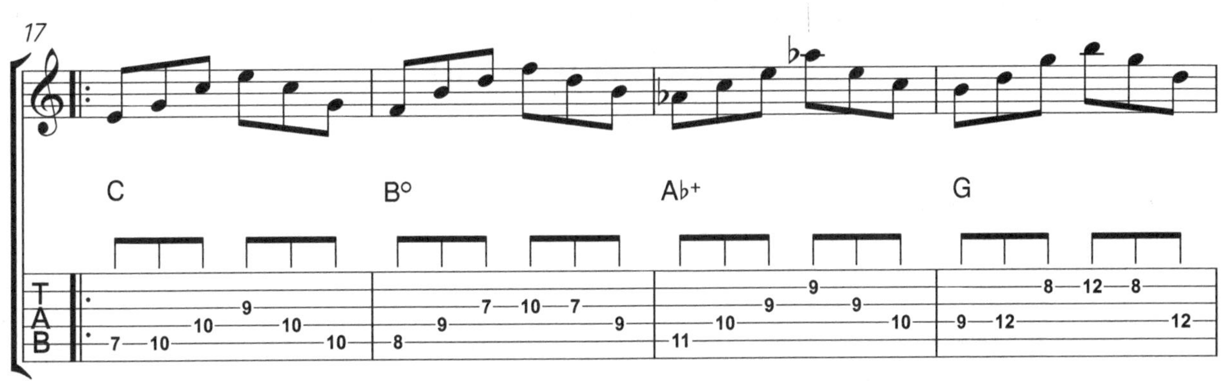
17
C
B°
A♭+
G

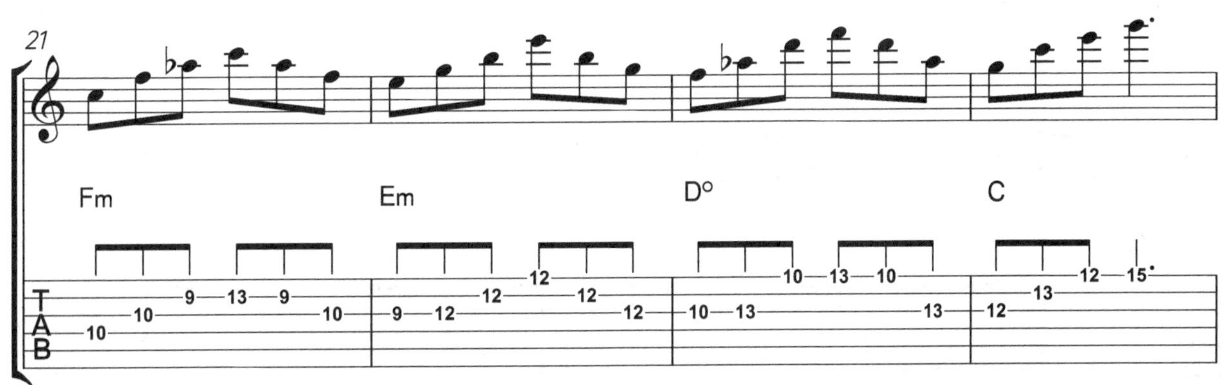
21
Fm
Em
D°
C

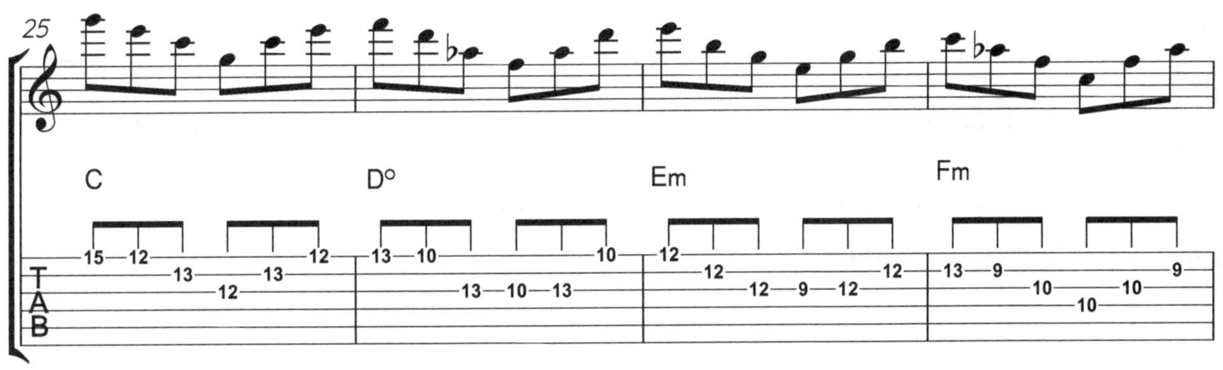
25
C
D°
Em
Fm

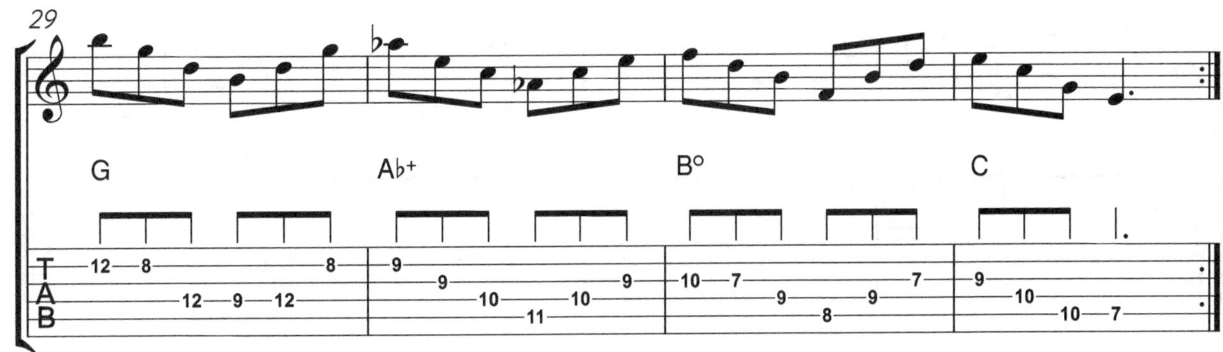
29
G
A♭+
B°
C

# C Harmonic Major Scale 6/8 Sequence ①
## Second Inversion

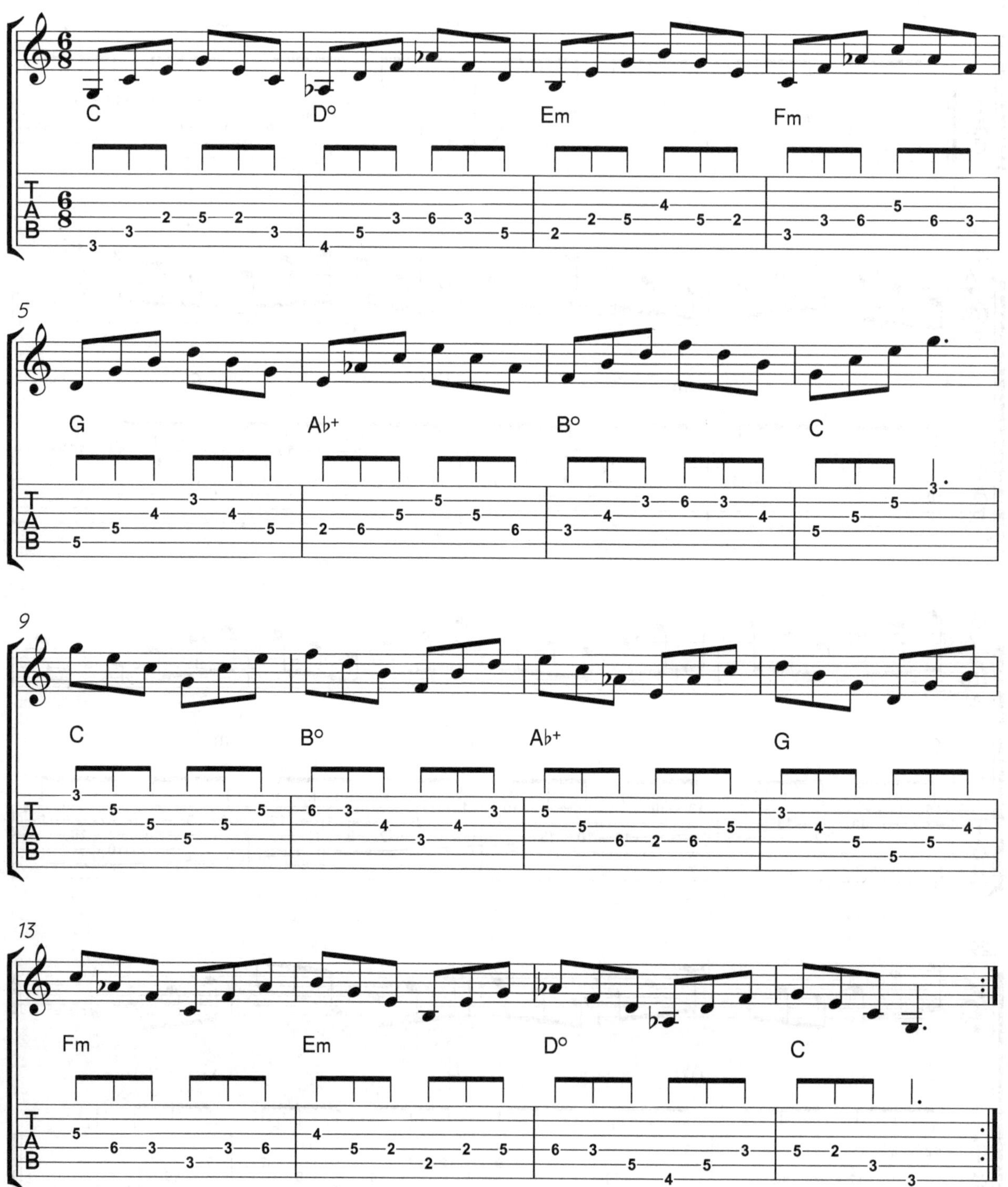

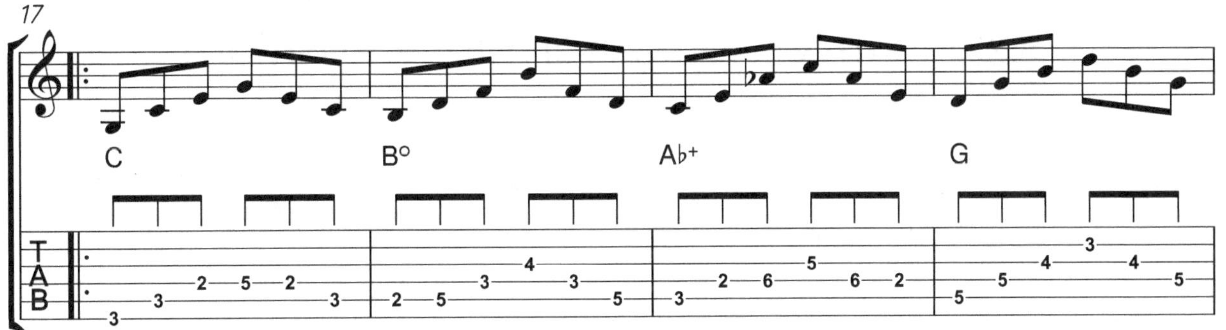
17
C
B°
A♭+
G

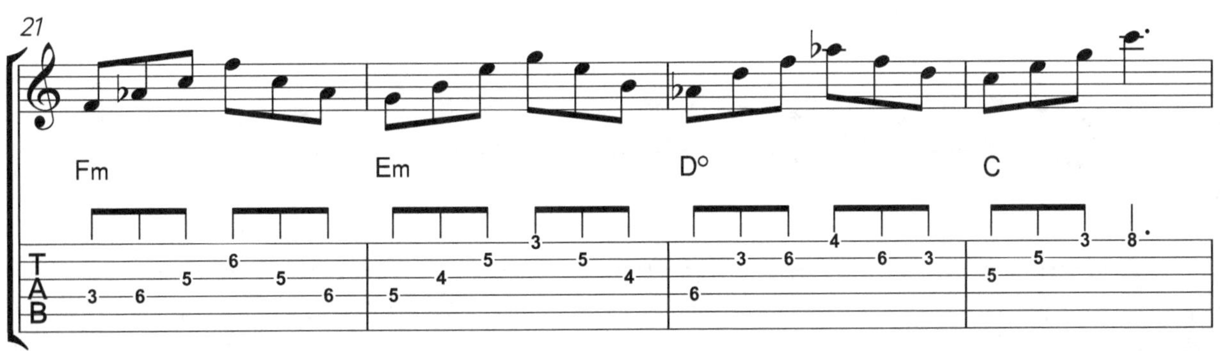
21
Fm
Em
D°
C

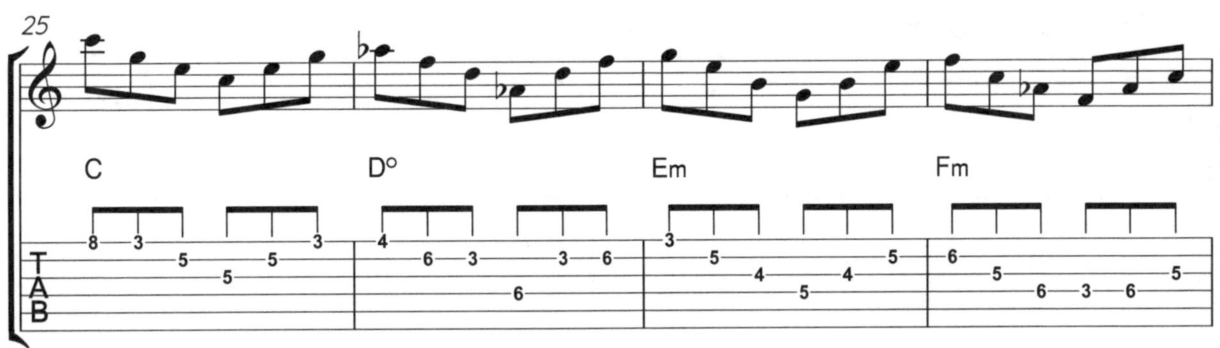
25
C
D°
Em
Fm

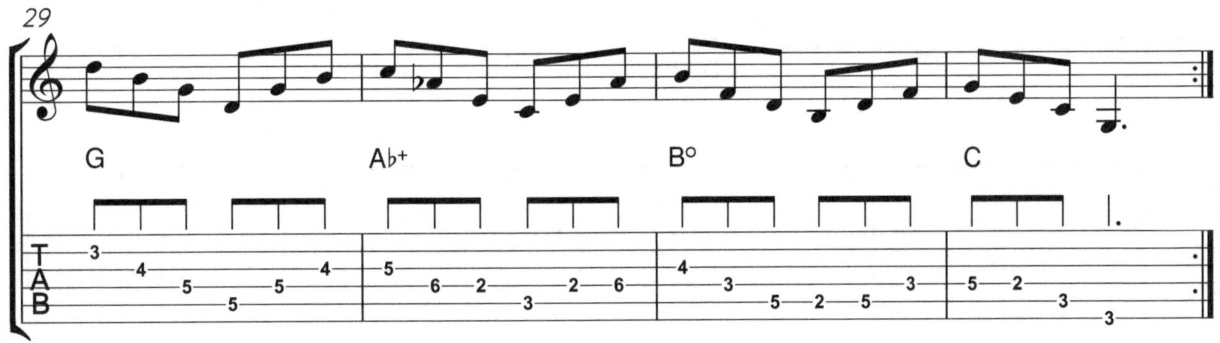
29
G
A♭+
B°
C

# C Harmonic Major Scale 6/8 Sequence ①
# Second Inversion (Alternative Position)

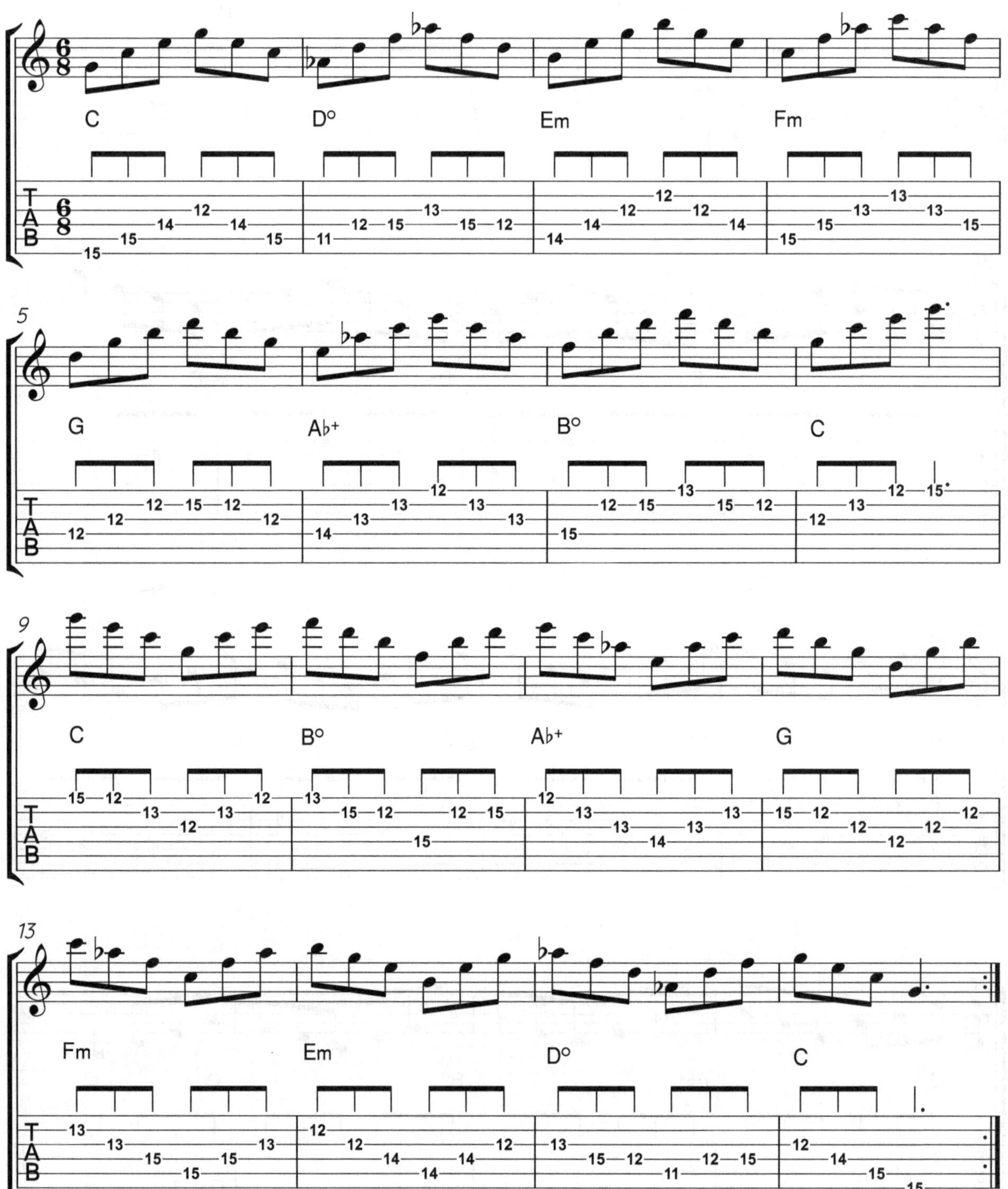

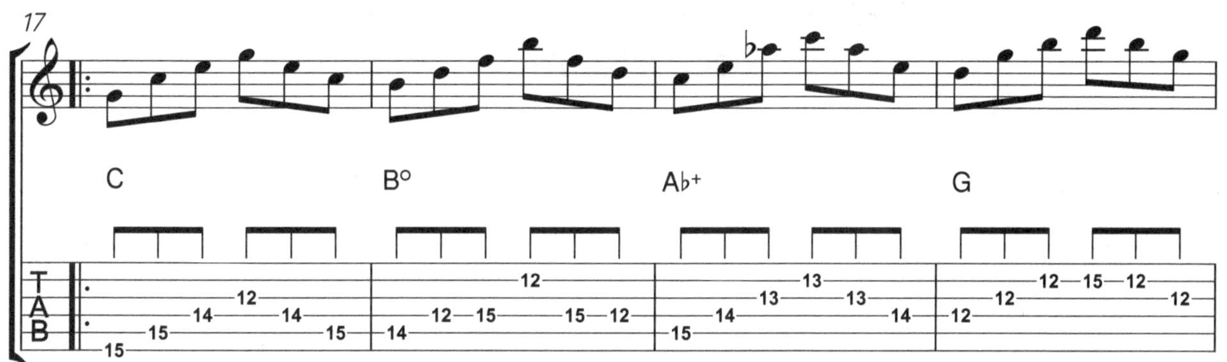
17
C
B°
A♭+
G
T
A
B

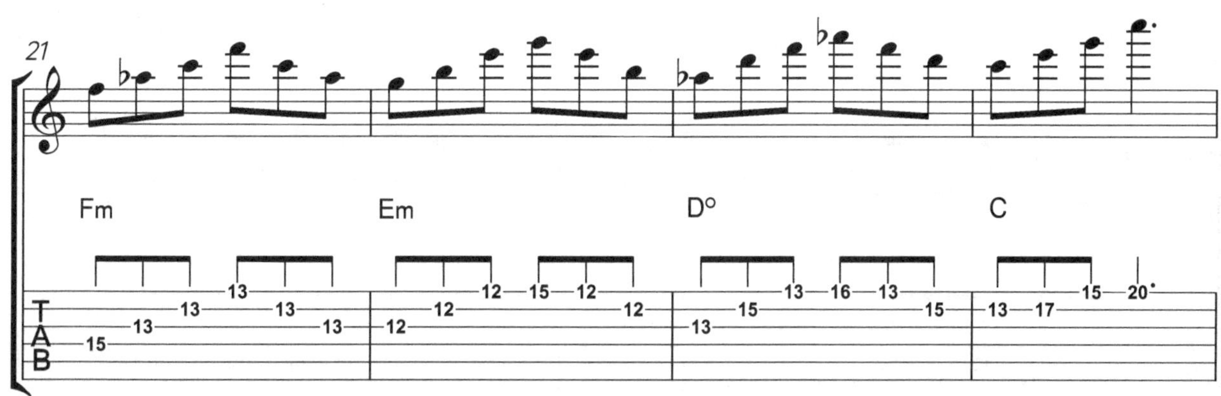
21
Fm
Em
D°
C
T
A
B

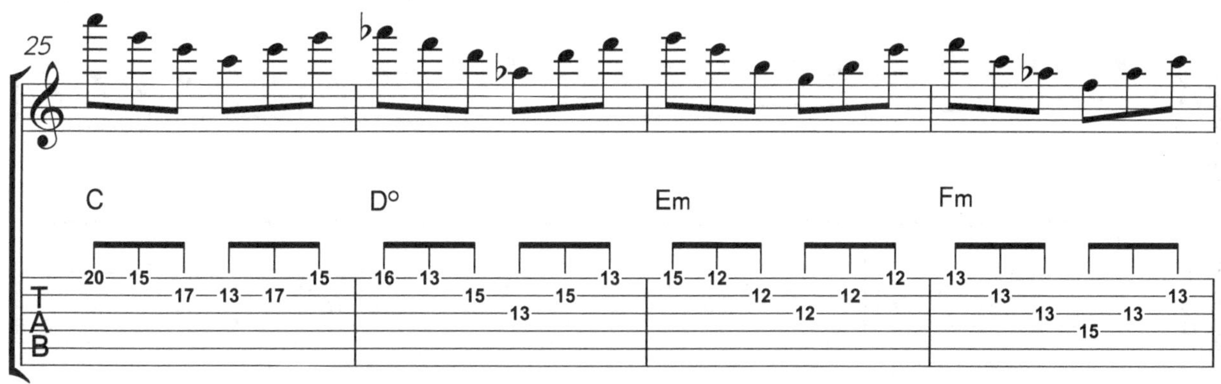
25
C
D°
Em
Fm
T
A
B

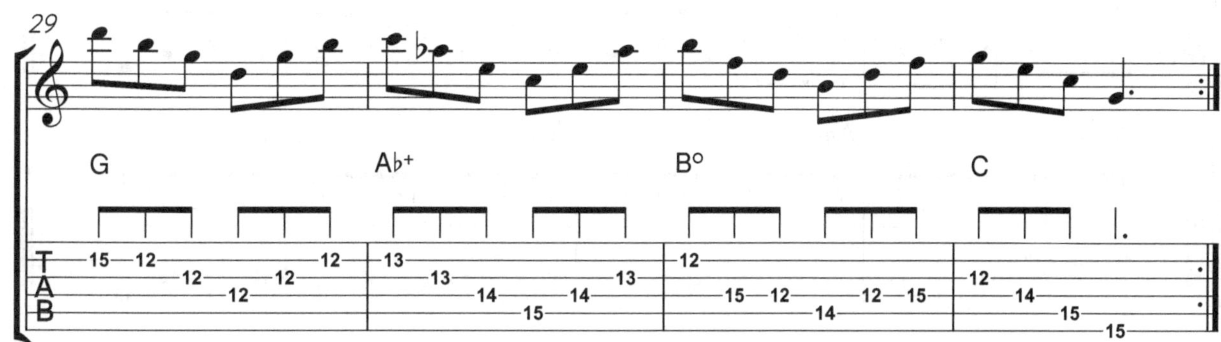
29
G
A♭+
B°
C
T
A
B

# F Major Scale 6/8 Sequence ②
## Root Position

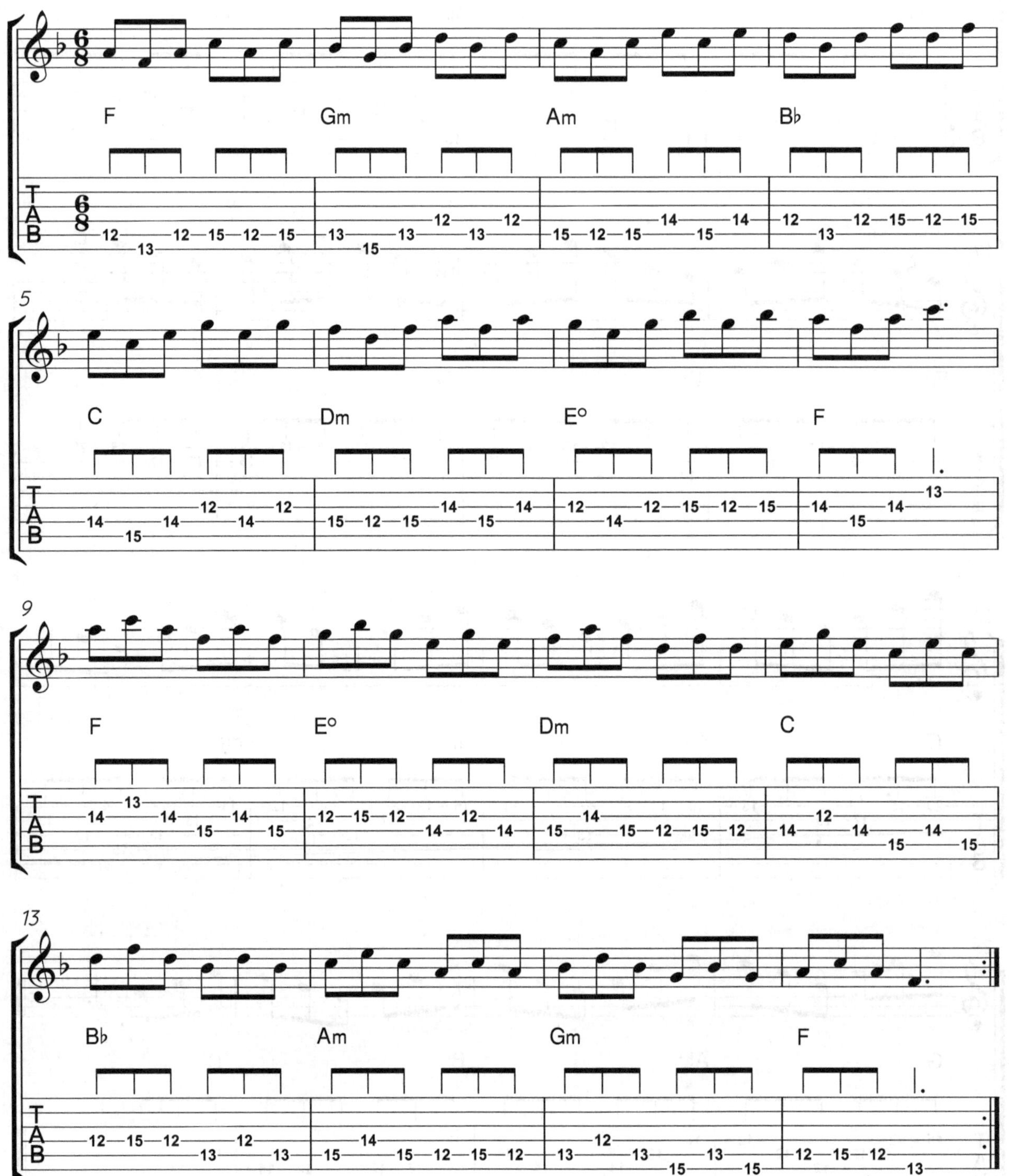

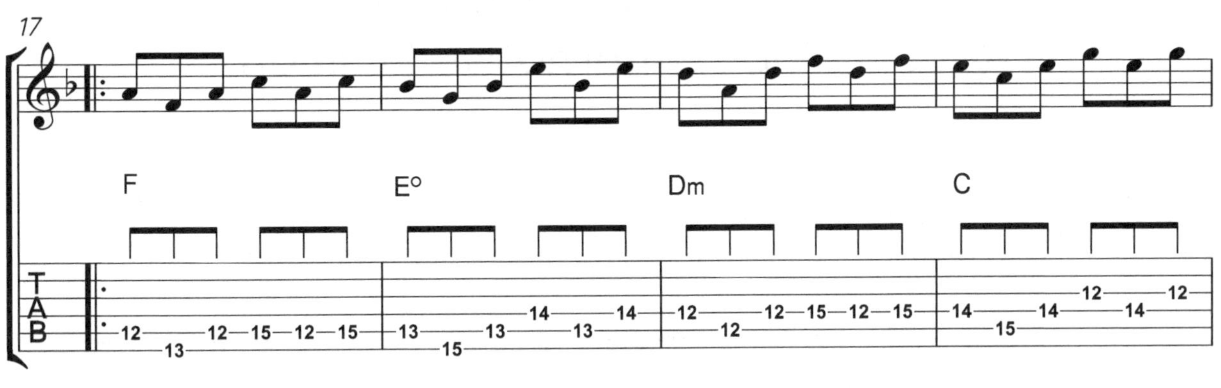
17
F
E°
Dm
C
TAB

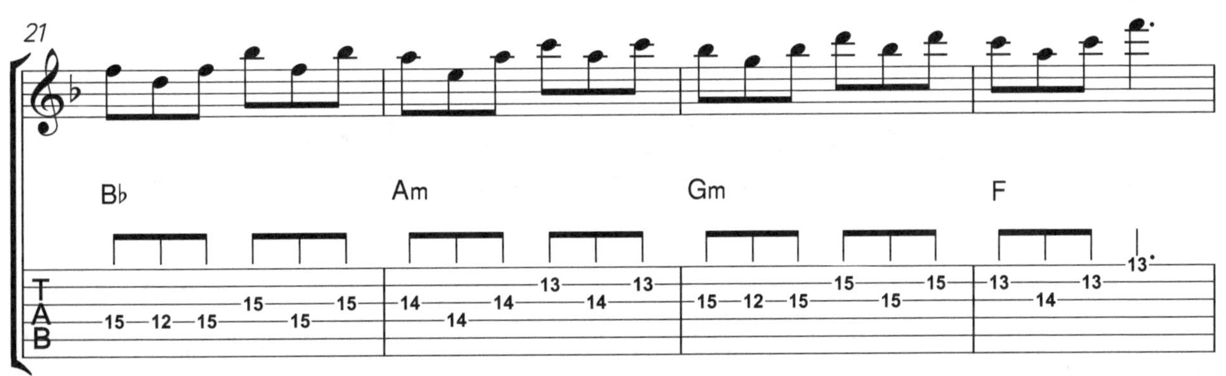
21
B♭
Am
Gm
F
TAB

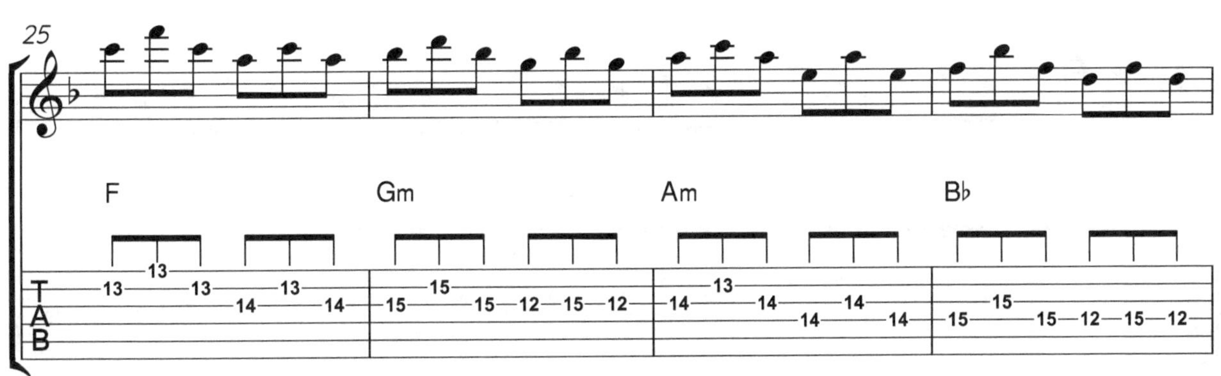
25
F
Gm
Am
B♭
TAB

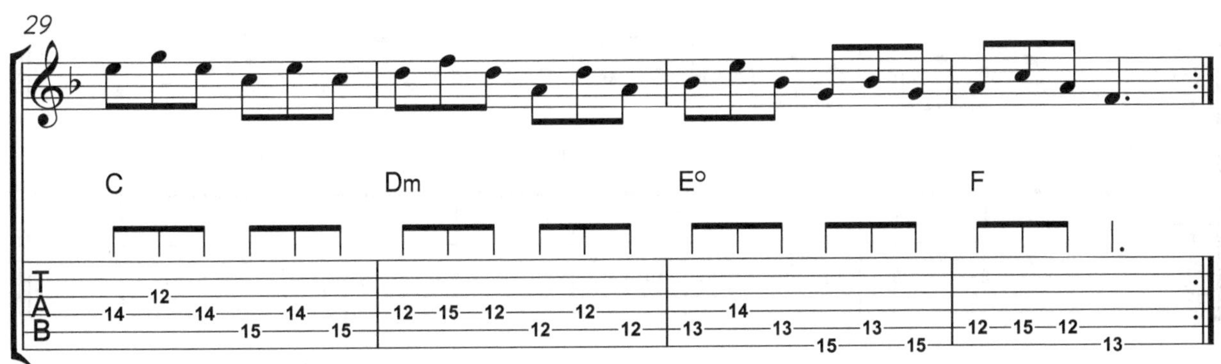
29
C
Dm
E°
F
TAB

# F Major Scale 6/8 Sequence ②
## Root Position (Alternative Position)

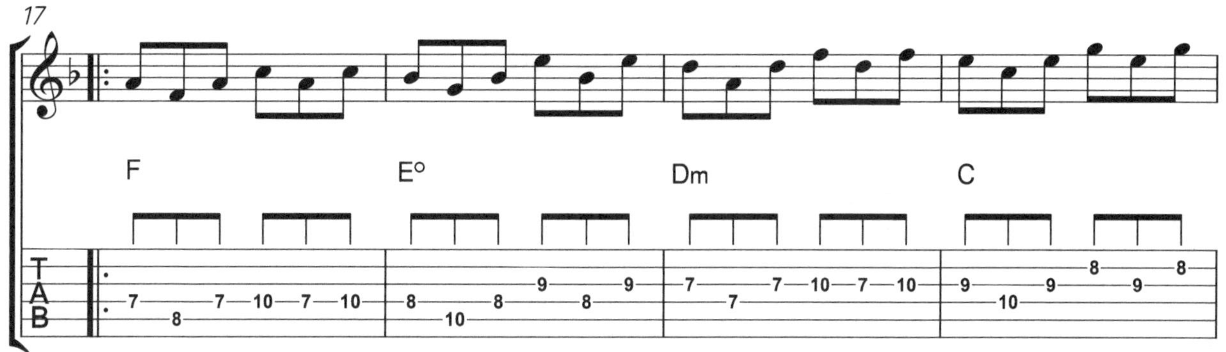
17
F
E°
Dm
C
TAB

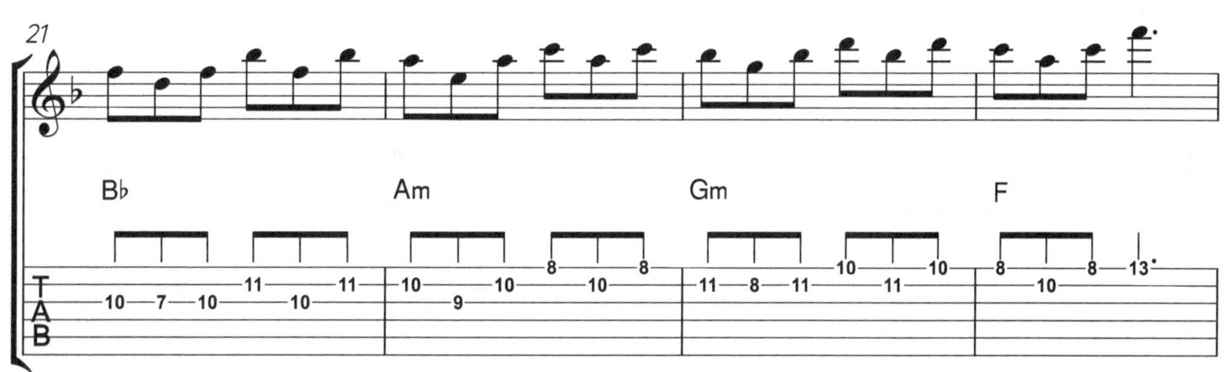
21
B♭
Am
Gm
F
TAB

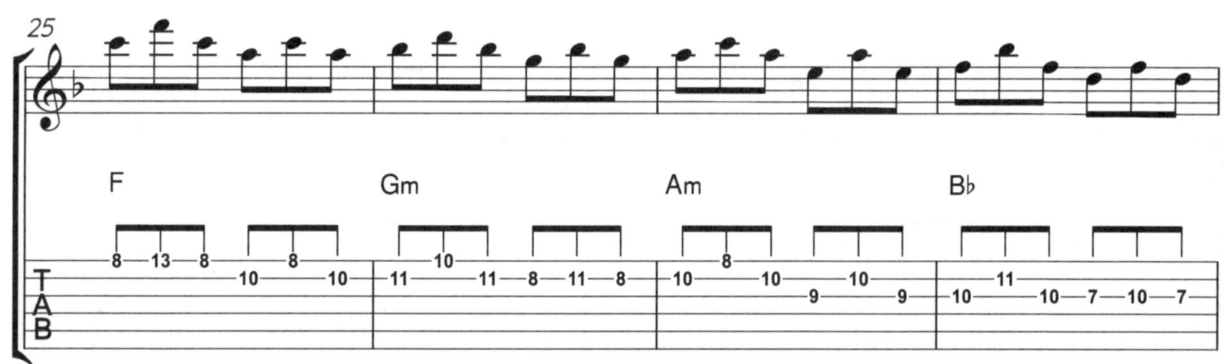
25
F
Gm
Am
B♭
TAB

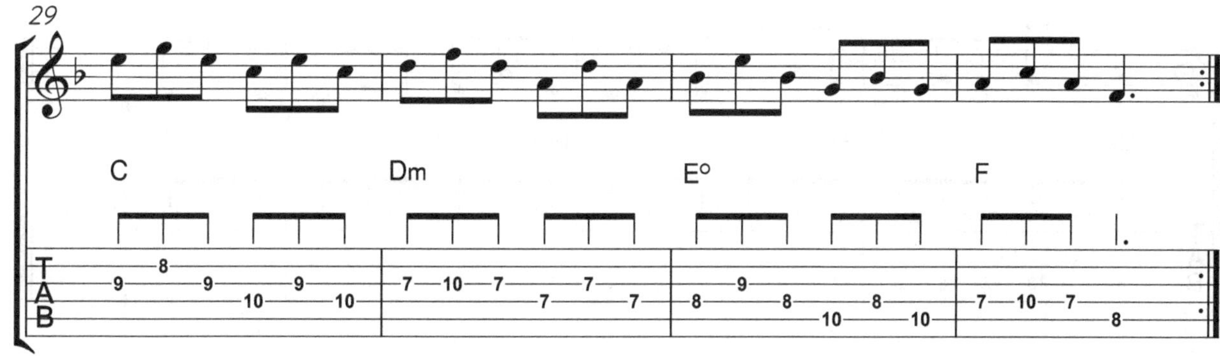
29
C
Dm
E°
F
TAB

# F Major Scale 6/8 Sequence ②
## First Inversion

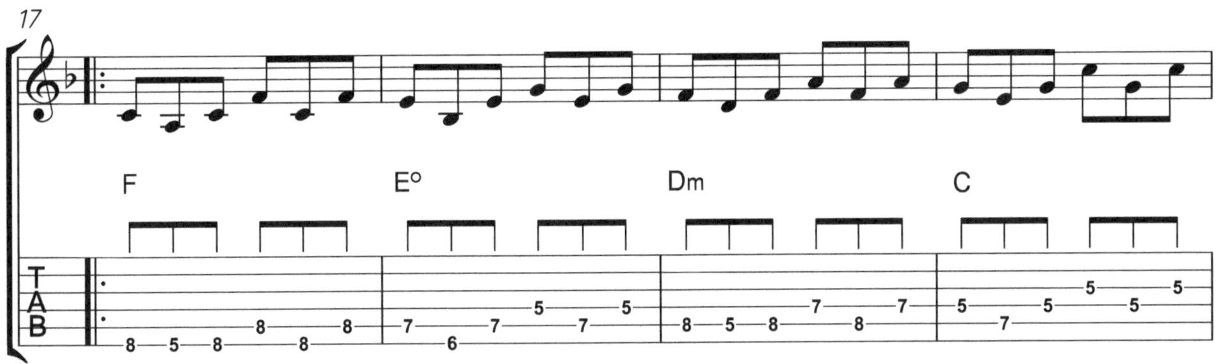
17
F
E°
Dm
C
TAB
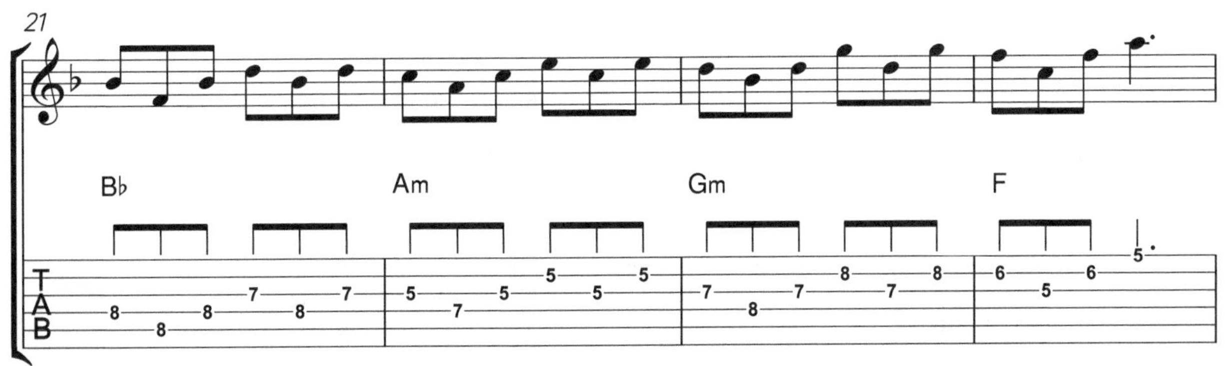
21
B♭
Am
Gm
F
TAB

25
F
Gm
Am
B♭
TAB
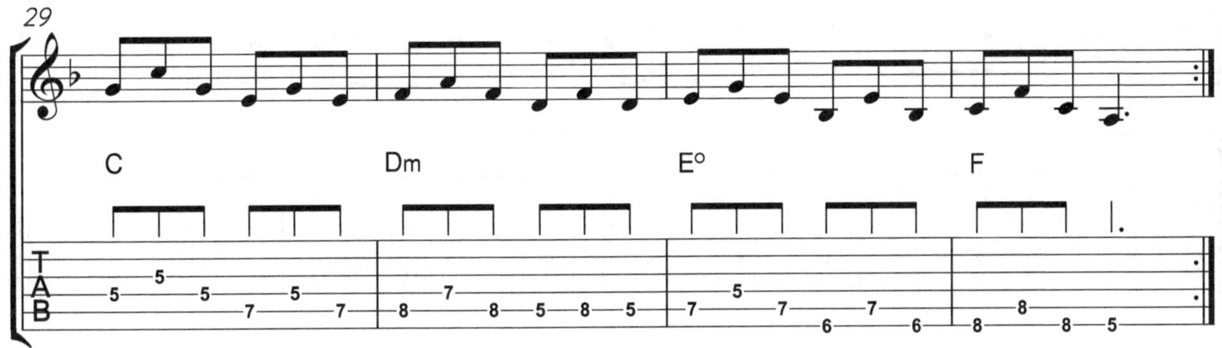
29
C
Dm
E°
F
TAB

# F Major Scale 6/8 Sequence ②
# First Inversion (Alternative Position)

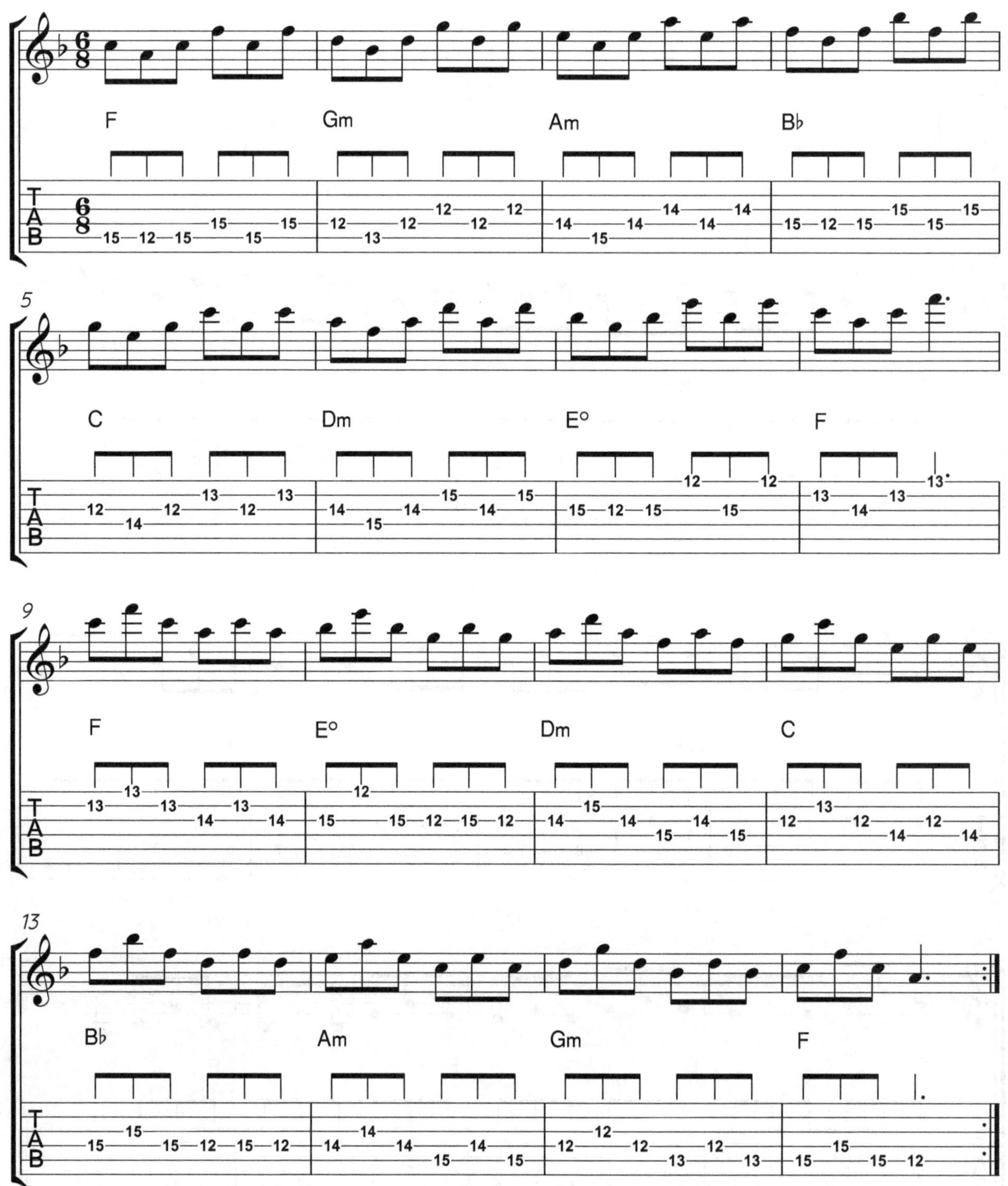

17
F
E°
Dm
C
T
A
B

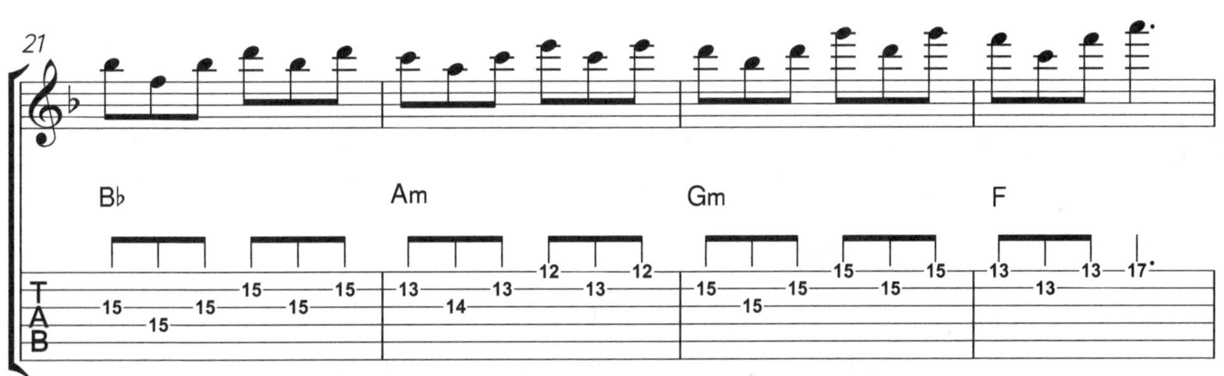
21
B♭
Am
Gm
F
T
A
B

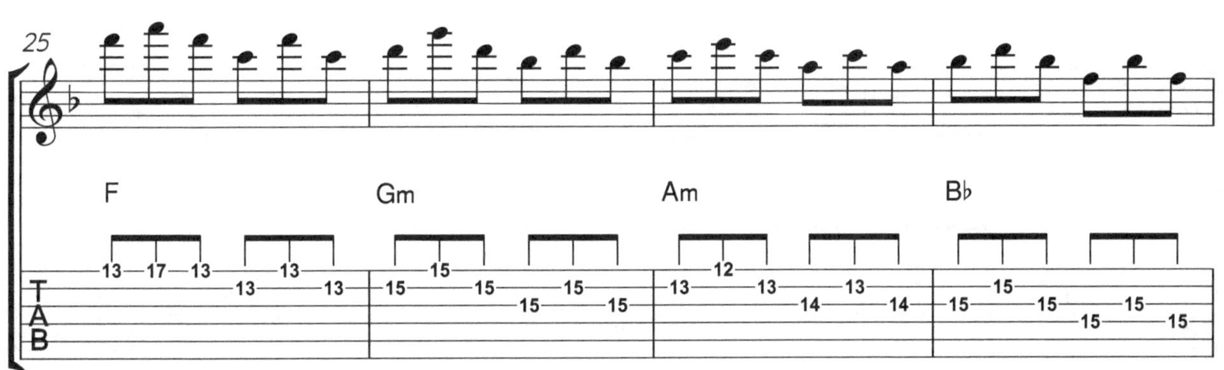
25
F
Gm
Am
B♭
T
A
B

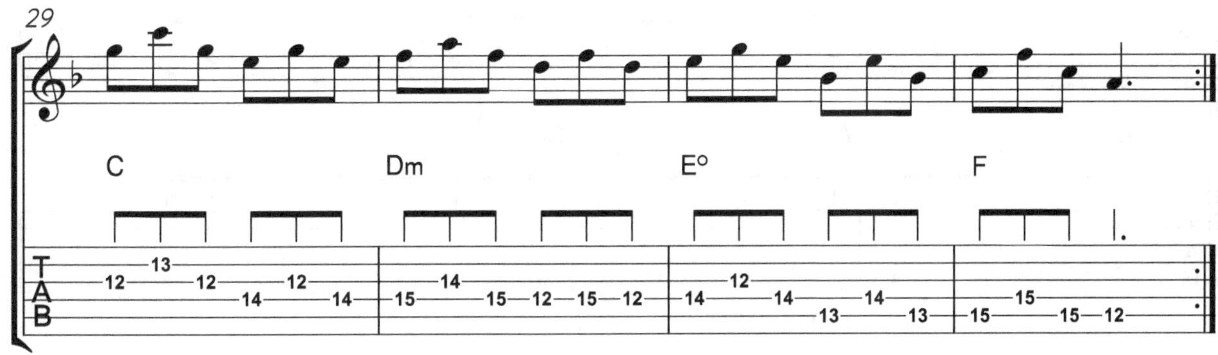
29
C
Dm
E°
F
T
A
B

# F Major Scale 6/8 Sequence ②
# Second Inversion

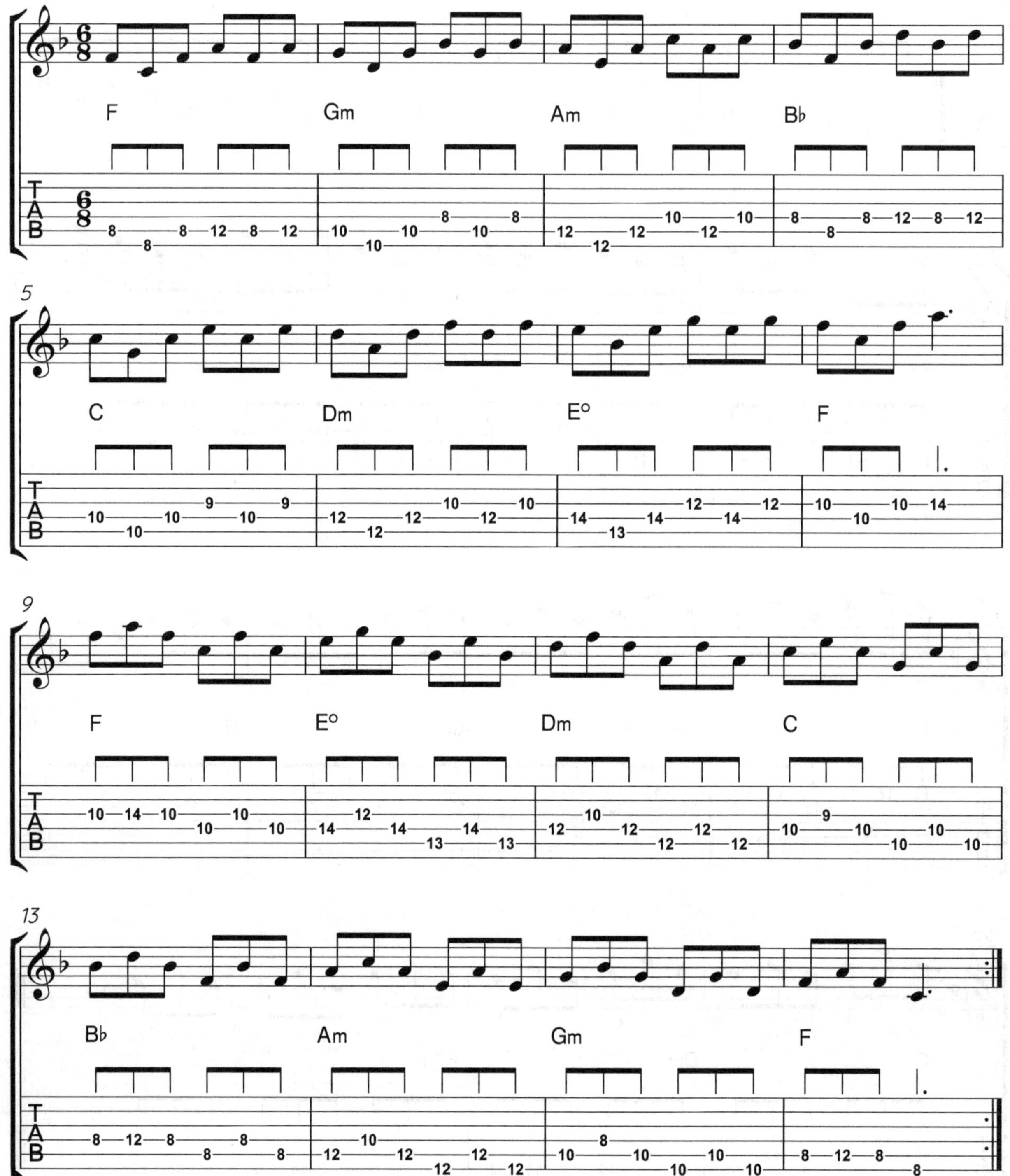

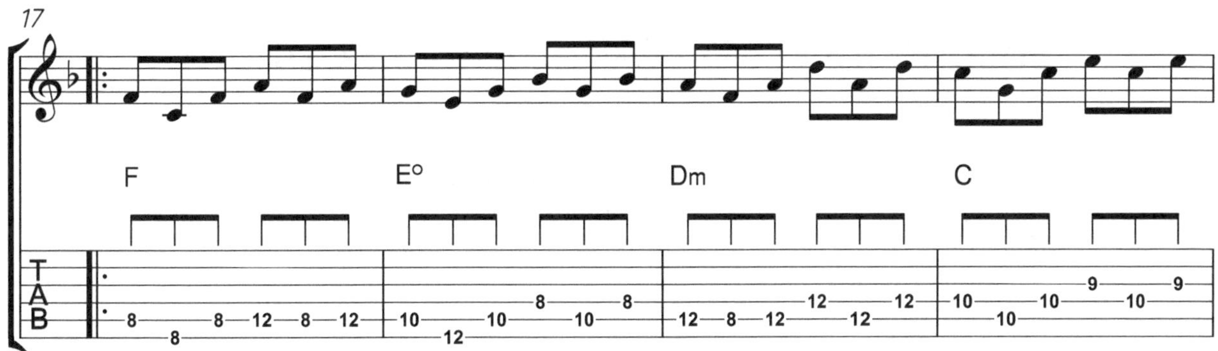
17
F
E°
Dm
C
TAB

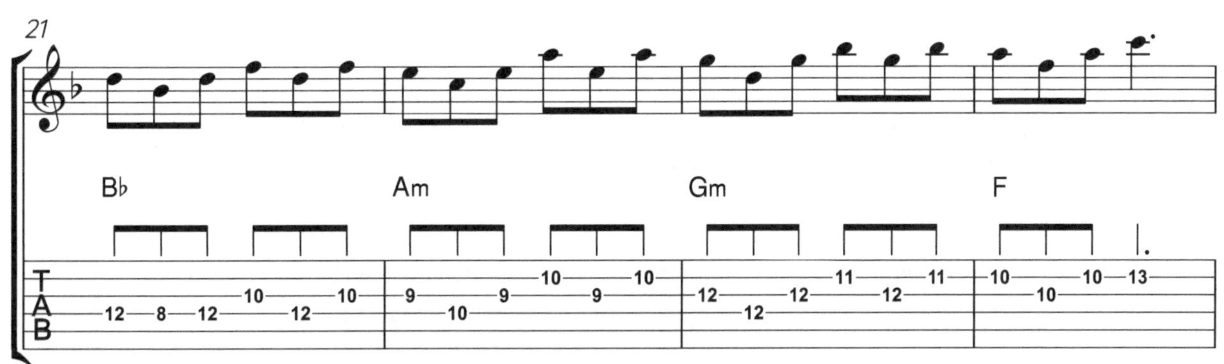
21
B♭
Am
Gm
F
TAB

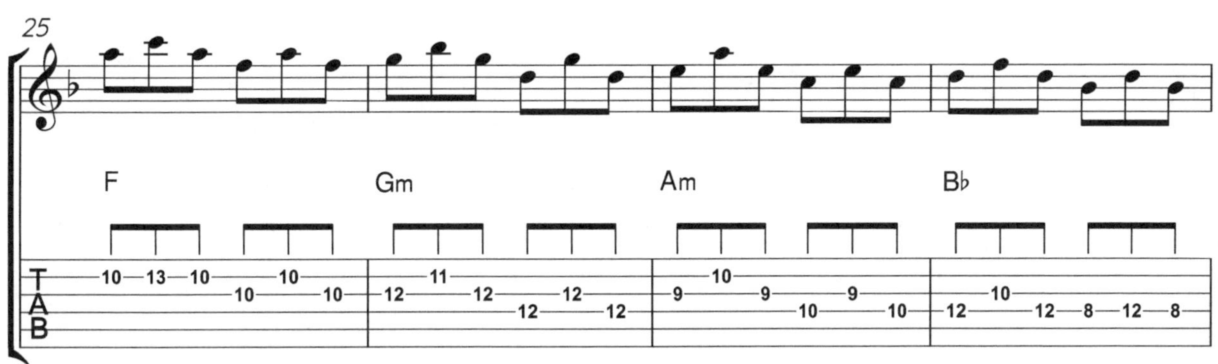
25
F
Gm
Am
B♭
TAB

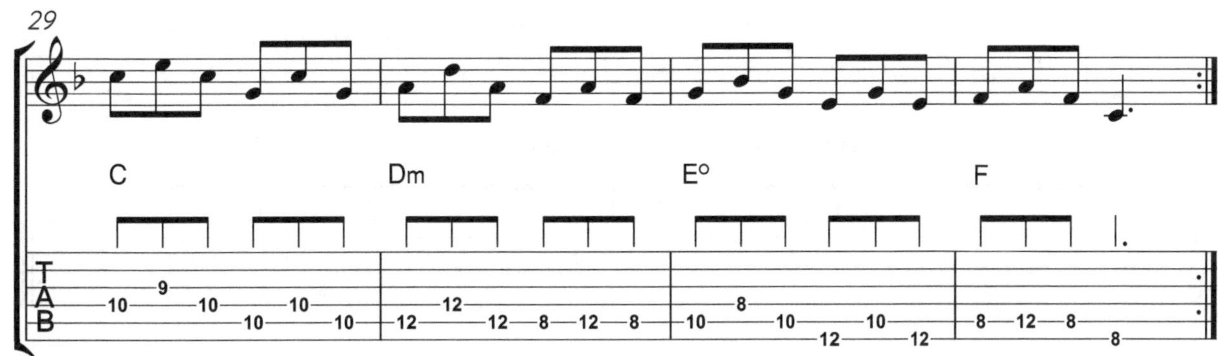
29
C
Dm
E°
F
TAB

# F Major Scale 6/8 Sequence ②
# Second Inversion (Alternative Position)

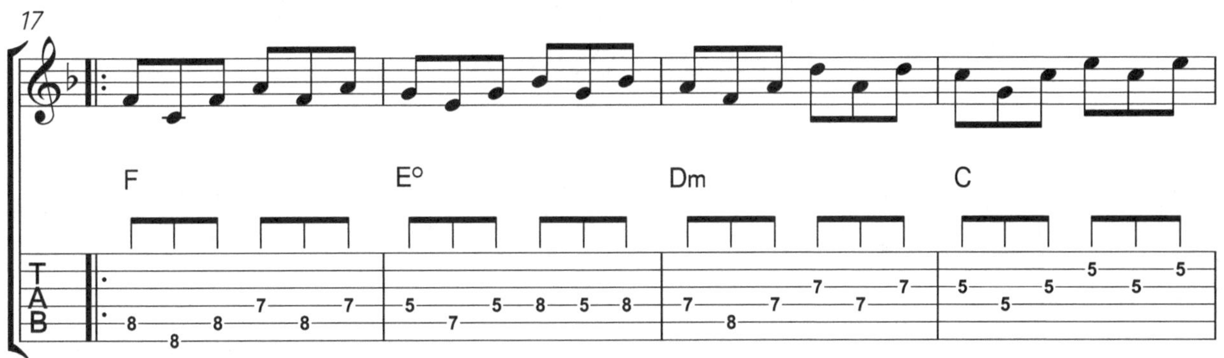
17
F
E°
Dm
C
T
A
B

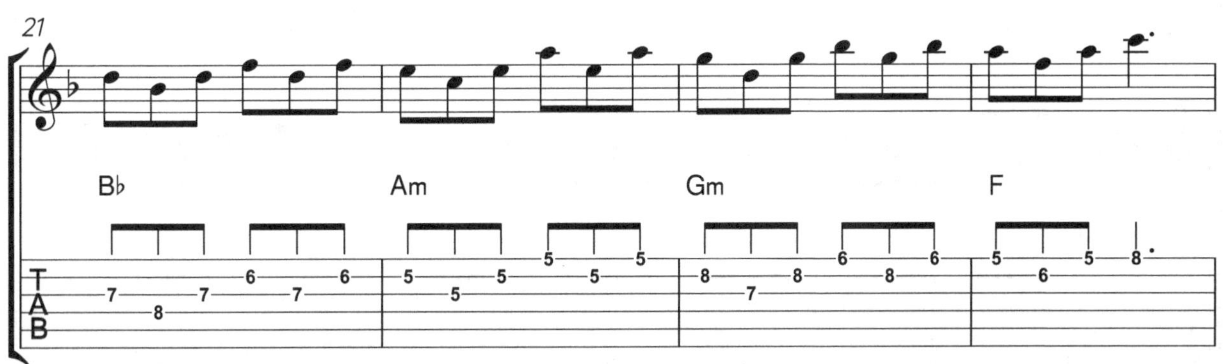
21
B♭
Am
Gm
F
T
A
B

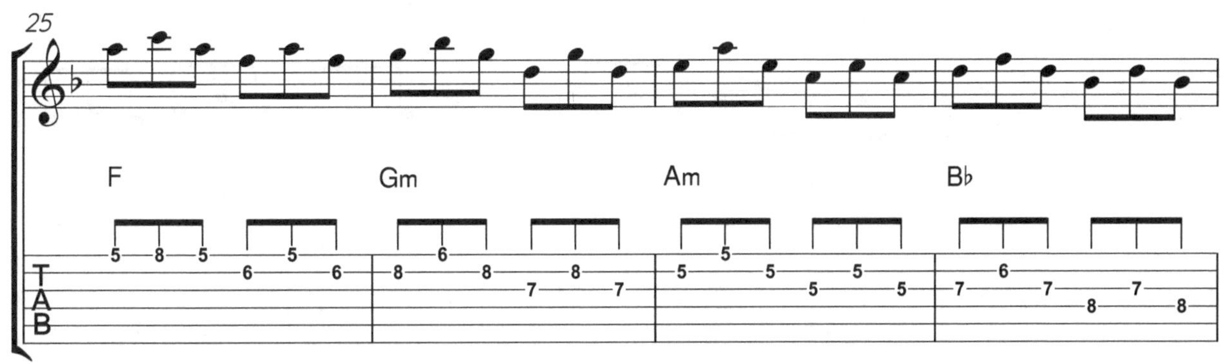
25
F
Gm
Am
B♭
T
A
B

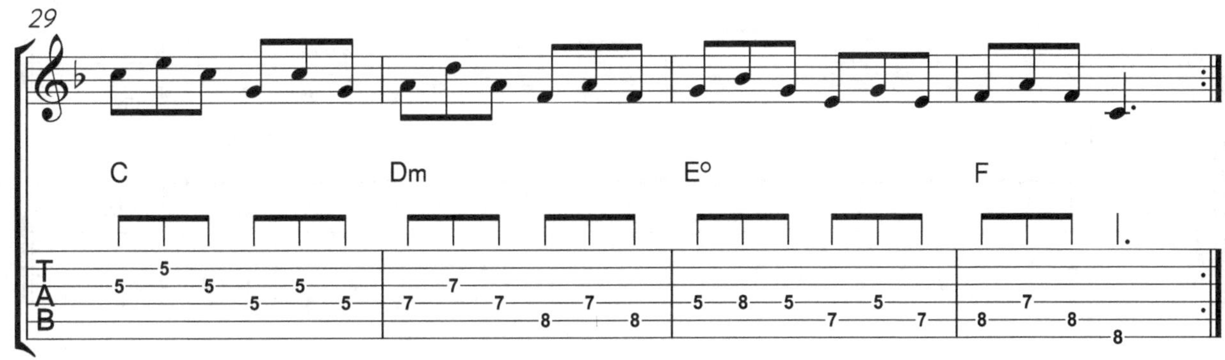
29
C
Dm
E°
F
T
A
B

# B ♭ Minor Scale 6/8 Sequence ②
# Root Position

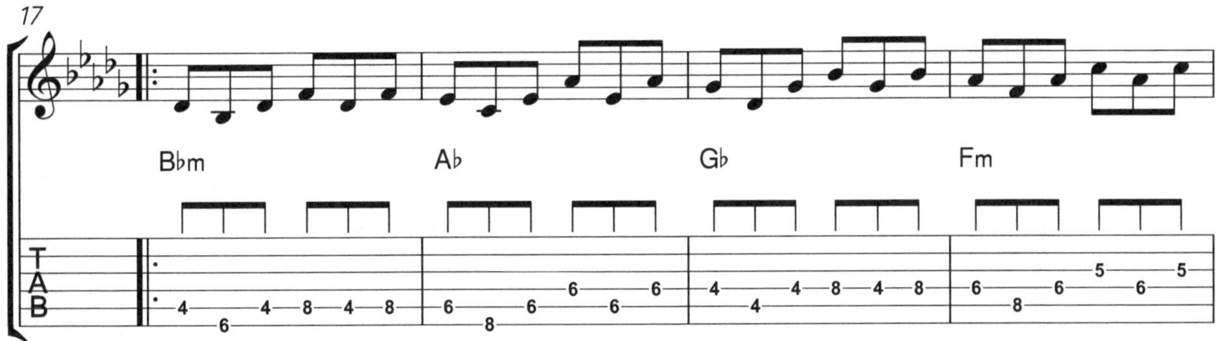
17
B♭m
A♭
G♭
Fm

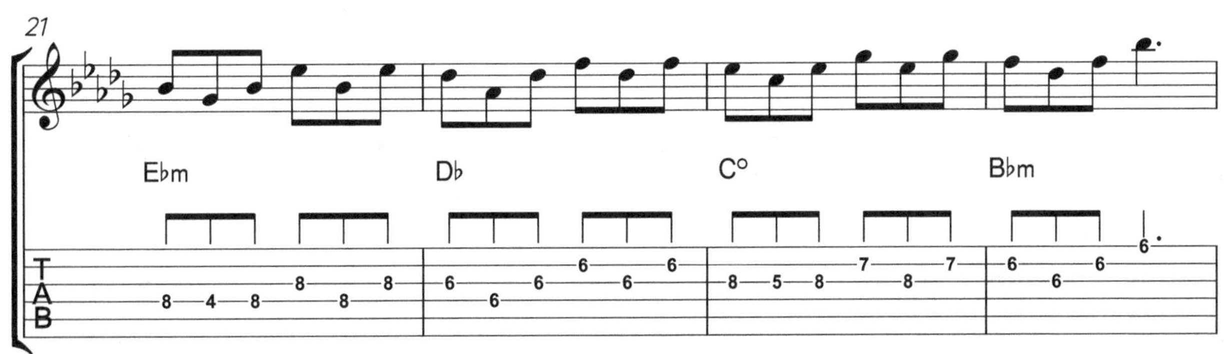
21
E♭m
D♭
C°
B♭m

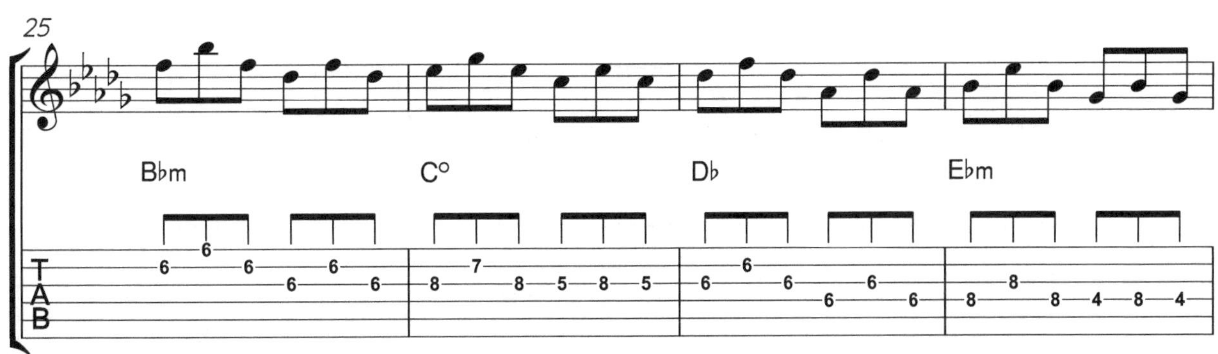
25
B♭m
C°
D♭
E♭m

29
Fm
G♭
A♭
B♭m

# B ♭ Minor Scale 6/8 Sequence ②
# Root Position (Alternative Position)

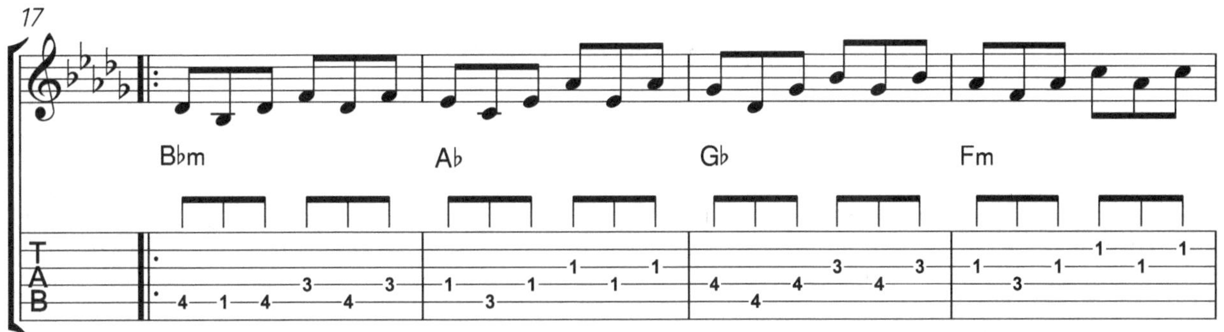
17
B♭m
A♭
G♭
Fm
T
A
B

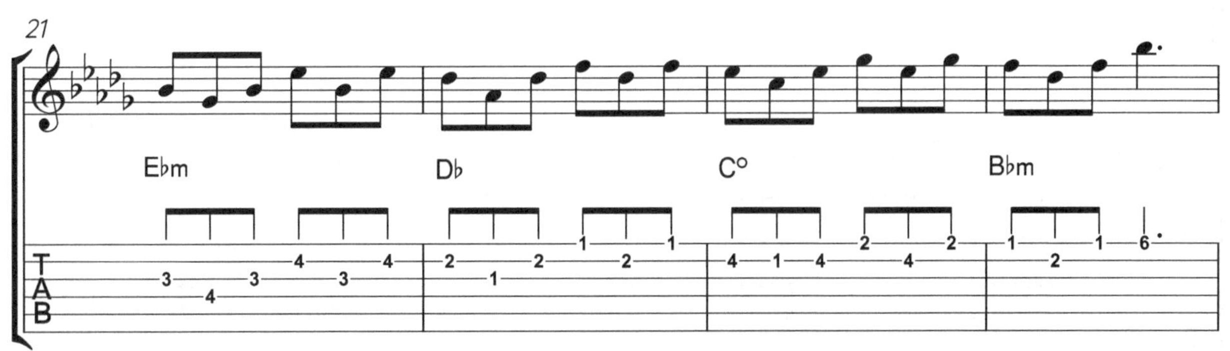
21
E♭m
D♭
C°
B♭m
T
A
B

25
B♭m
C°
D♭
E♭m
T
A
B

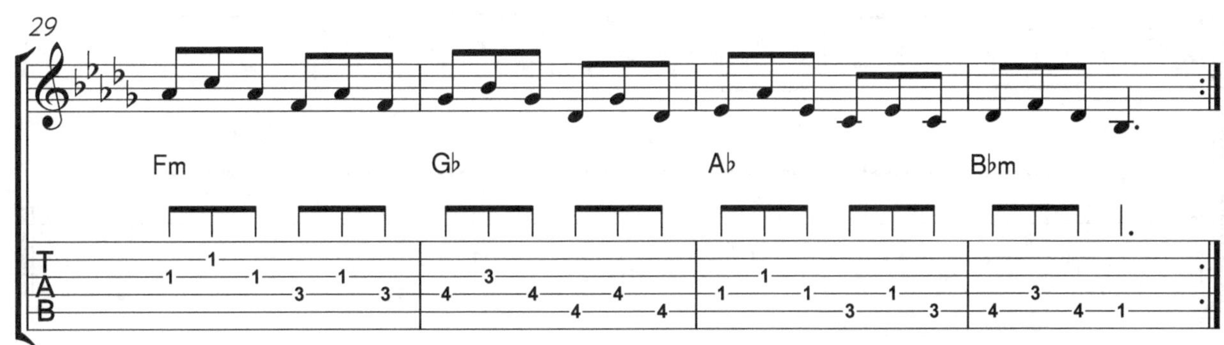
29
Fm
G♭
A♭
B♭m
T
A
B

# B ♭ Minor Scale 6/8 Sequence ②
## First Inversion

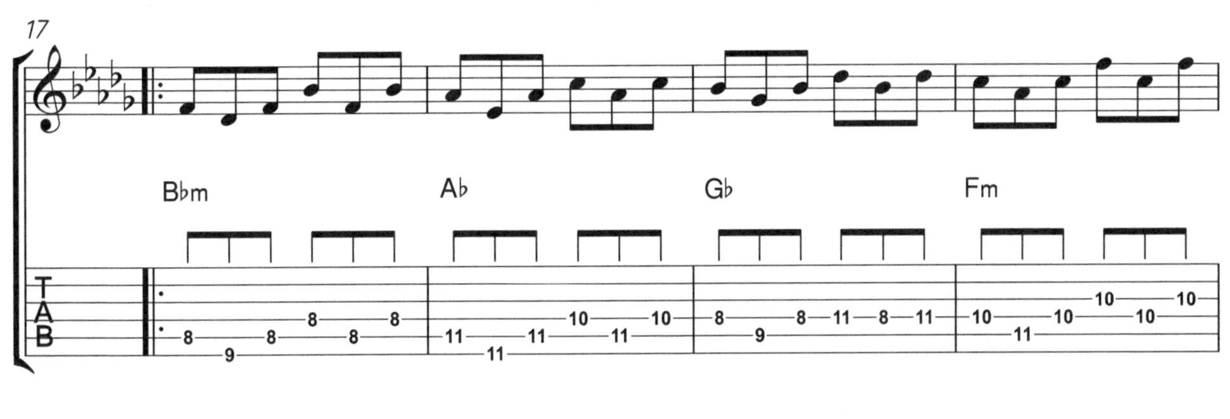
17
B♭m
A♭
G♭
Fm
T
A
B

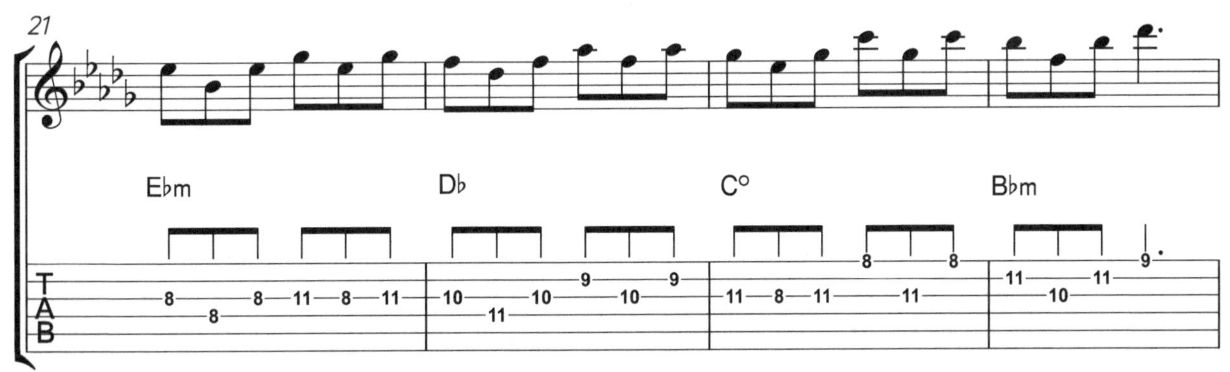
21
E♭m
D♭
C°
B♭m
T
A
B

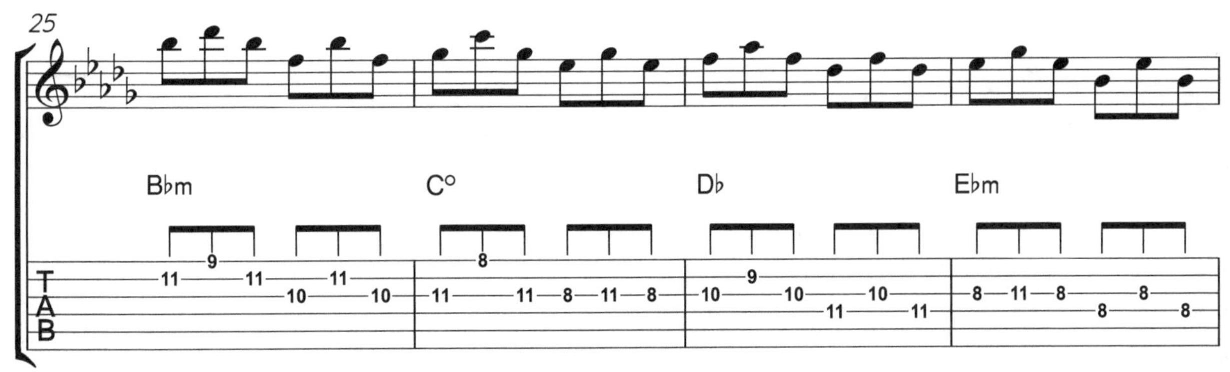
25
B♭m
C°
D♭
E♭m
T
A
B

29
Fm
G♭
A♭
B♭m
T
A
B

# B ♭ Minor Scale 6/8 Sequence ②
# First Inversion (Alternative Position)

17
B♭m
A♭
G♭
Fm
T
A
B
21
E♭m
D♭
C°
B♭m
25
B♭m
C°
D♭
E♭m
29
Fm
G♭
A♭
B♭m

# B ♭ Minor Scale 6/8 Sequence ②
# Second Inversion

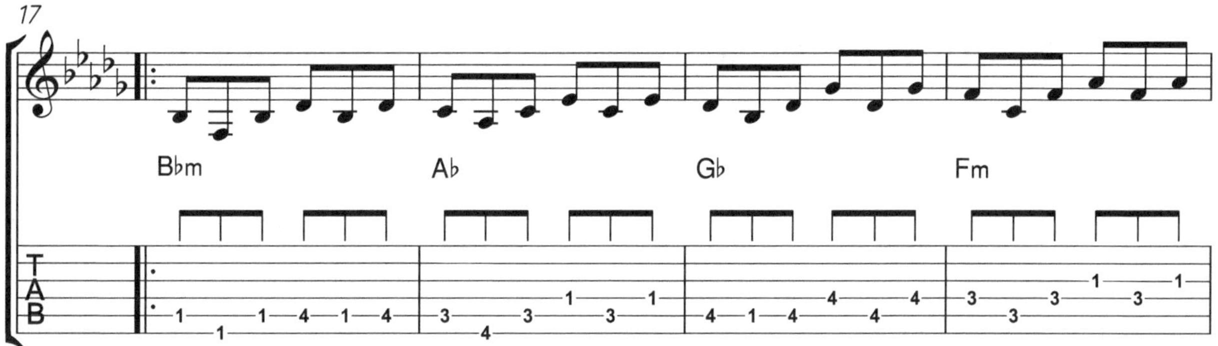
17
B♭m
A♭
G♭
Fm

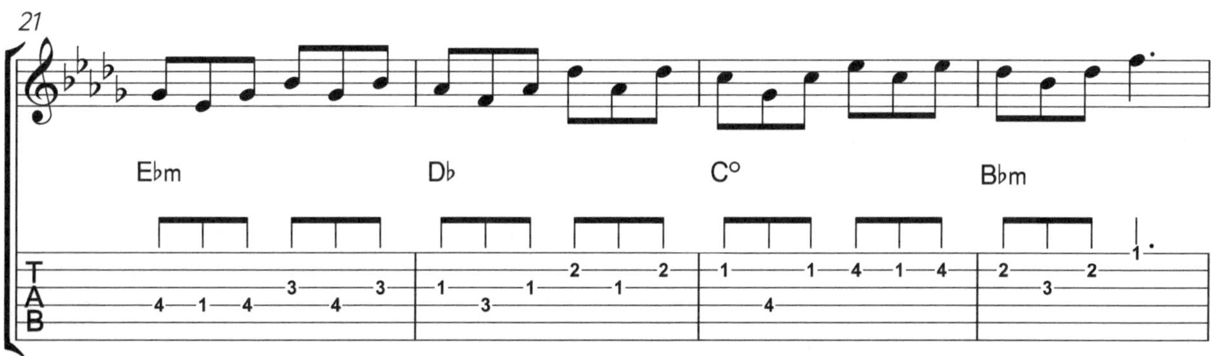
21
E♭m
D♭
C°
B♭m

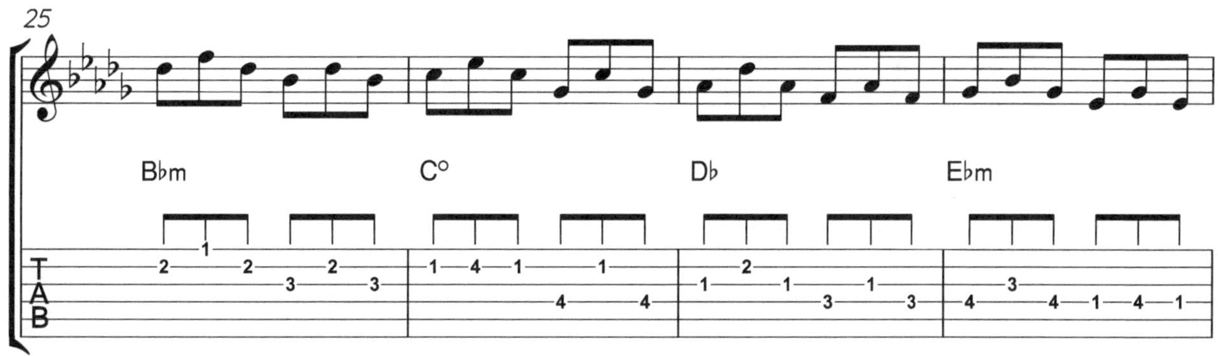
25
B♭m
C°
D♭
E♭m

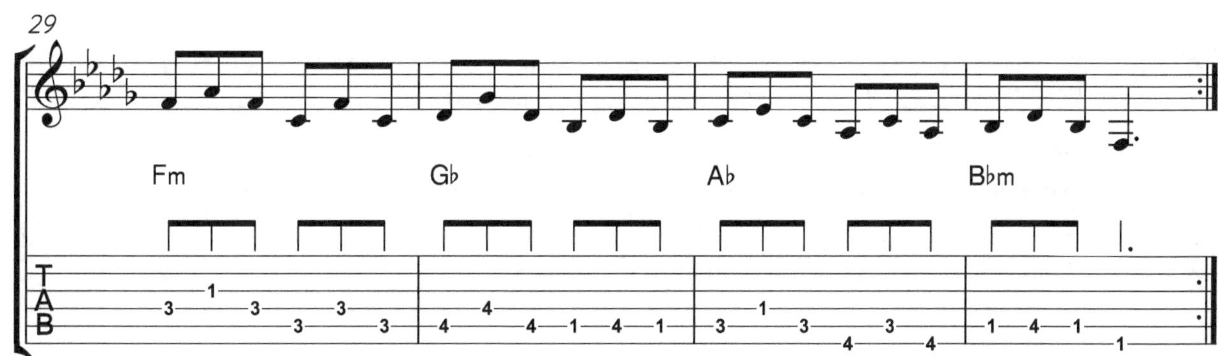
29
Fm
G♭
A♭
B♭m

# B♭ Minor Scale 6/8 Sequence ②
# Second Inversion (Alternative Position)

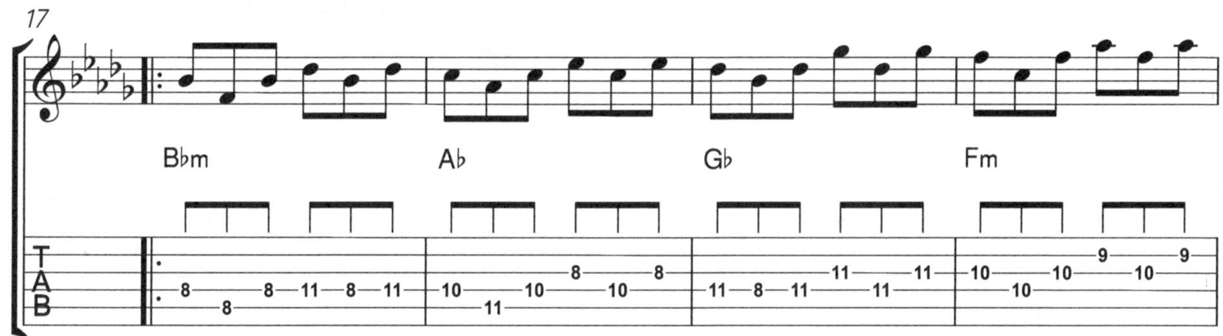
17
B♭m
A♭
G♭
Fm
T
A
B

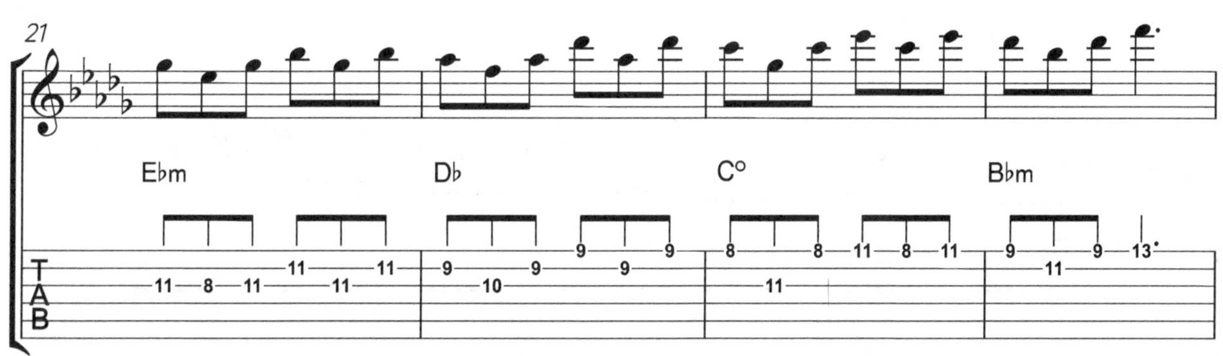
21
E♭m
D♭
C°
B♭m
T
A
B

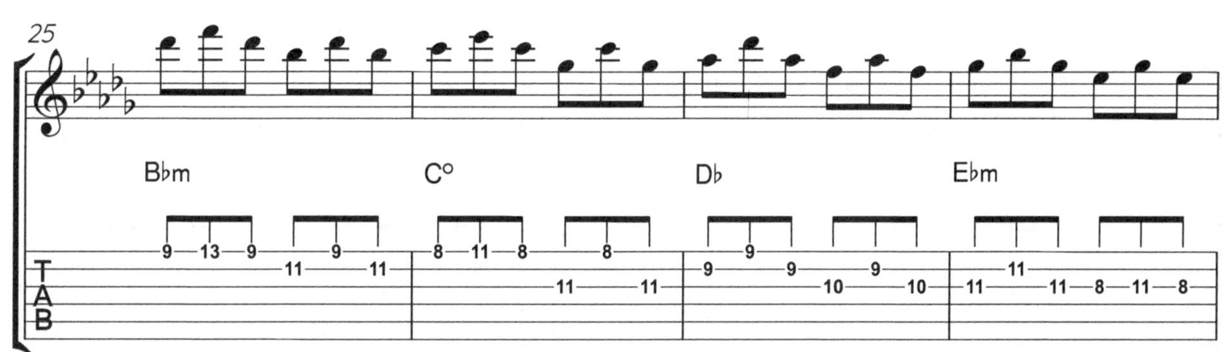
25
B♭m
C°
D♭
E♭m
T
A
B

29
Fm
G♭
A♭
B♭m
T
A
B

# E ♭ Harmonic Minor Scale 6/8 Sequence ②
## Root Position

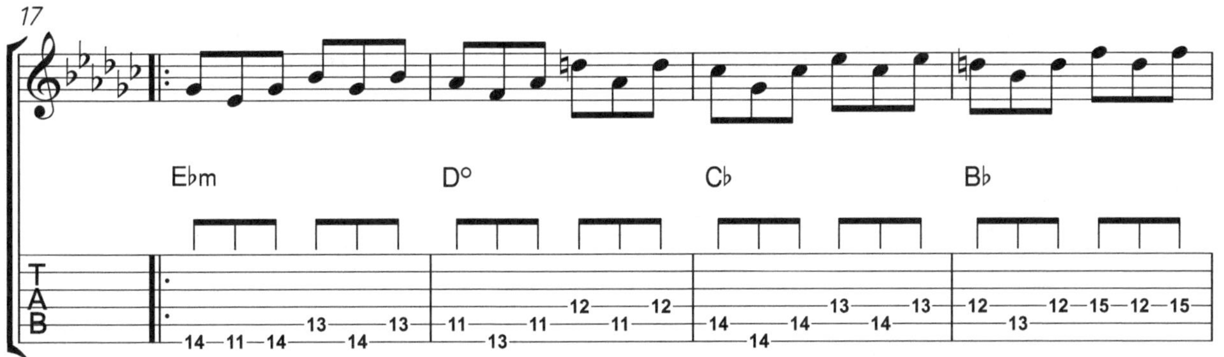
17
E♭m
D°
C♭
B♭
TAB

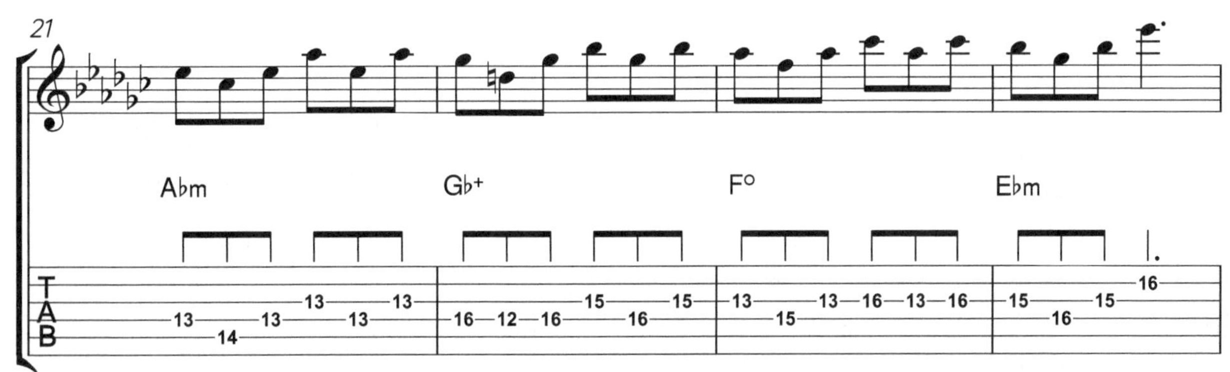
21
A♭m
G♭+
F°
E♭m
TAB

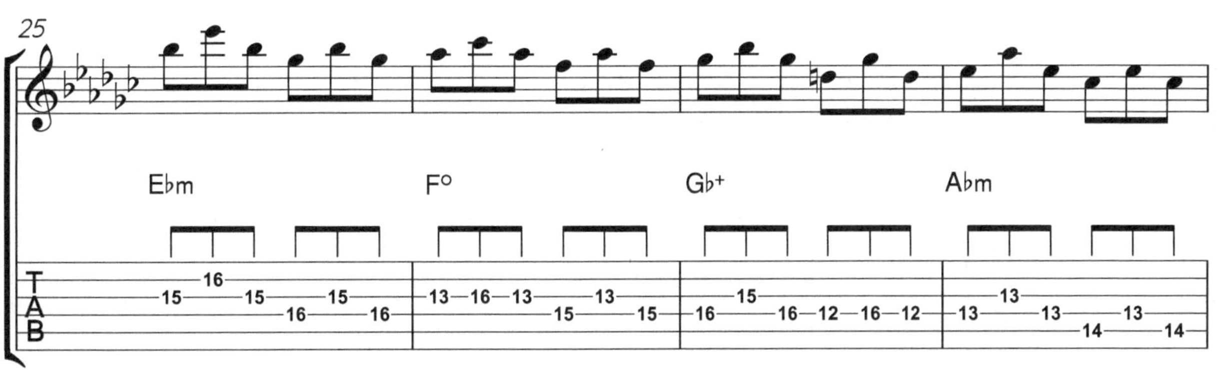
25
E♭m
F°
G♭+
A♭m
TAB

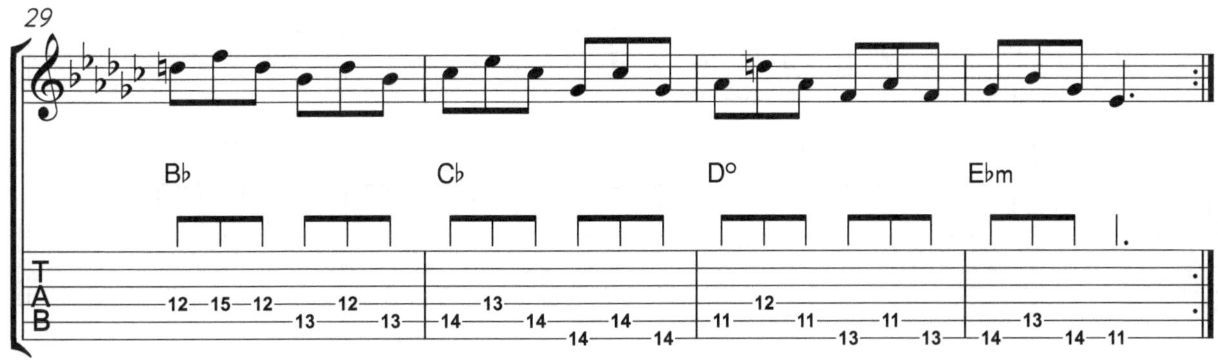
29
B♭
C♭
D°
E♭m
TAB

# E♭ Harmonic Minor Scale 6/8 Sequence ②
## Root Position (Alternative Position)

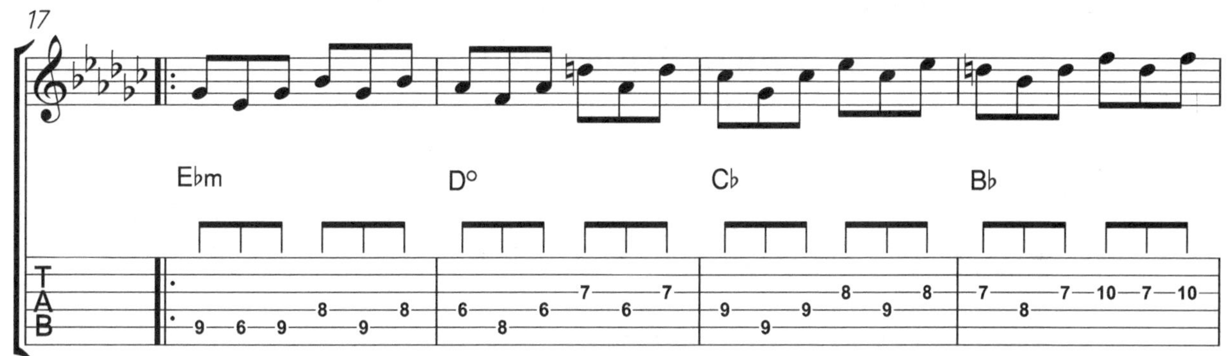
17
Ebm
Do
Cb
Bb

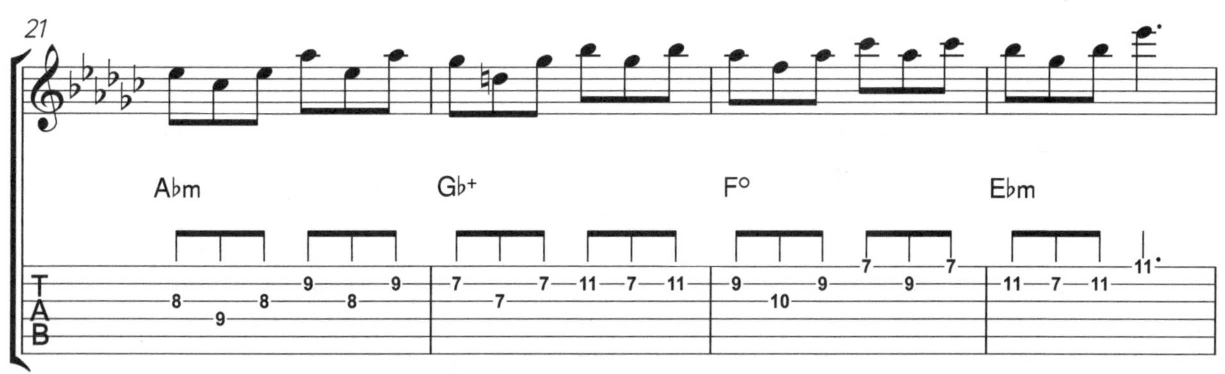
21
Abm
Gb+
Fo
Ebm

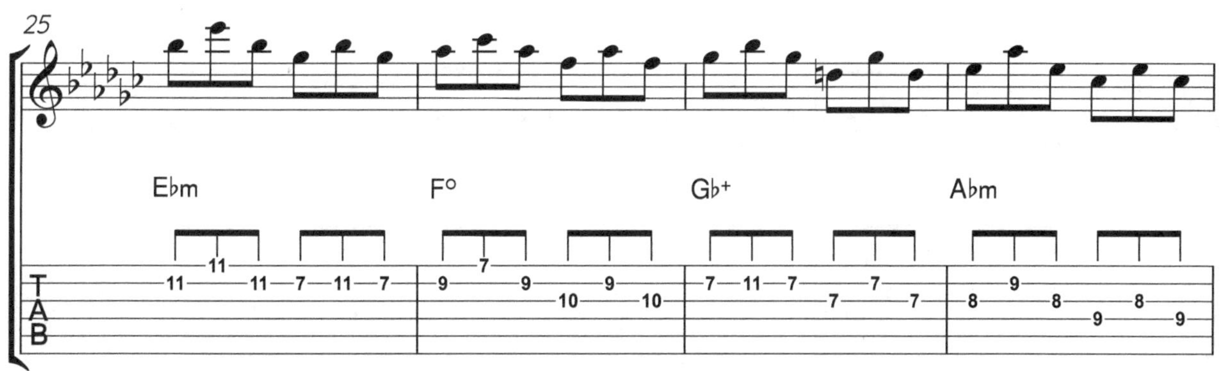
25
Ebm
Fo
Gb+
Abm

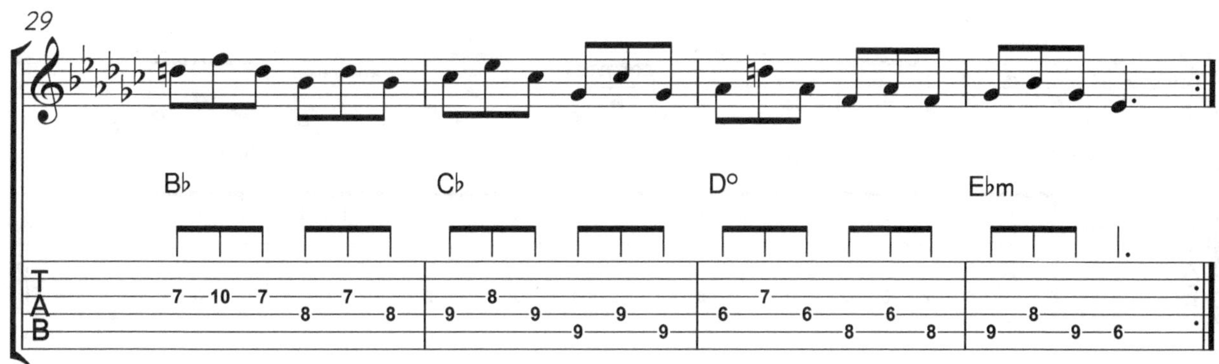
29
Bb
Cb
Do
Ebm

# E♭ Harmonic Minor Scale 6/8 Sequence ②
# First Inversion

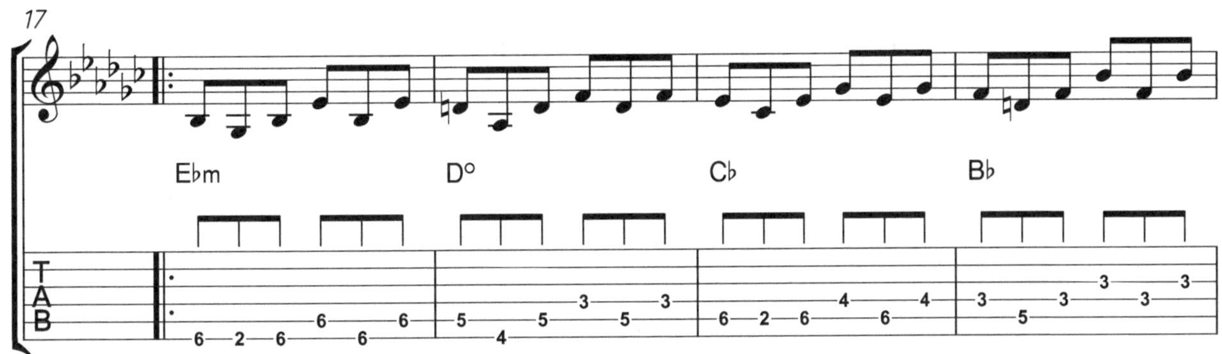
17
E♭m
D°
C♭
B♭
T
A
B

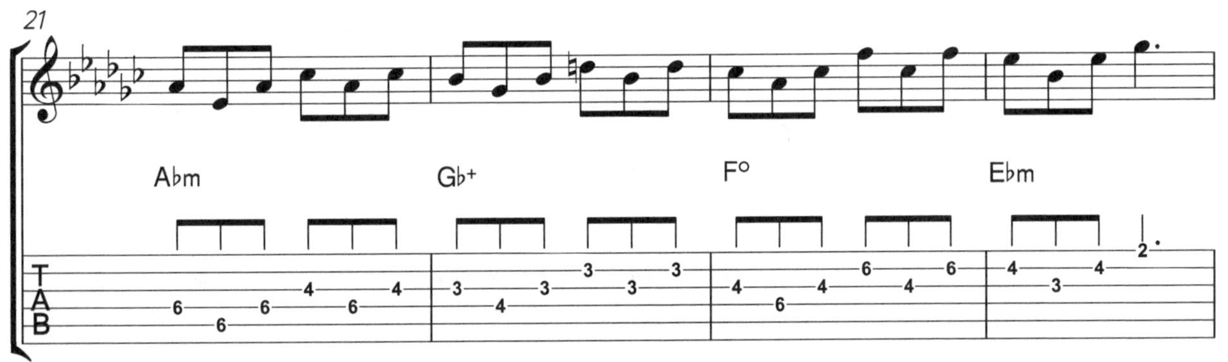
21
A♭m
G♭+
F°
E♭m
T
A
B

25
E♭m
F°
G♭+
A♭m
T
A
B

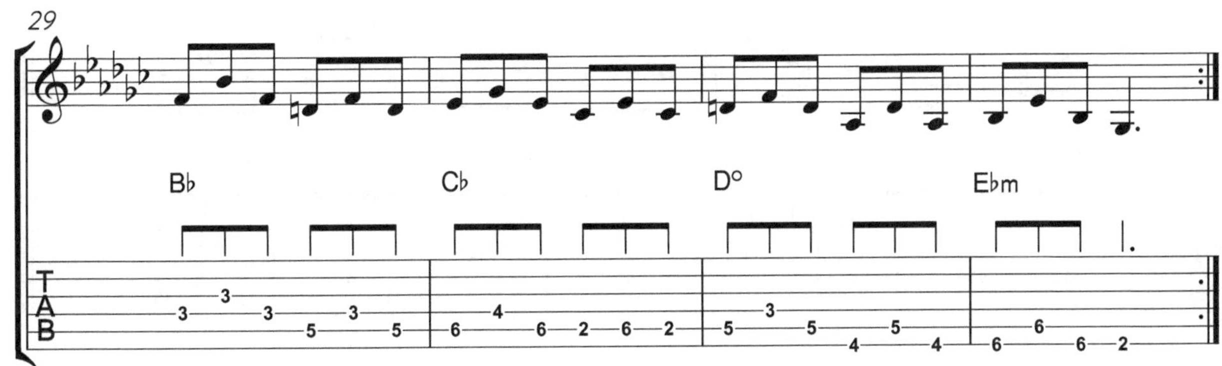
29
B♭
C♭
D°
E♭m
T
A
B

# E♭ Harmonic Minor Scale 6/8 Sequence ②
# First Inversion (Alternative Position)

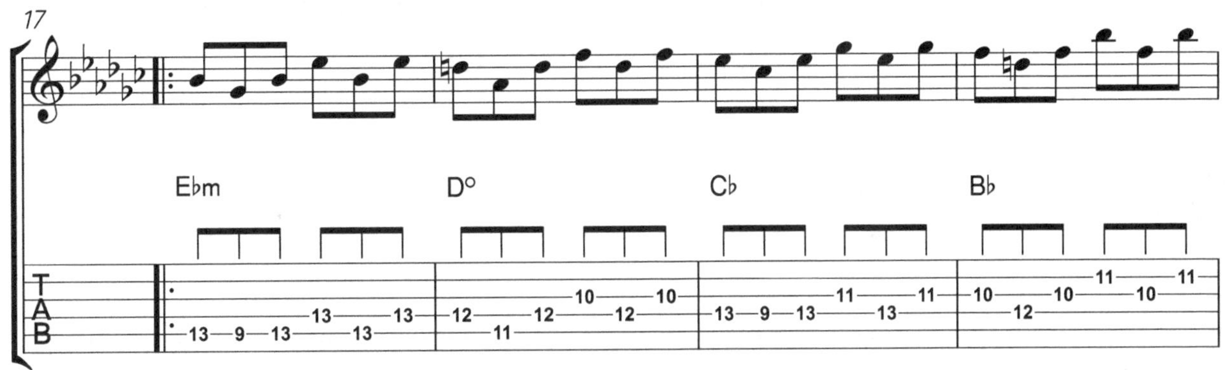
17
E♭m
D°
C♭
B♭
T
A
B

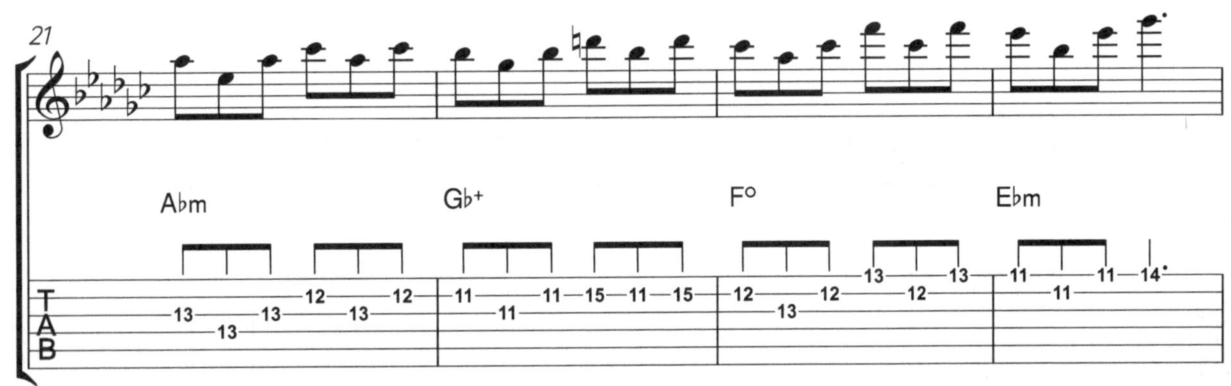
21
A♭m
G♭+
F°
E♭m
T
A
B

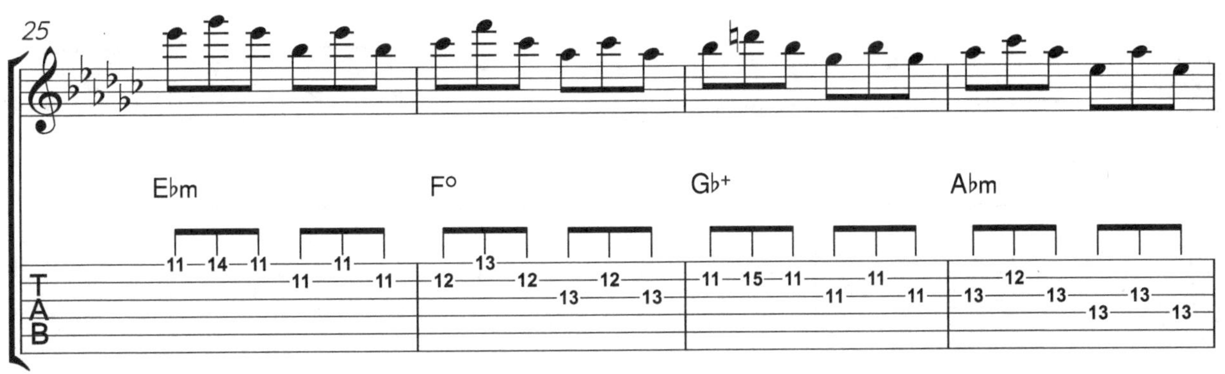
25
E♭m
F°
G♭+
A♭m
T
A
B

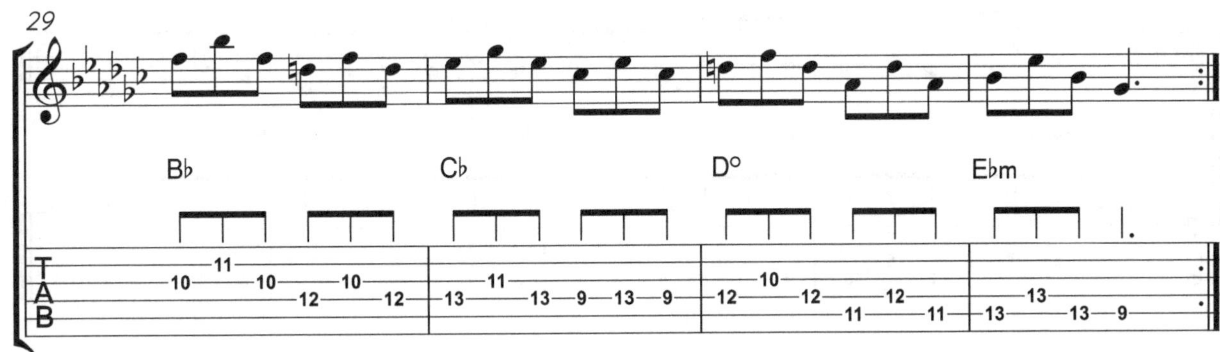
29
B♭
C♭
D°
E♭m
T
A
B

# E ♭ Harmonic Minor Scale 6/8 Sequence ②
## Second Inversion

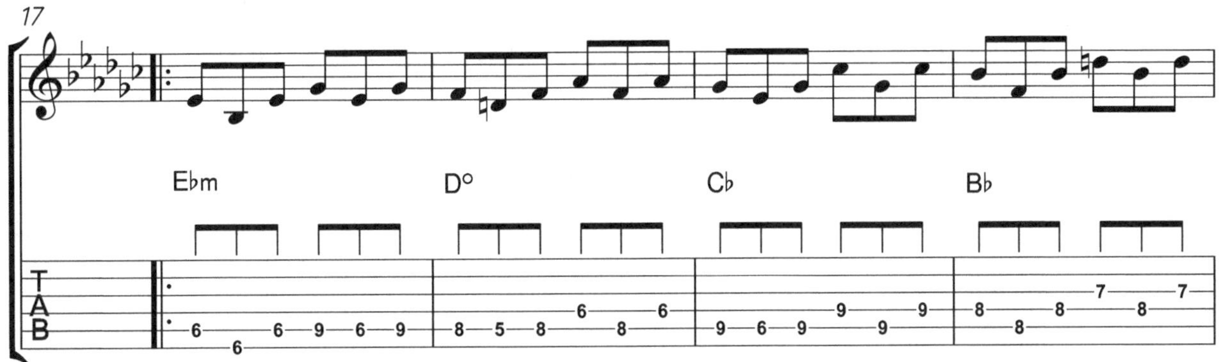
17
E♭m
D°
C♭
B♭
T
A
B

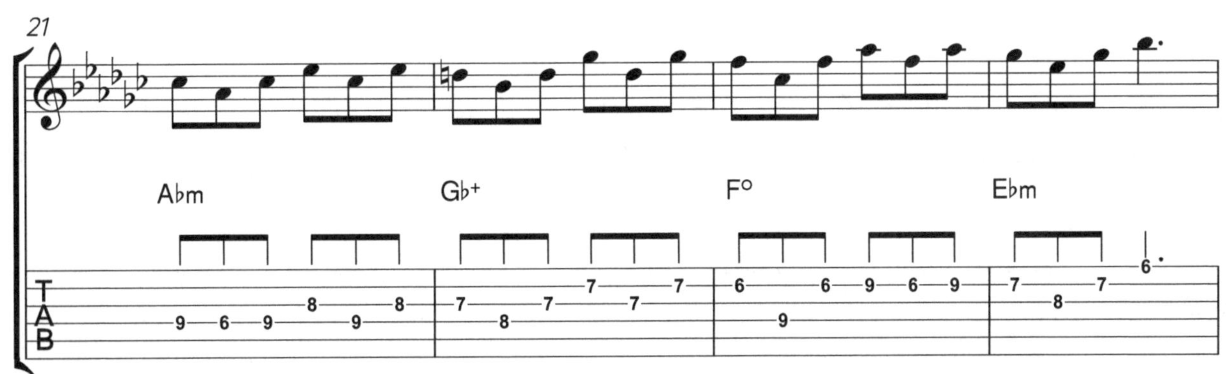
21
A♭m
G♭+
F°
E♭m
T
A
B

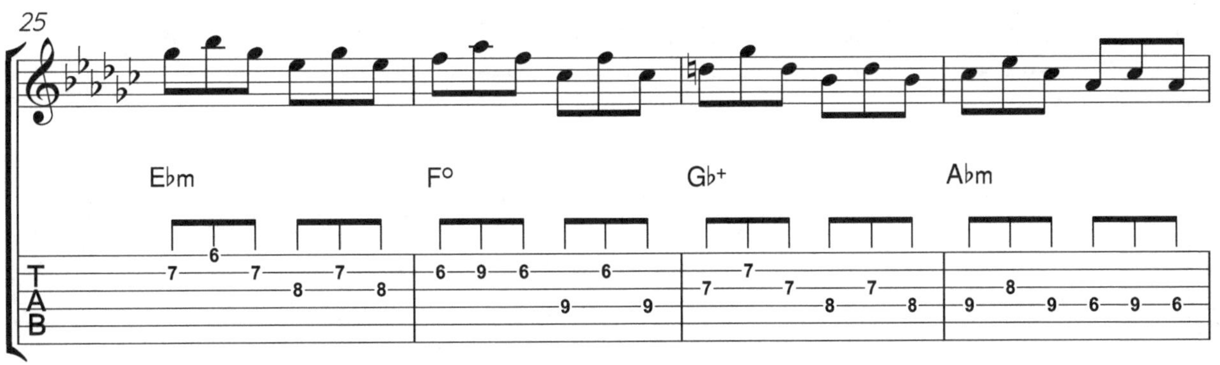
25
E♭m
F°
G♭+
A♭m
T
A
B

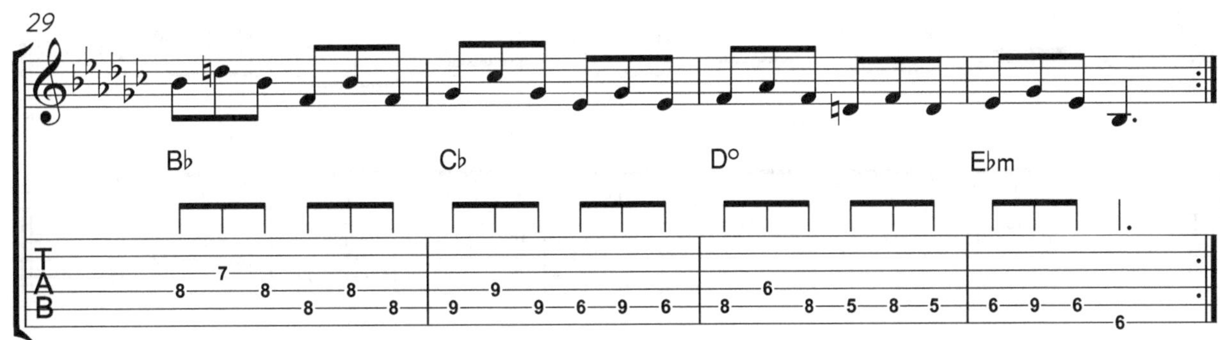
29
B♭
C♭
D°
E♭m
T
A
B

# E ♭ Harmonic Minor Scale 6/8 Sequence ②
# Second Inversion (Alternative Position)

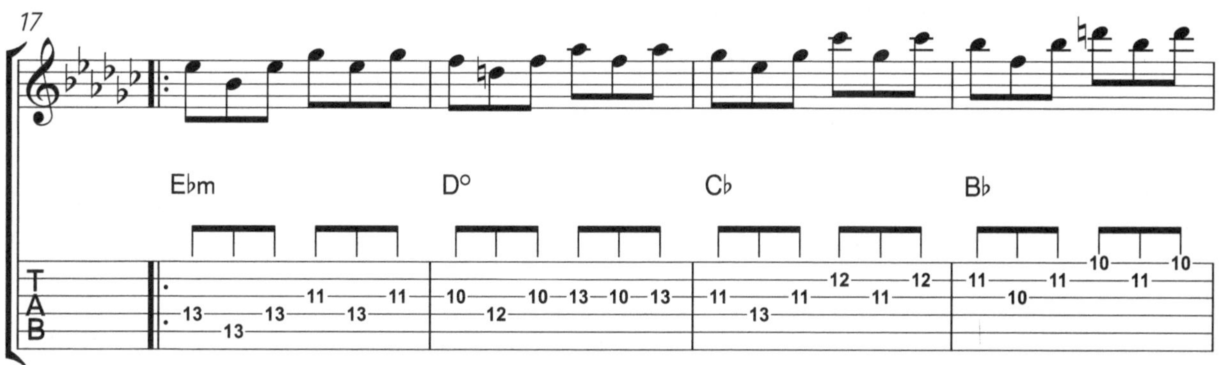
17
E♭m
D°
C♭
B♭
T
A
B

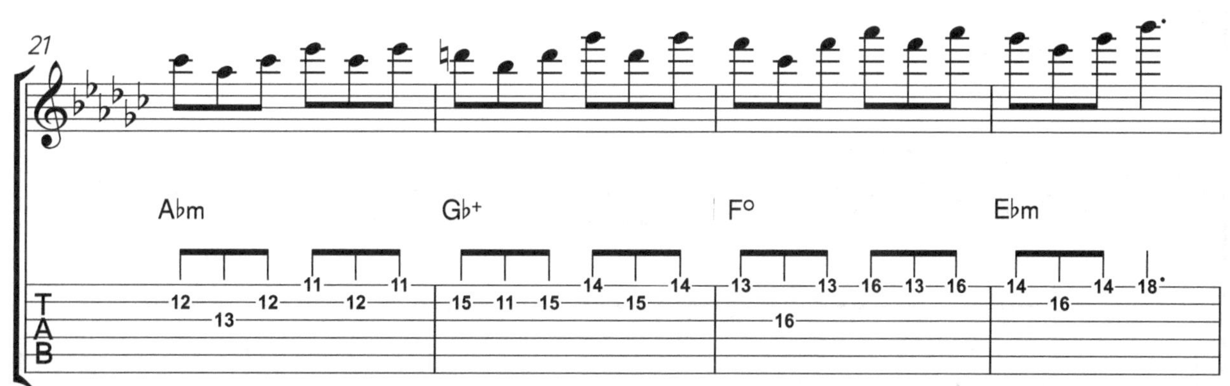
21
A♭m
G♭+
F°
E♭m
T
A
B

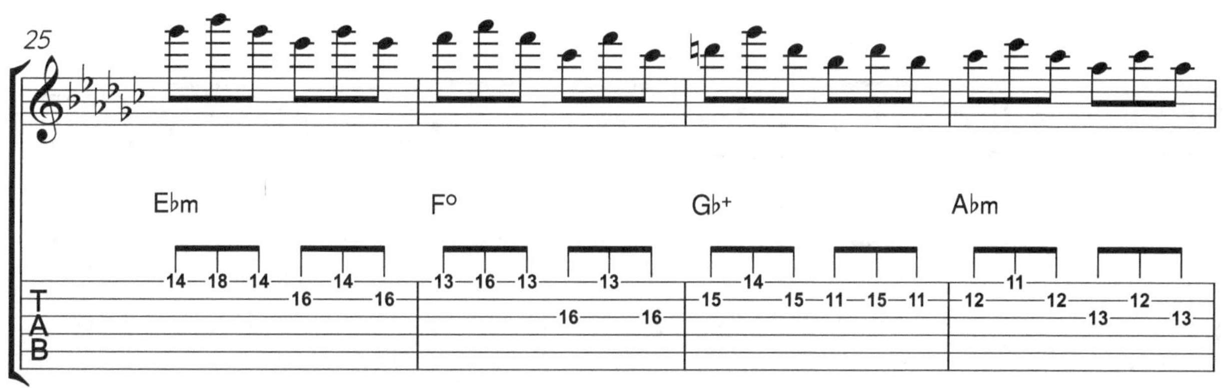
25
E♭m
F°
G♭+
A♭m
T
A
B

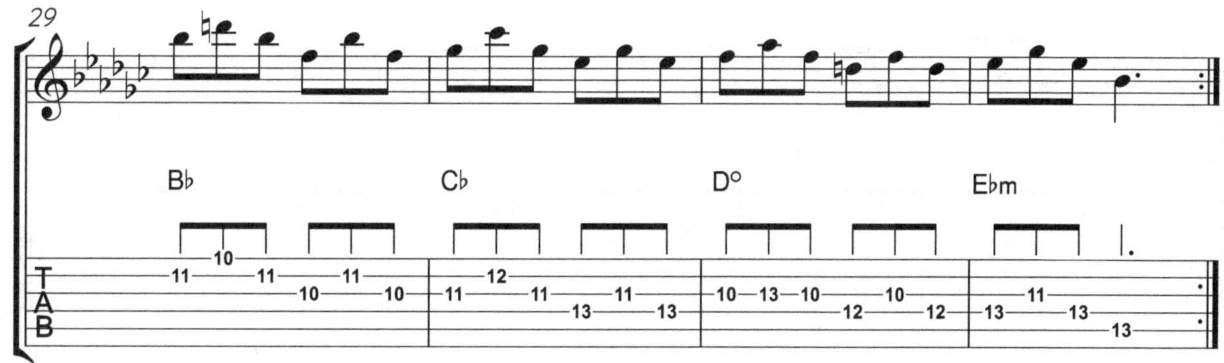
29
B♭
C♭
D°
E♭m
T
A
B

# A♭ Melodic Minor Scale 6/8 Sequence ②
# Root Position

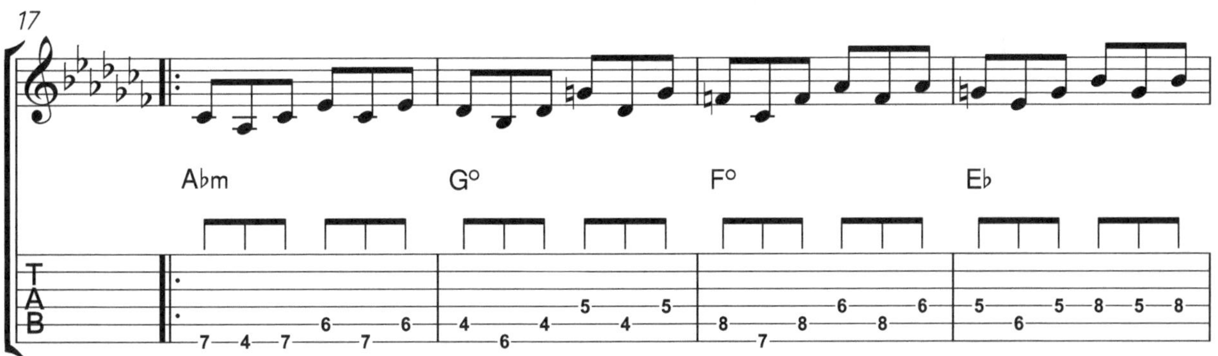
17
A♭m
G°
F°
E♭

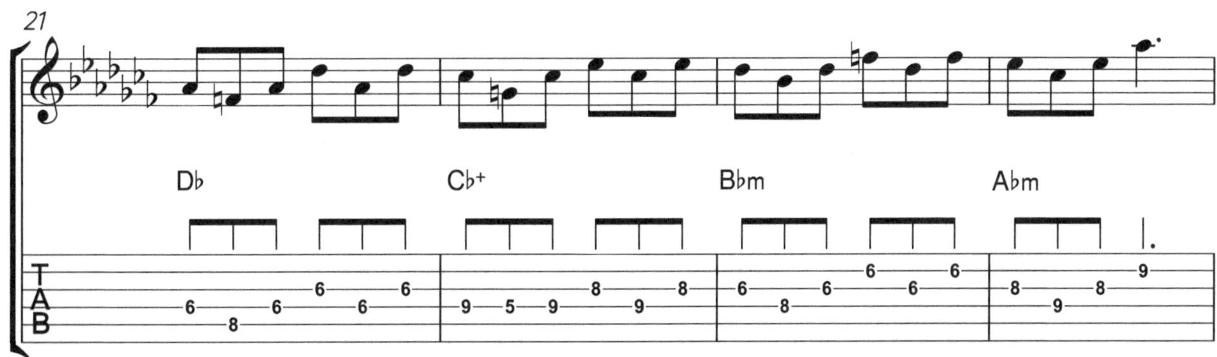
21
D♭
C♭+
B♭m
A♭m

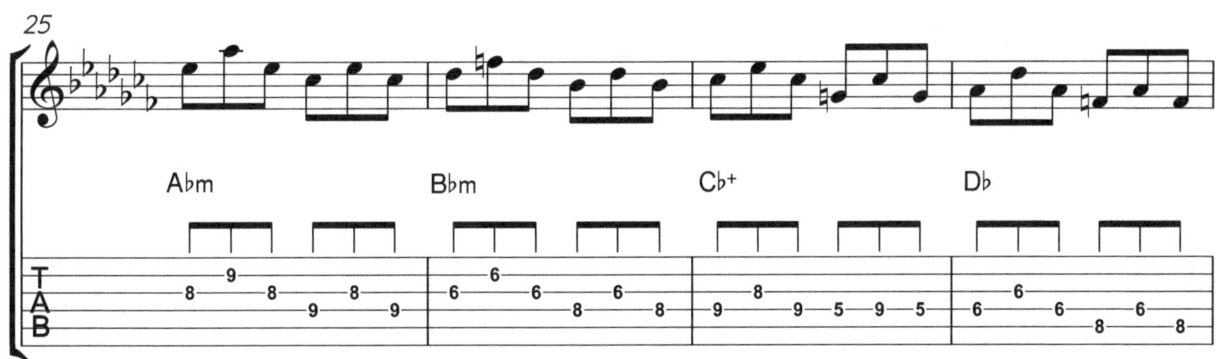
25
A♭m
B♭m
C♭+
D♭

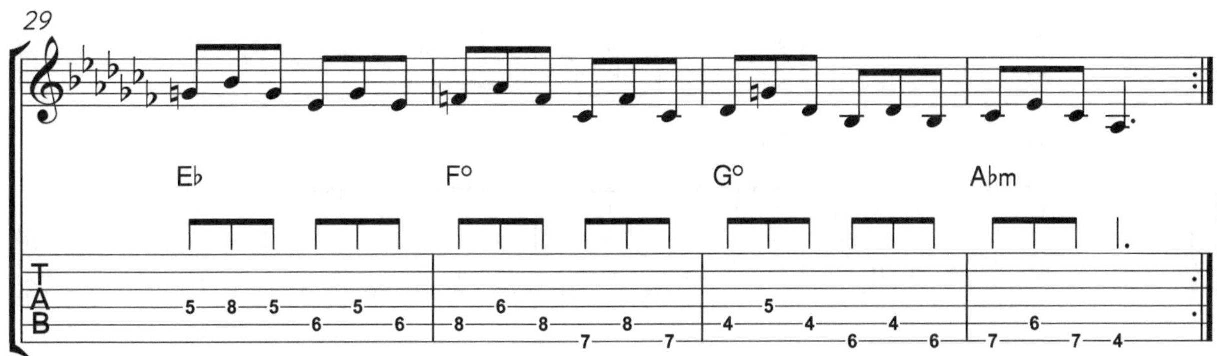
29
E♭
F°
G°
A♭m

# A♭ Melodic Minor Scale 6/8 Sequence ②
# Root Position (Alternative Position)

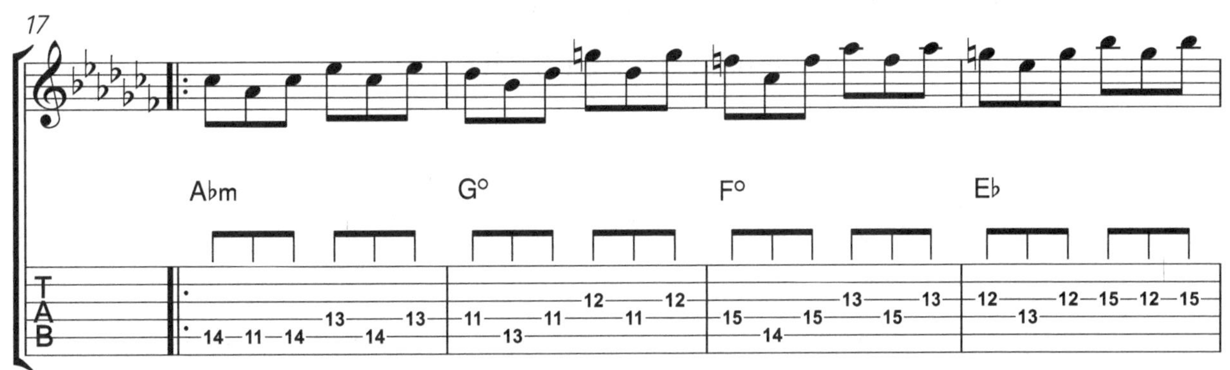
17
Abm
G°
F°
Eb
TAB

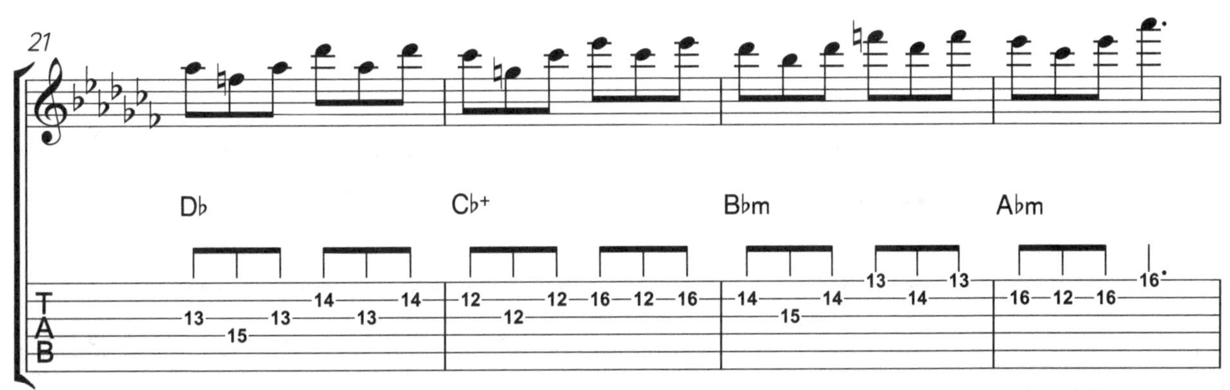
21
Db
Cb+
Bbm
Abm
TAB

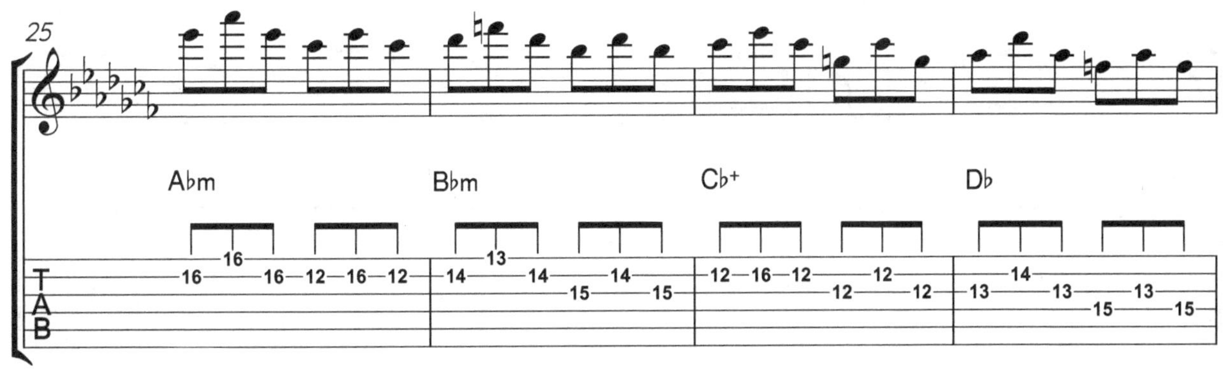
25
Abm
Bbm
Cb+
Db
TAB

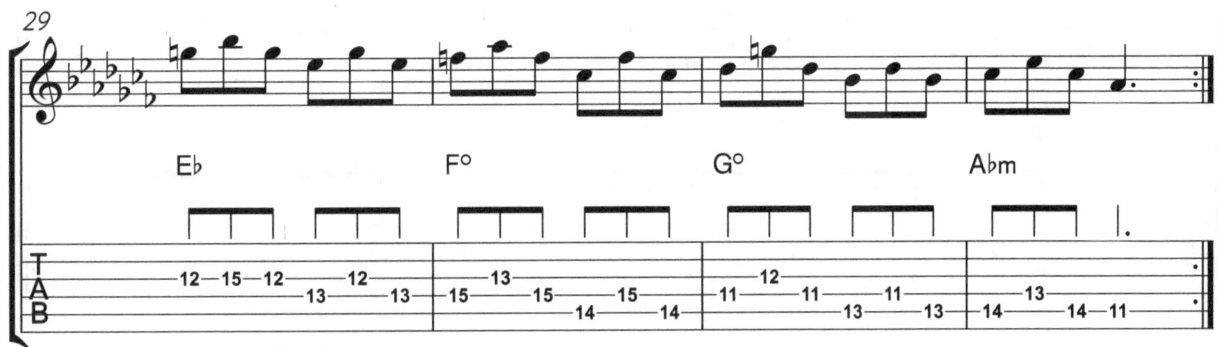
29
Eb
F°
G°
Abm
TAB

## A ♭ Melodic Minor Scale 6/8 Sequence ②
## First Inversion

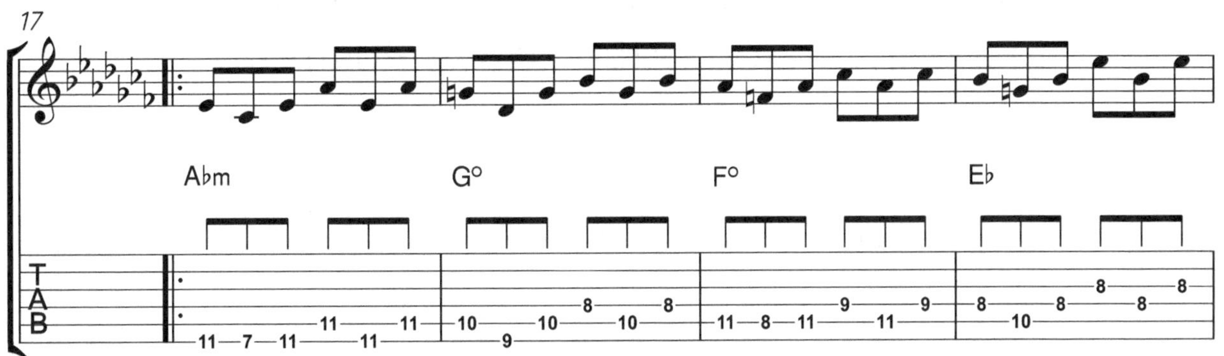
17
Abm
G°
F°
Eb
T
A
B
11 7 11 11 11 11
10 9 10 8 10 8
11 8 11 9 11 9
8 10 8 8 8 8

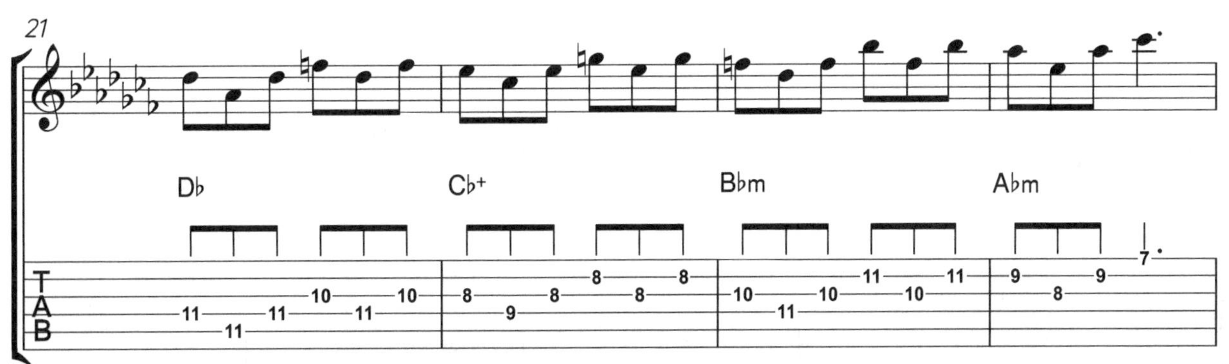
21
Db
Cb+
Bbm
Abm
T
A
B
11 11 11 10 11 10
8 9 8 8 8 8
10 11 10 11 10 11
9 8 9 7

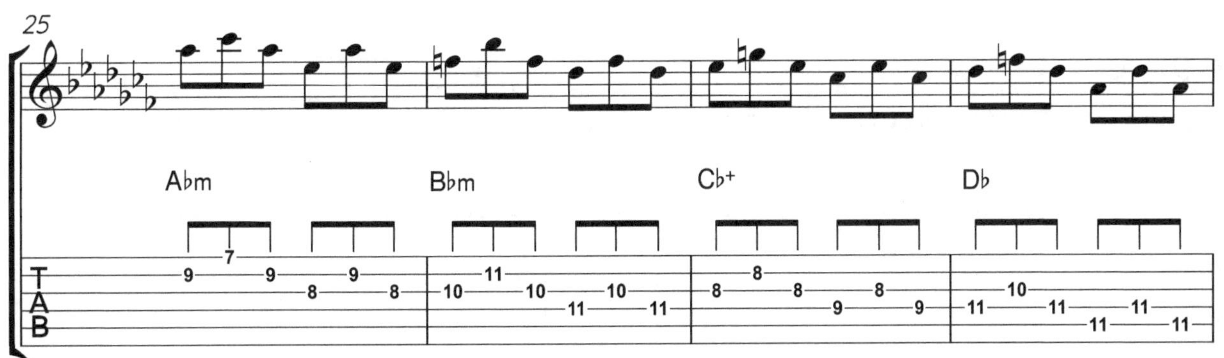
25
Abm
Bbm
Cb+
Db
T
A
B
9 7 9 8 9 8
10 11 10 11 10 11
8 8 8 9 8 9
11 10 11 11 11 11

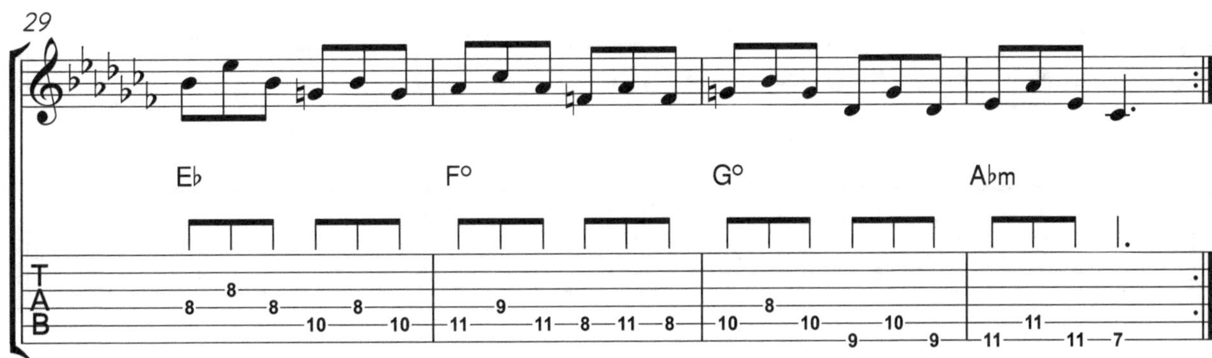
29
Eb
F°
G°
Abm
T
A
B
8 8 8 10 8 10
11 9 11 8 11 8
10 8 10 9 10 9
11 11 11 7

# A ♭ Melodic Minor Scale 6/8 Sequence ②
# First Inversion (Alternative Position)

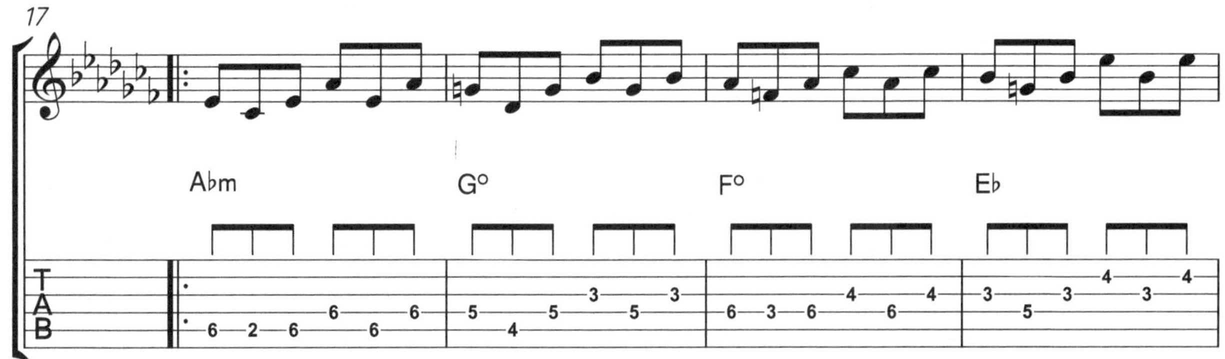
17
A♭m
G°
F°
E♭

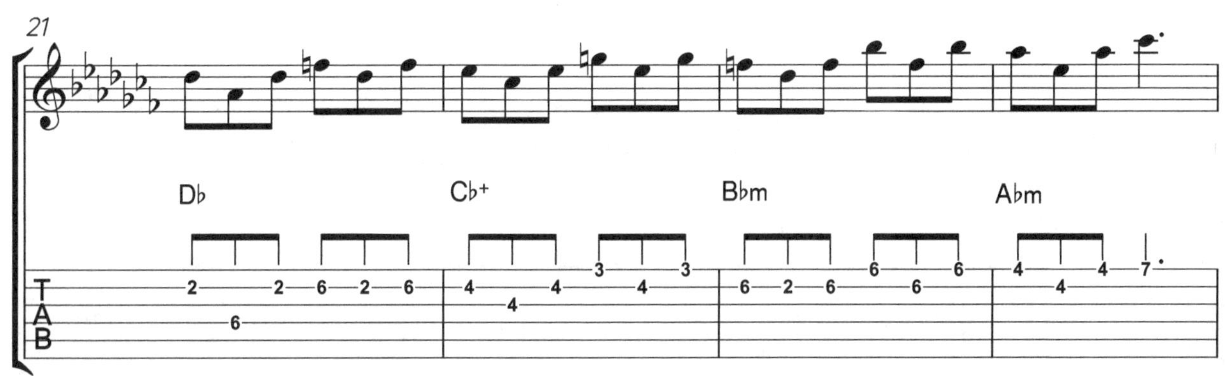
21
D♭
C♭+
B♭m
A♭m

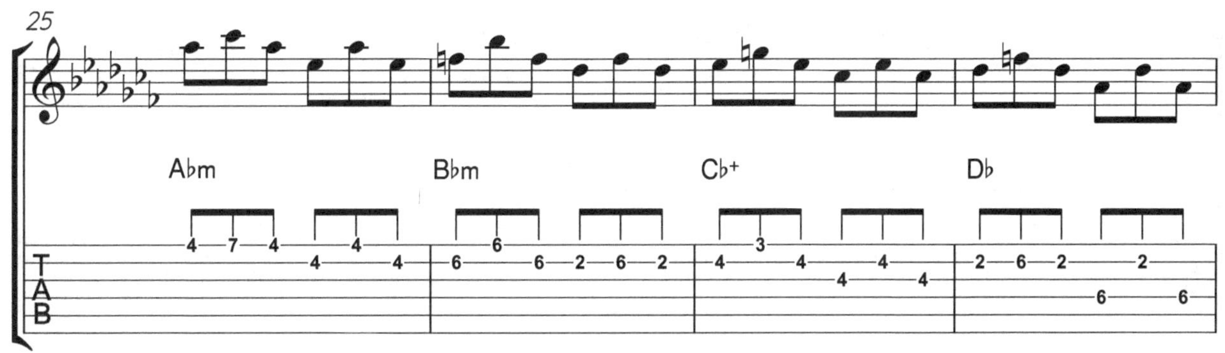
25
A♭m
B♭m
C♭+
D♭

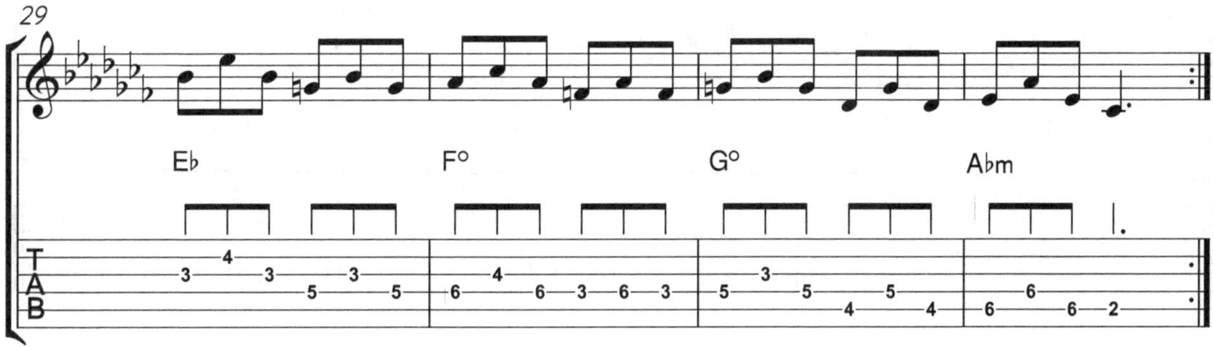
29
E♭
F°
G°
A♭m

# A♭ Melodic Minor Scale 6/8 Sequence ②
# Second Inversion

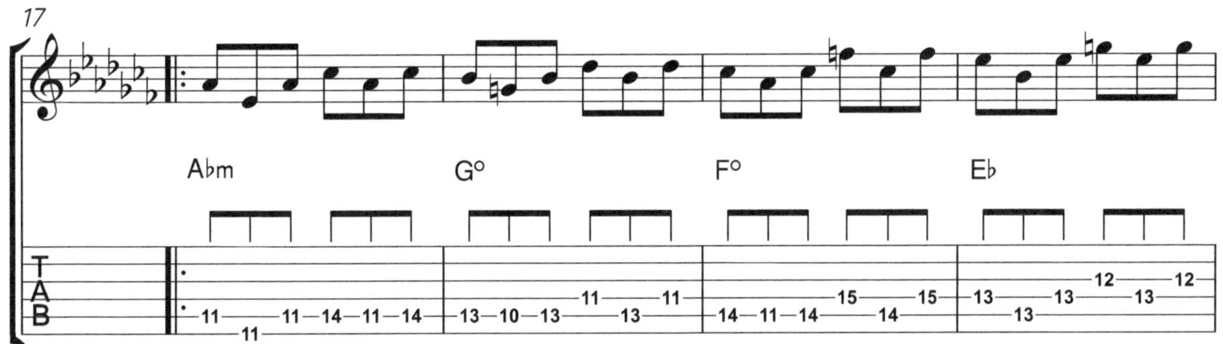
17
A♭m
G°
F°
E♭

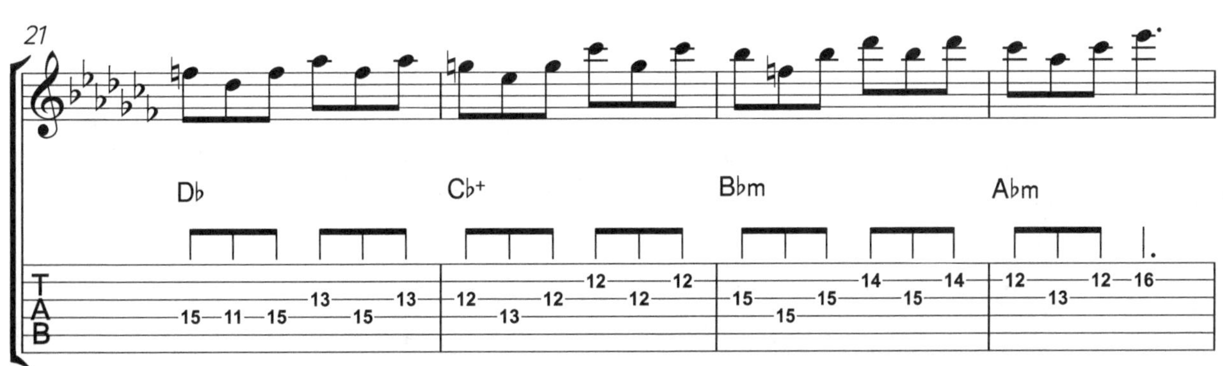
21
D♭
C♭+
B♭m
A♭m

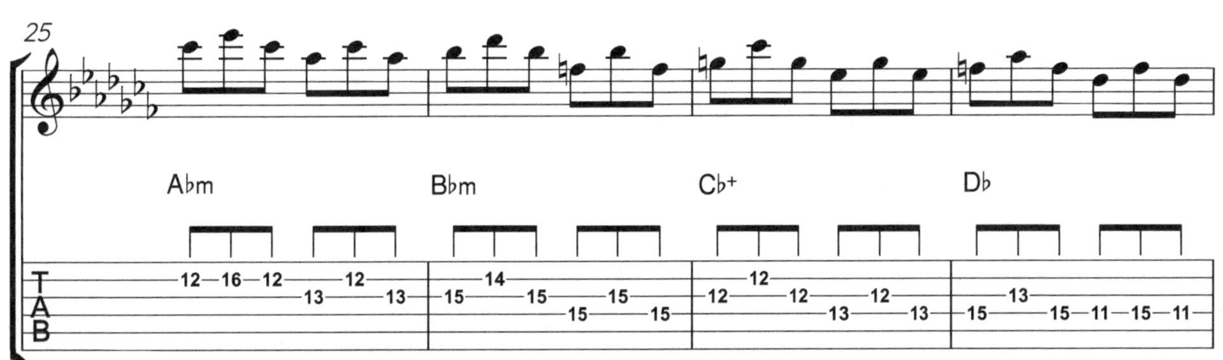
25
A♭m
B♭m
C♭+
D♭

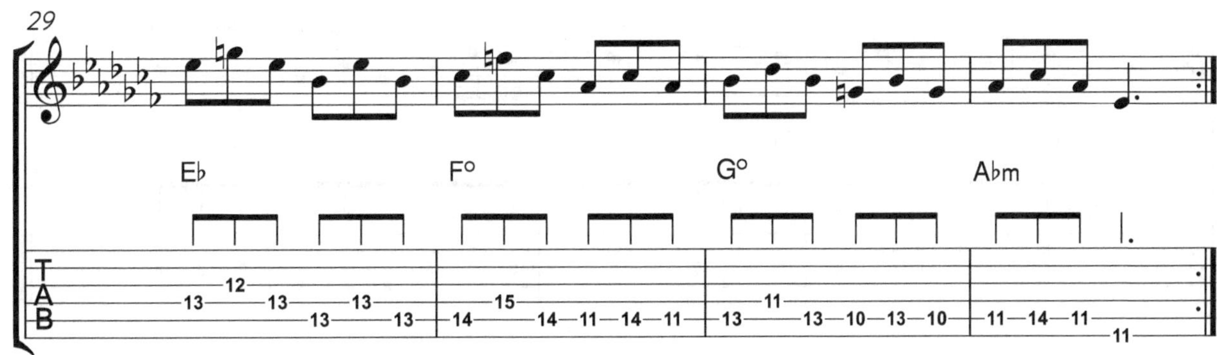
29
E♭
F°
G°
A♭m

# A♭ Melodic Minor Scale 6/8 Sequence ②
# Second Inversion (Alternative Position)

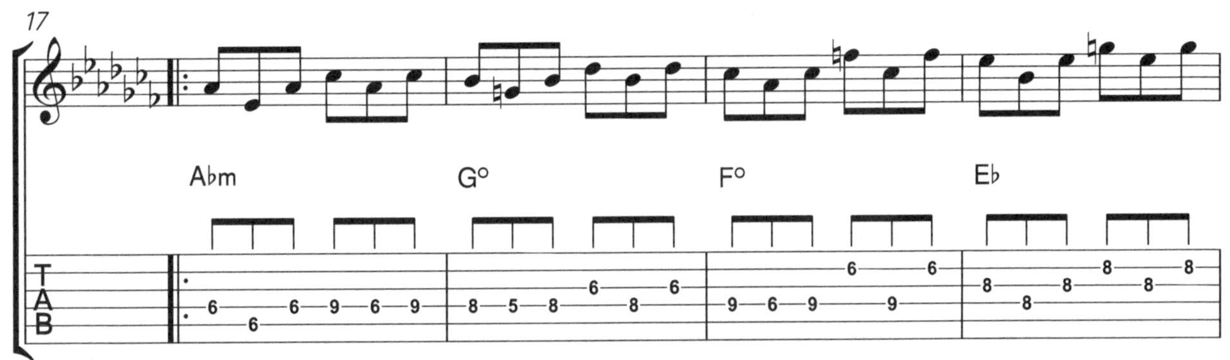
17
A♭m
G°
F°
E♭
T
A
B
6 6 6 9 6 9
8 5 8 6 8 6
9 6 9 6 9 6
8 8 8 8 8 8

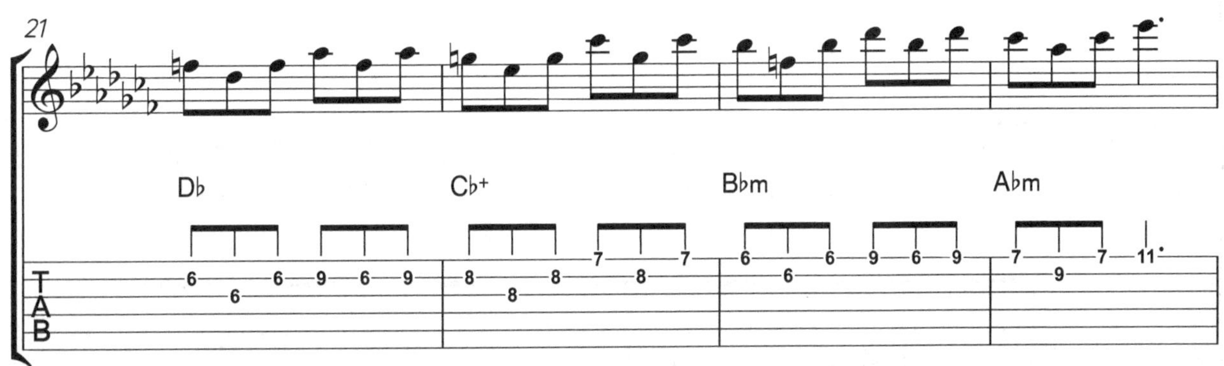
21
D♭
C♭+
B♭m
A♭m
T
A
B
6 6 6 9 6 9
8 8 8 7 8 7
6 6 6 9 6 9
7 9 7 11

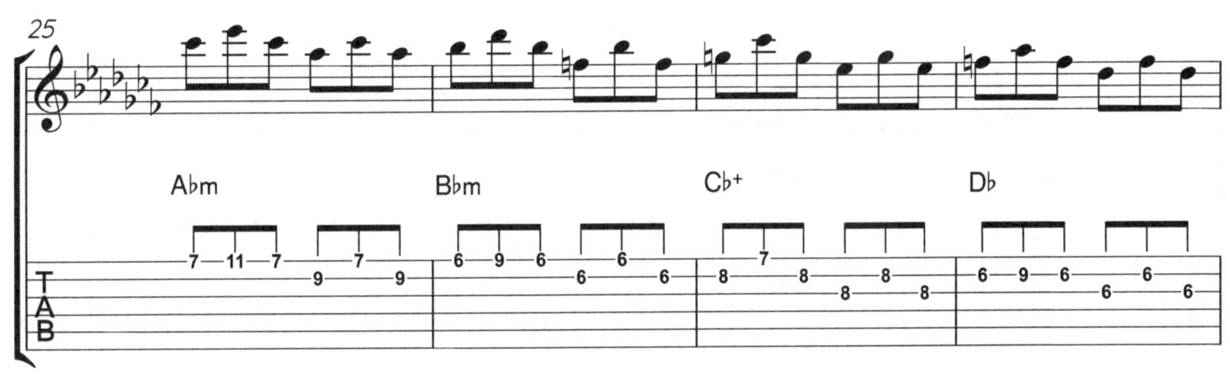
25
A♭m
B♭m
C♭+
D♭
T
A
B
7 11 7 9 7 9
6 9 6 6 6 6
8 7 8 8 8 8
6 9 6 6 6 6

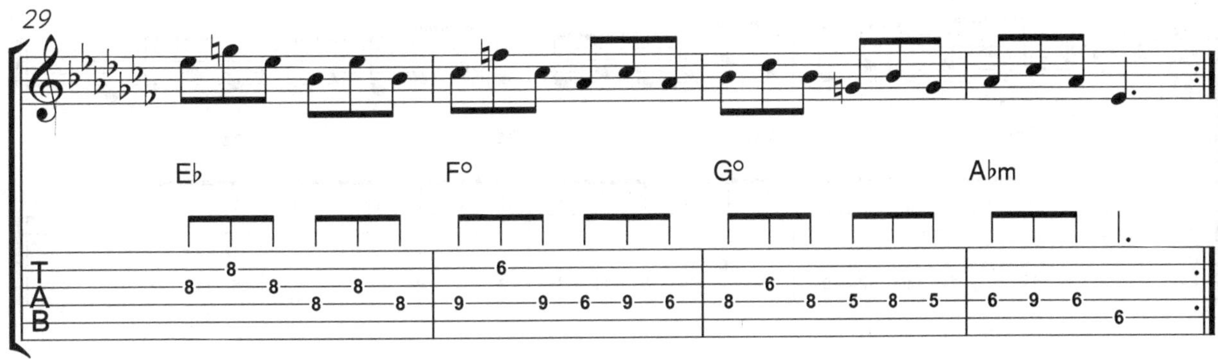
29
E♭
F°
G°
A♭m
T
A
B
8 8 8 8 8 8
9 6 9 6 9 6
8 6 8 5 8 5
6 9 6 6

# C♯Harmonic Major Scale 6/8 Sequence ②
## Root Position

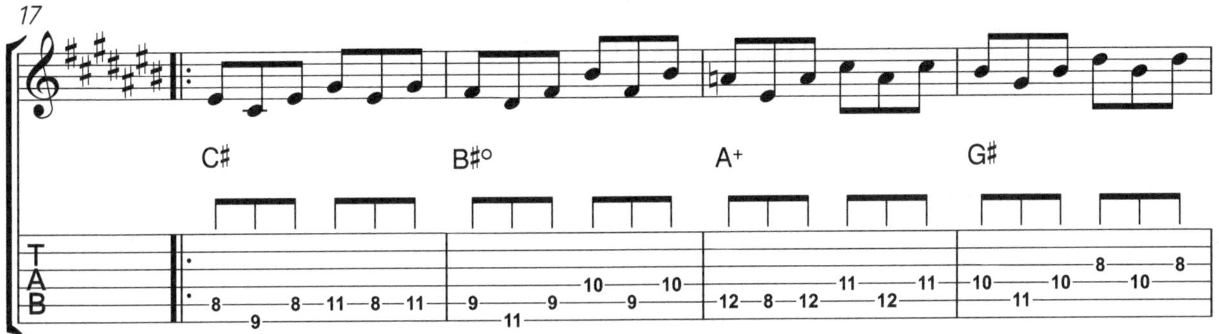
17
C♯
B♯o
A+
G♯
TAB

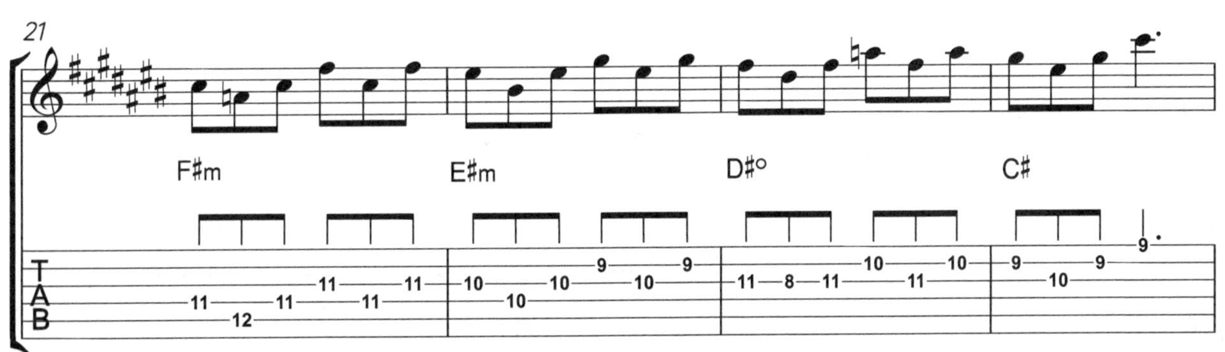
21
F♯m
E♯m
D♯o
C♯
TAB

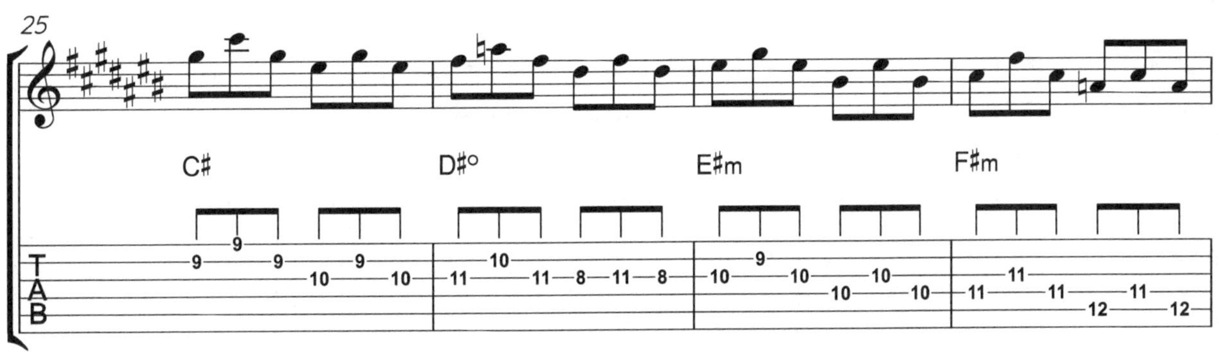
25
C♯
D♯o
E♯m
F♯m
TAB

29
G♯
A+
B♯o
C♯
TAB

# C♯ Harmonic Major Scale 6/8 Sequence ②
## Root Position (Alternative Position)

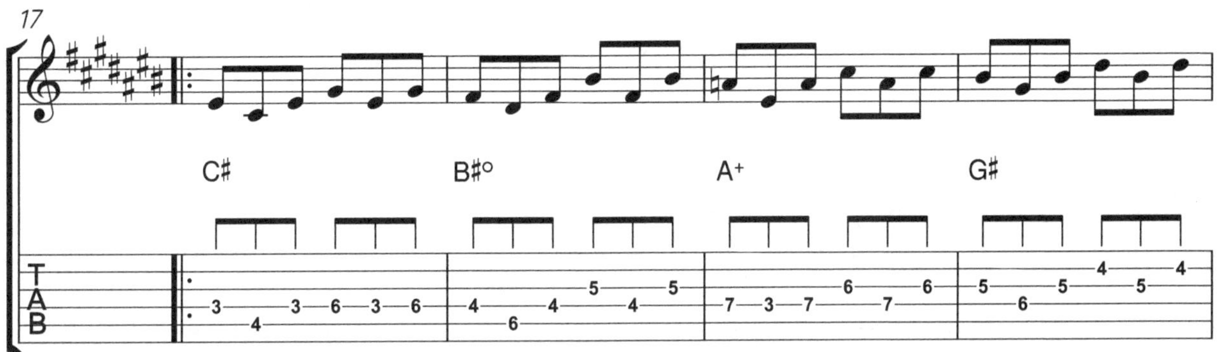
17
C♯
B♯°
A+
G♯
T
A
B

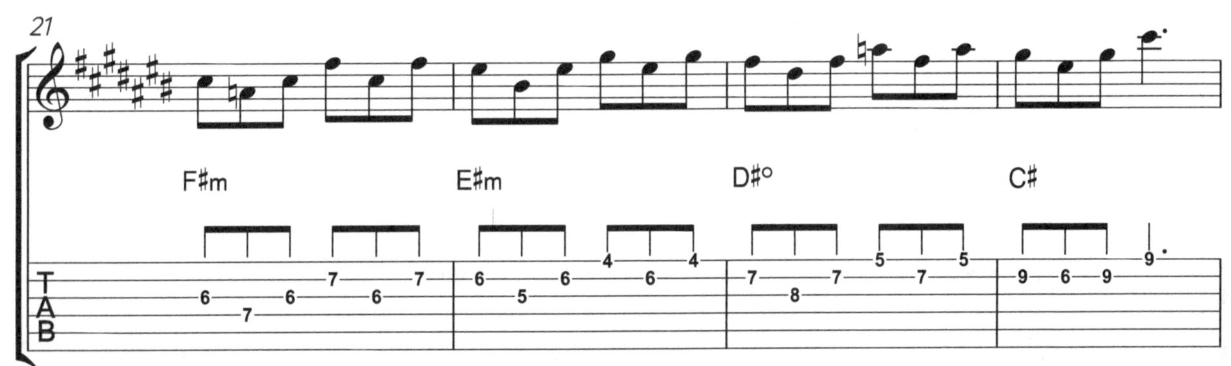
21
F♯m
E♯m
D♯°
C♯
T
A
B

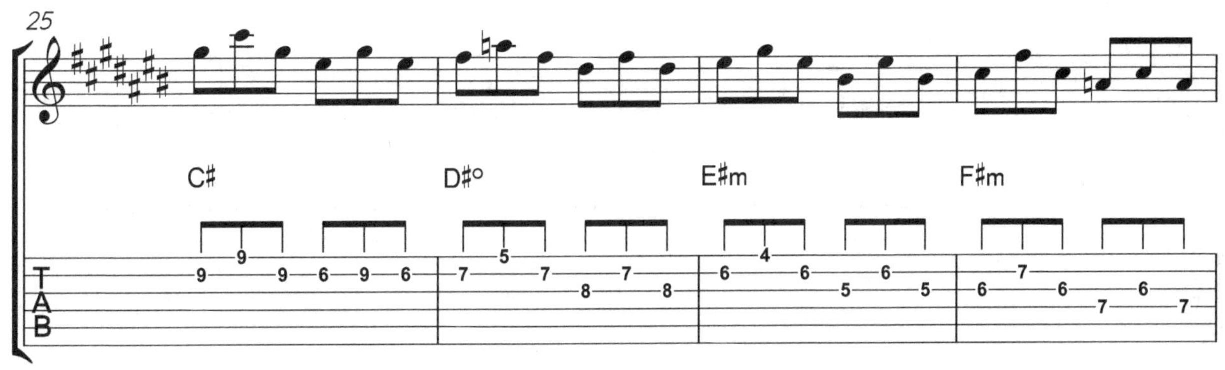
25
C♯
D♯°
E♯m
F♯m
T
A
B

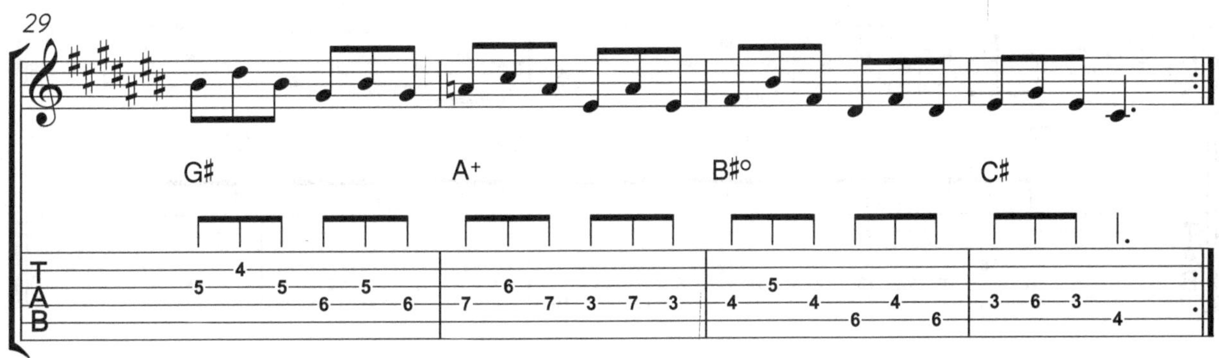
29
G♯
A+
B♯°
C♯
T
A
B

# C♯Harmonic Major Scale 6/8 Sequence ②
## First Inversion

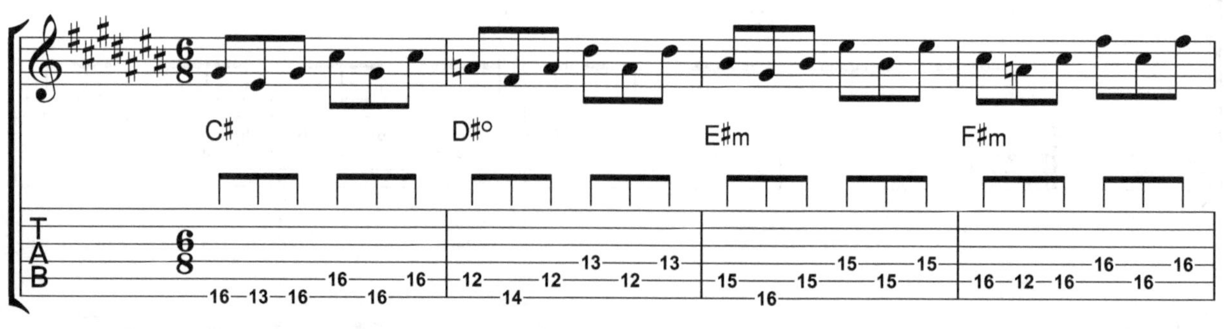


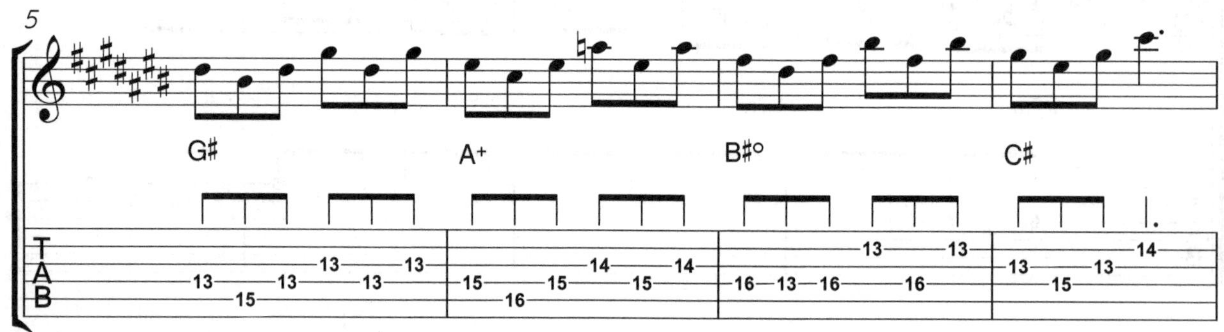


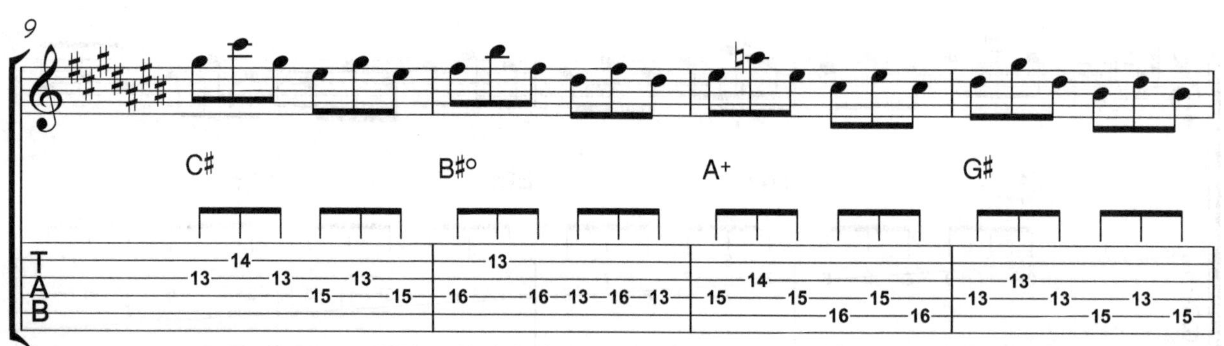


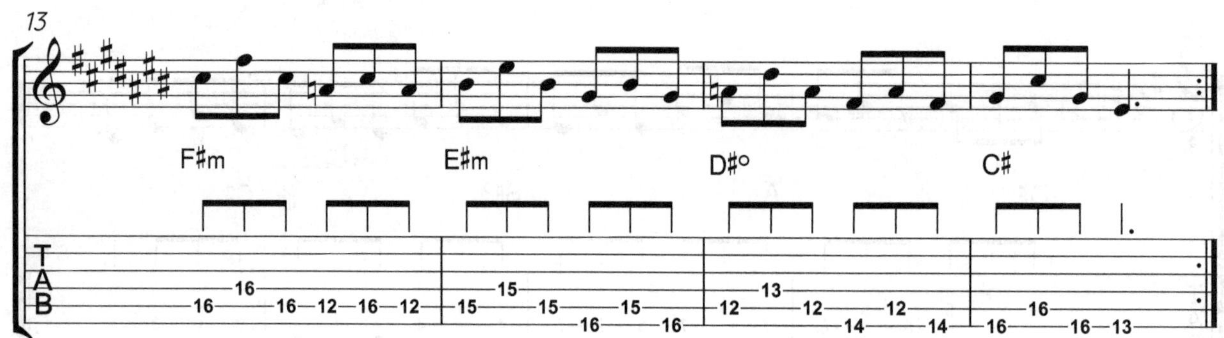

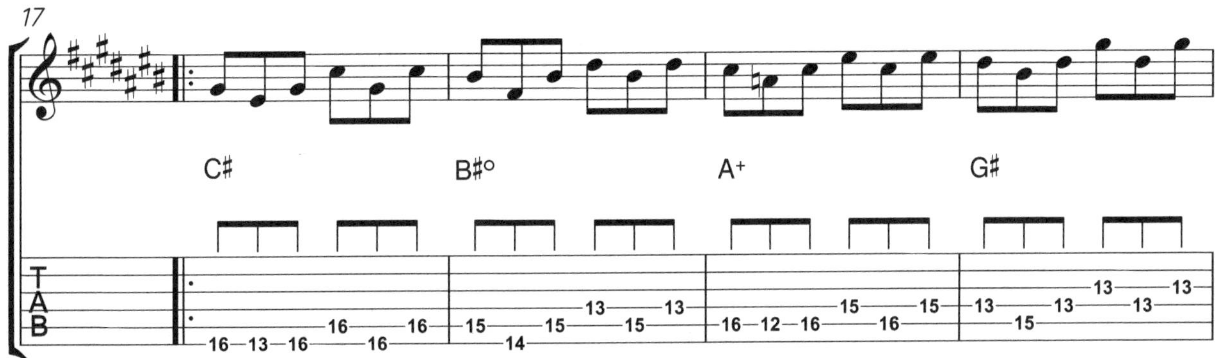
17
C♯
B♯○
A+
G♯
TAB

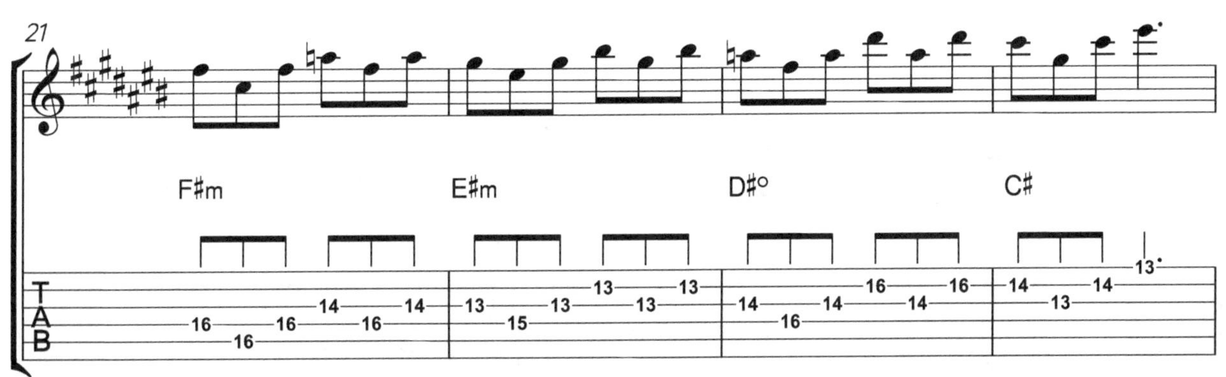
21
F♯m
E♯m
D♯○
C♯
TAB

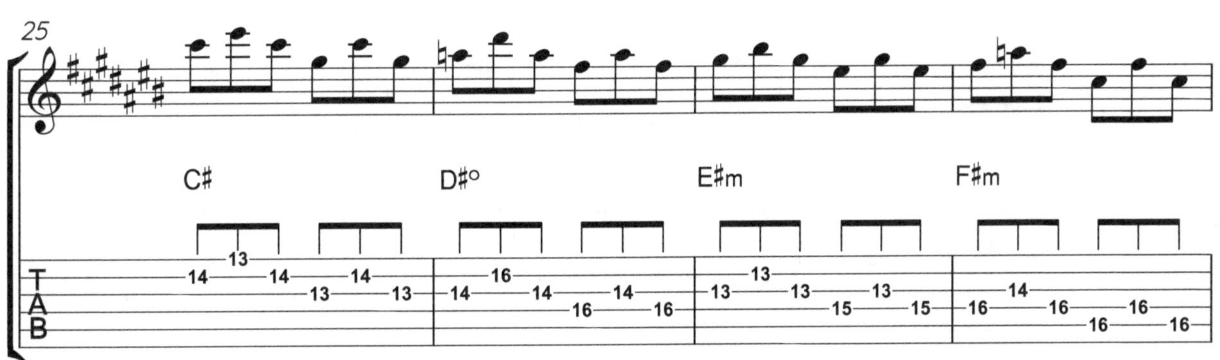
25
C♯
D♯○
E♯m
F♯m
TAB

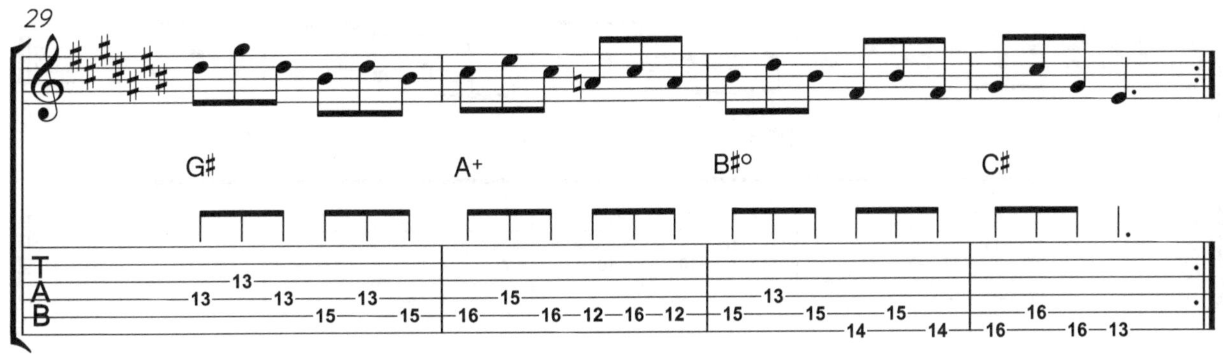
29
G♯
A+
B♯○
C♯
TAB

# C♯Harmonic Major Scale 6/8 Sequence ②
# First Inversion (Alternative Position)

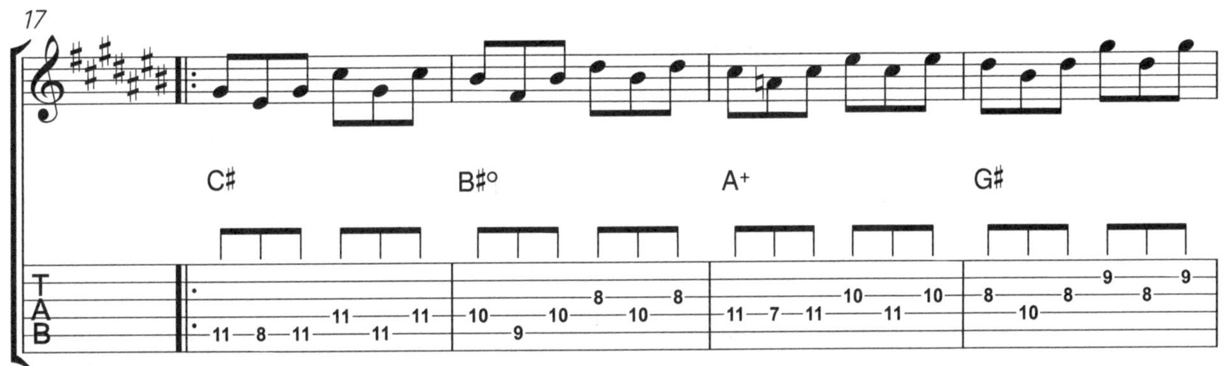
17
C♯
B♯°
A+
G♯
TAB

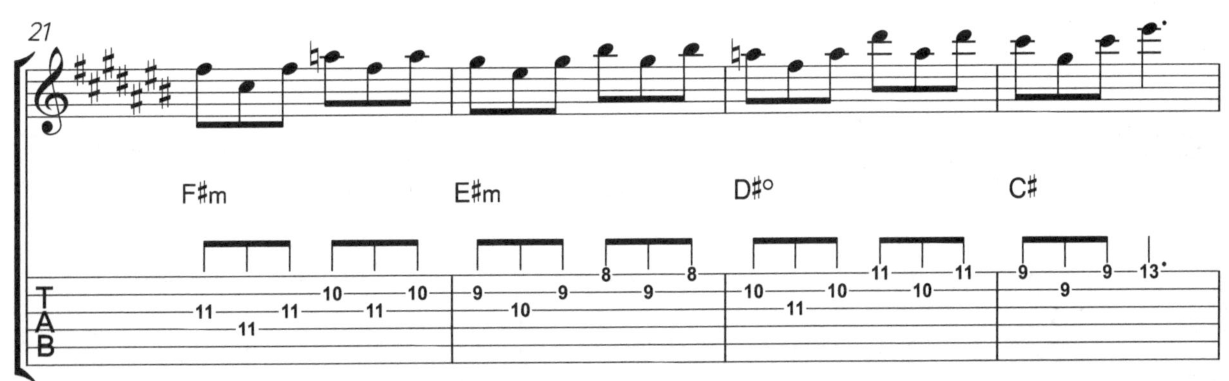
21
F♯m
E♯m
D♯°
C♯
TAB

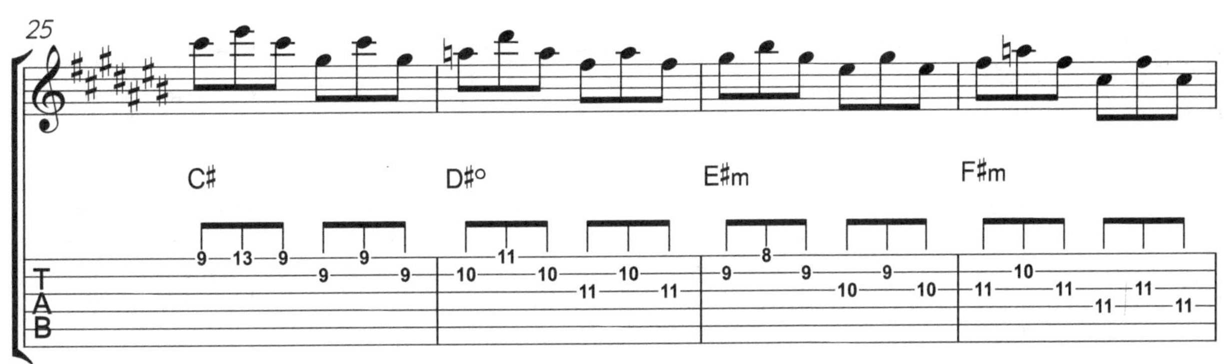
25
C♯
D♯°
E♯m
F♯m
TAB

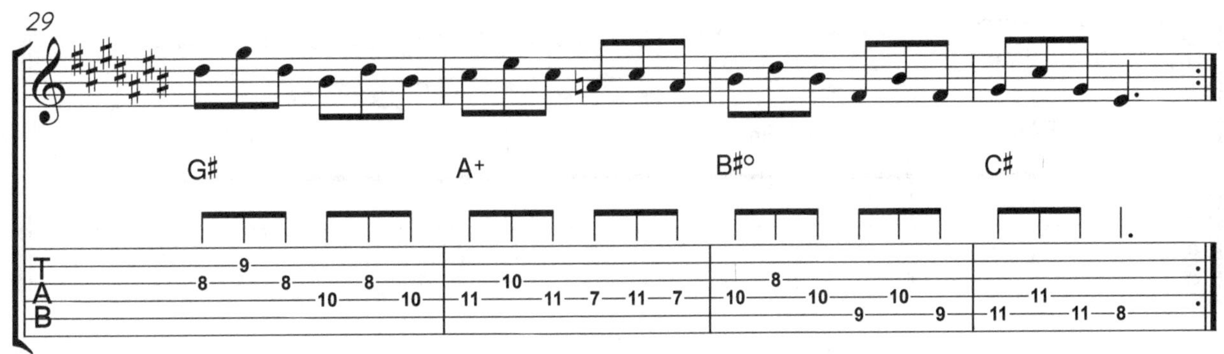
29
G♯
A+
B♯°
C♯
TAB

# C♯ Harmonic Major Scale 6/8 Sequence ②
## Second Inversion

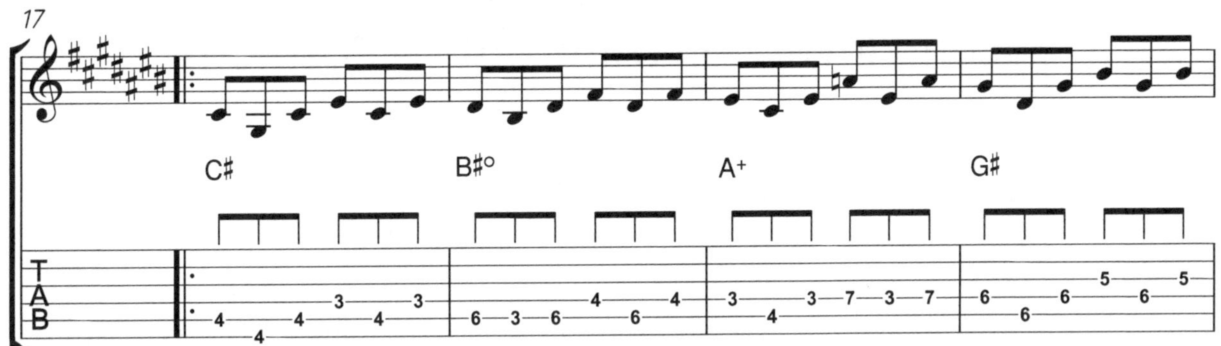
17
C♯
B♯o
A+
G♯
TAB

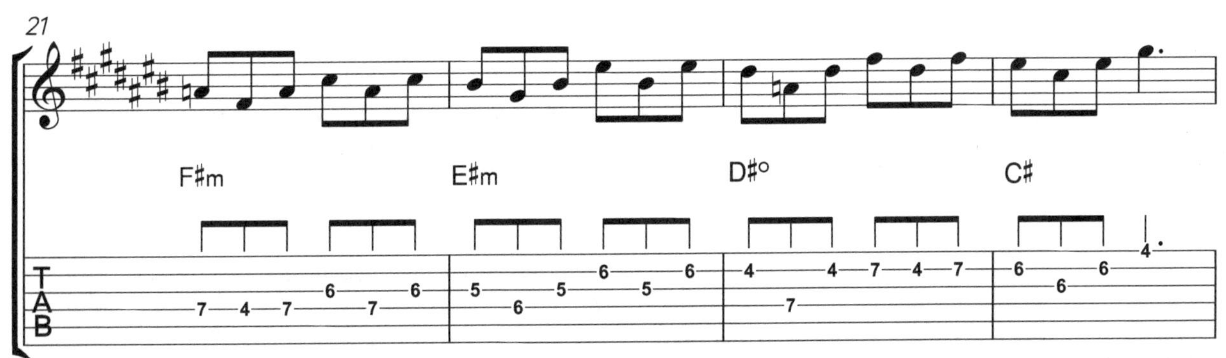
21
F♯m
E♯m
D♯o
C♯
TAB

25
C♯
D♯o
E♯m
F♯m
TAB

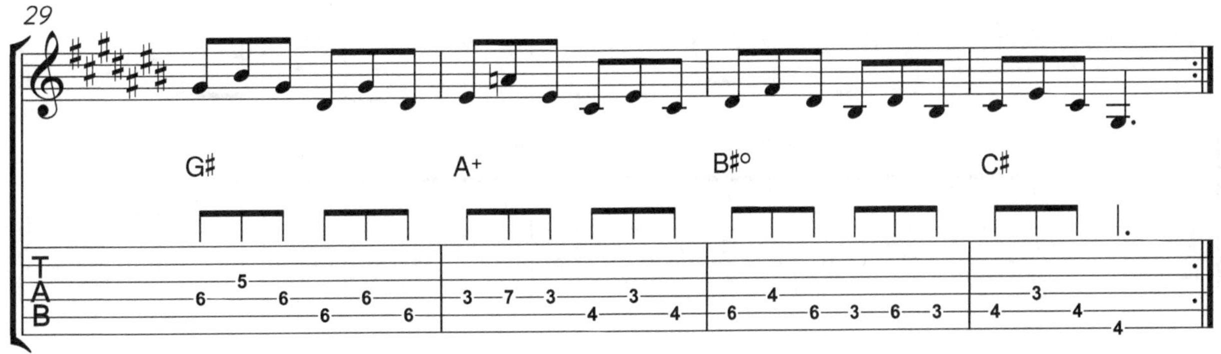
29
G♯
A+
B♯o
C♯
TAB

# C♯Harmonic Major Scale 6/8 Sequence ②
# Second Inversion (Alternative Position)

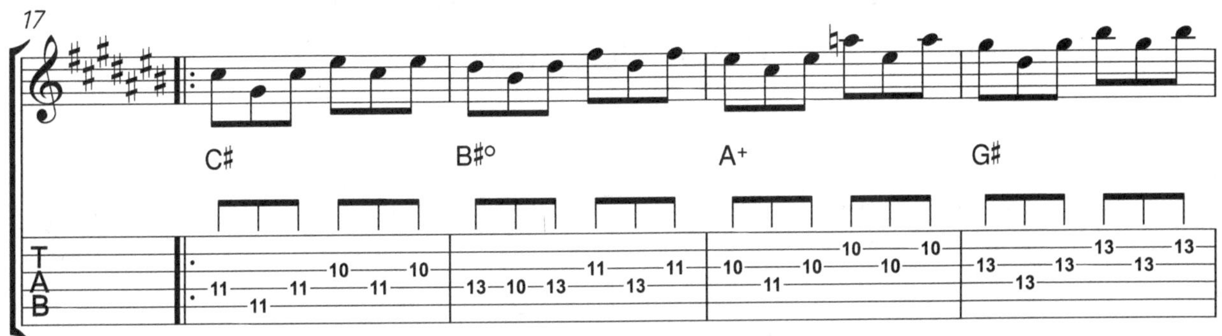
17
C♯
B♯°
A+
G♯
TAB

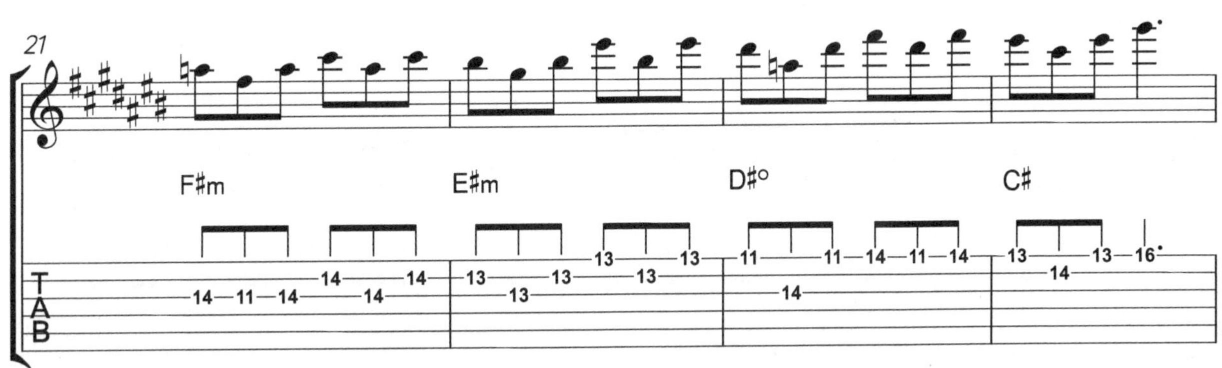
21
F♯m
E♯m
D♯°
C♯
TAB

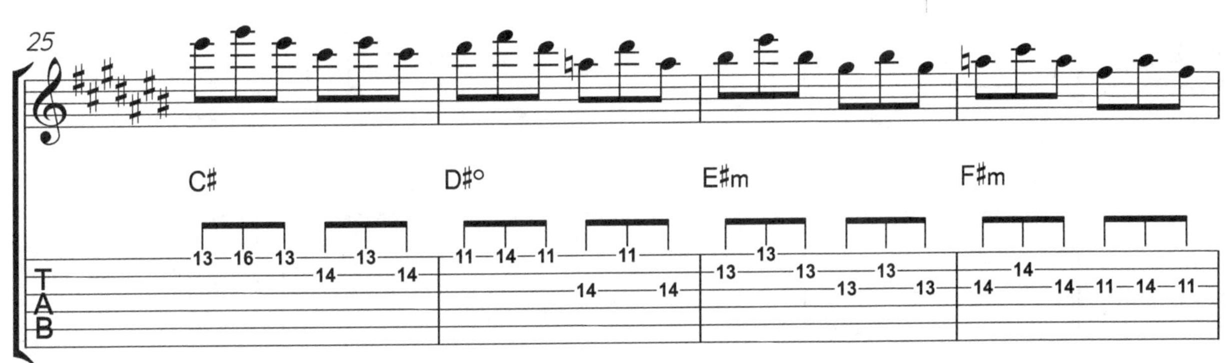
25
C♯
D♯°
E♯m
F♯m
TAB

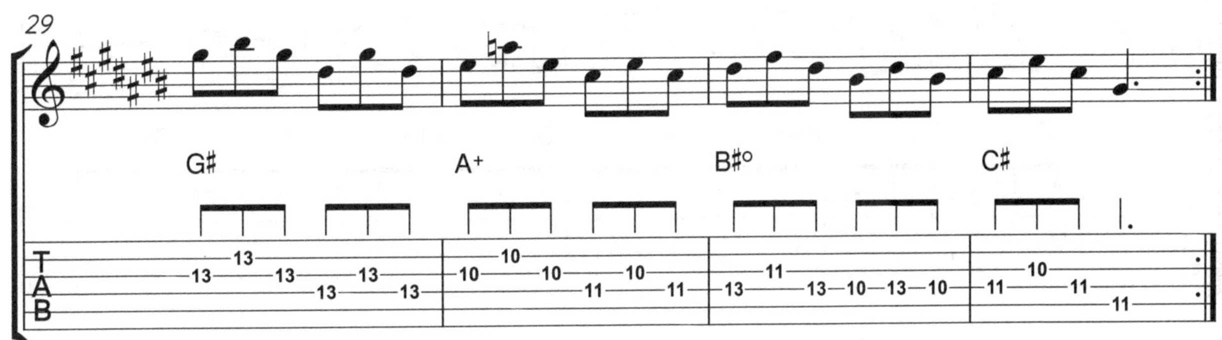
29
G♯
A+
B♯°
C♯
TAB

# G ♭ Major Scale 6/8 Sequence ③
## Root Position

# G♭ Major Scale 6/8 Sequence ③
# Root Position (Alternative Position)

# G ♭ Major Scale 6/8 Sequence ③
# First Inversion

# G♭ Major Scale 6/8 Sequence ③
# First Inversion (Alternative Position)

# G♭ Major Scale 6/8 Sequence ③
## Second Inversion

# G♭ Major Scale 6/8 Sequence ③
# Second Inversion (Alternative Position)

# B Minor Scale 6/8 Sequence ③
## Root Position

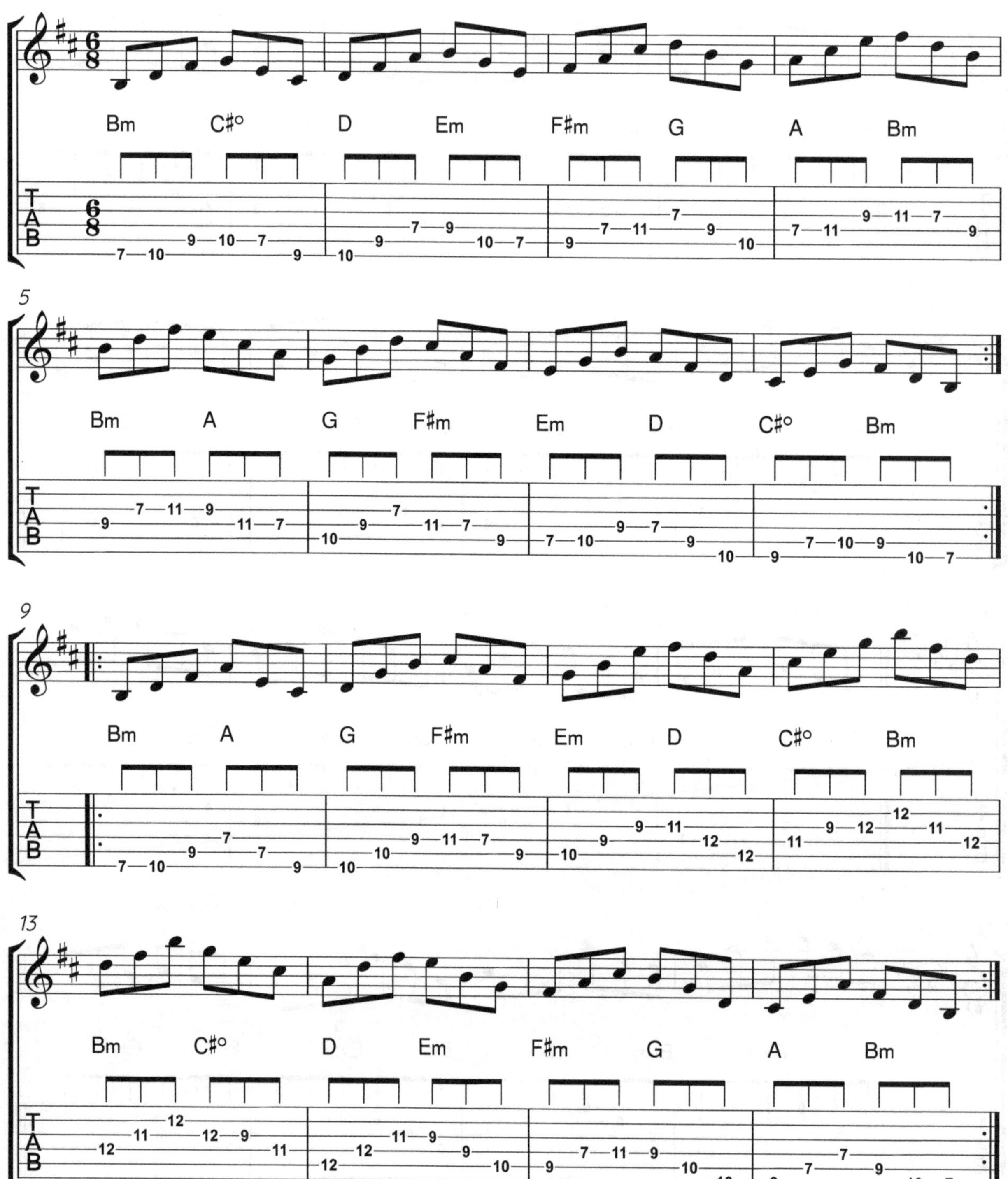

# B Minor Scale 6/8 Sequence ③
# Root Position (Alternative Position)

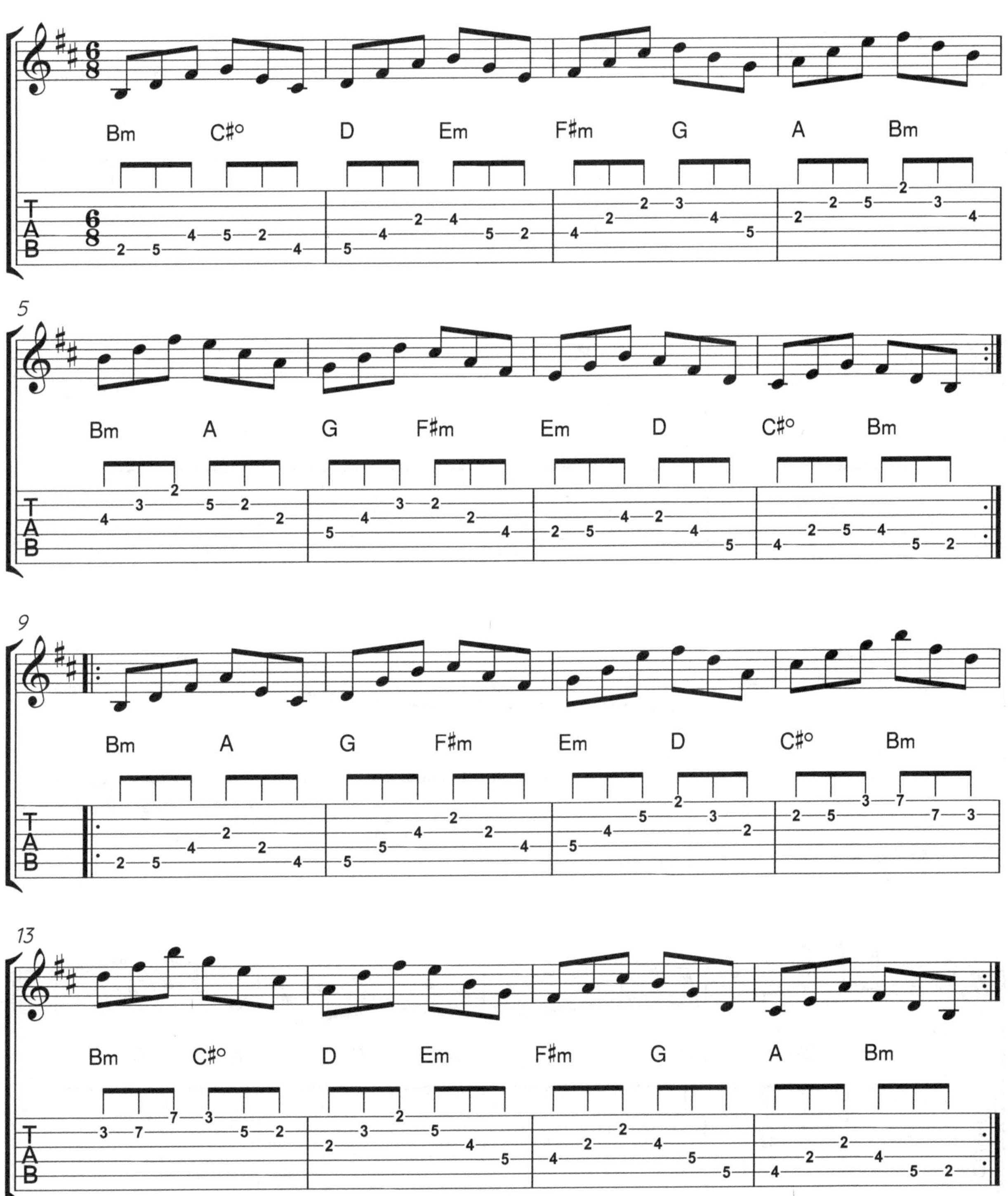

# B Minor Scale 6/8 Sequence ③
## First Inversion

# B Minor Scale 6/8 Sequence ③
# First Inversion (Alternative Position)

# B Minor Scale 6/8 Sequence ③
## Second Inversion

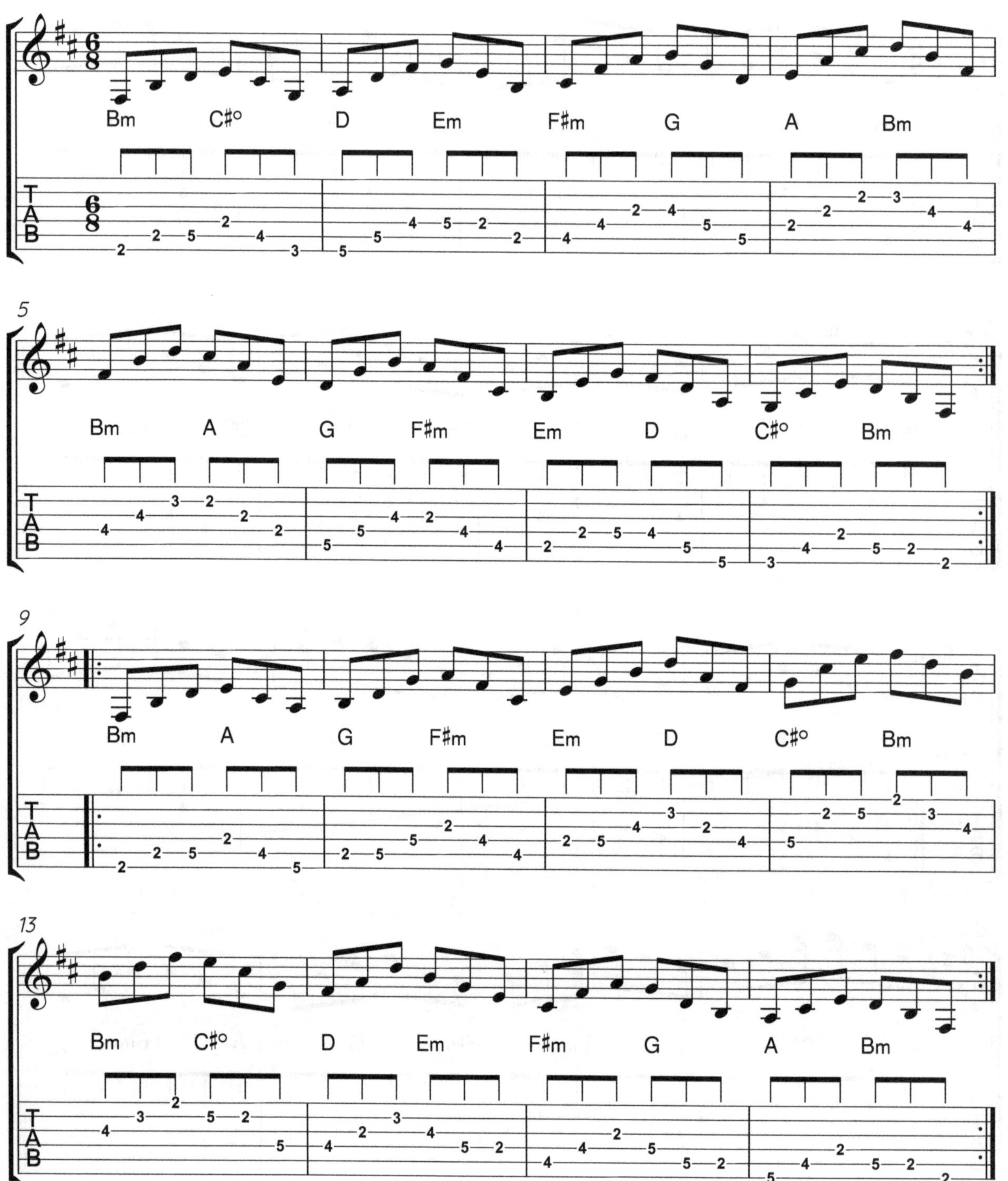

# B Minor Scale 6/8 Sequence ③
# Second Inversion (Alternative Position)

# E Harmonic Minor Scale 6/8 Sequence ③
# Root Position

# E Harmonic Minor Scale 6/8 Sequence ③
# Root Position (Alternative Position)

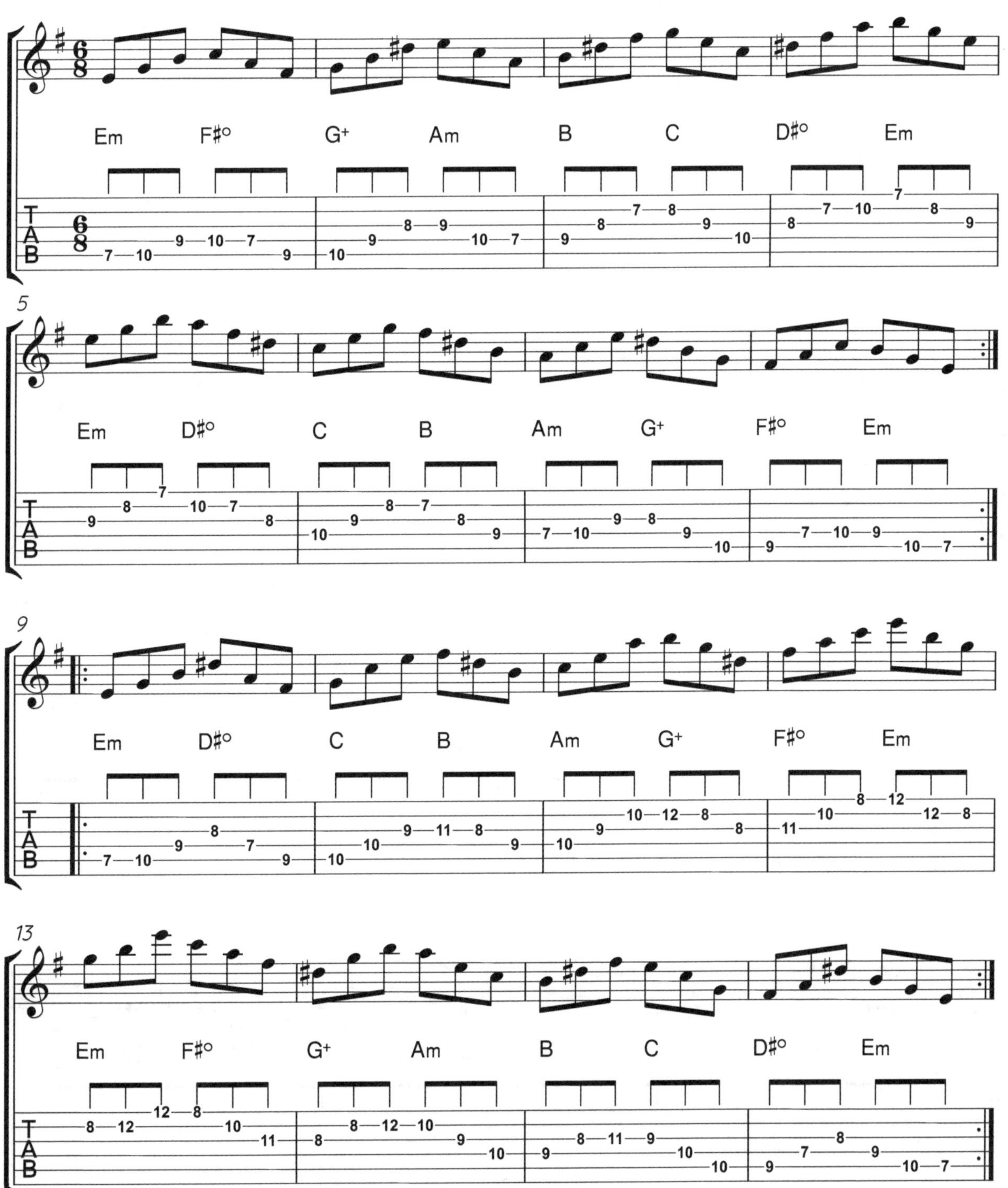

# E Harmonic Minor Scale 6/8 Sequence ③
# First Inversion

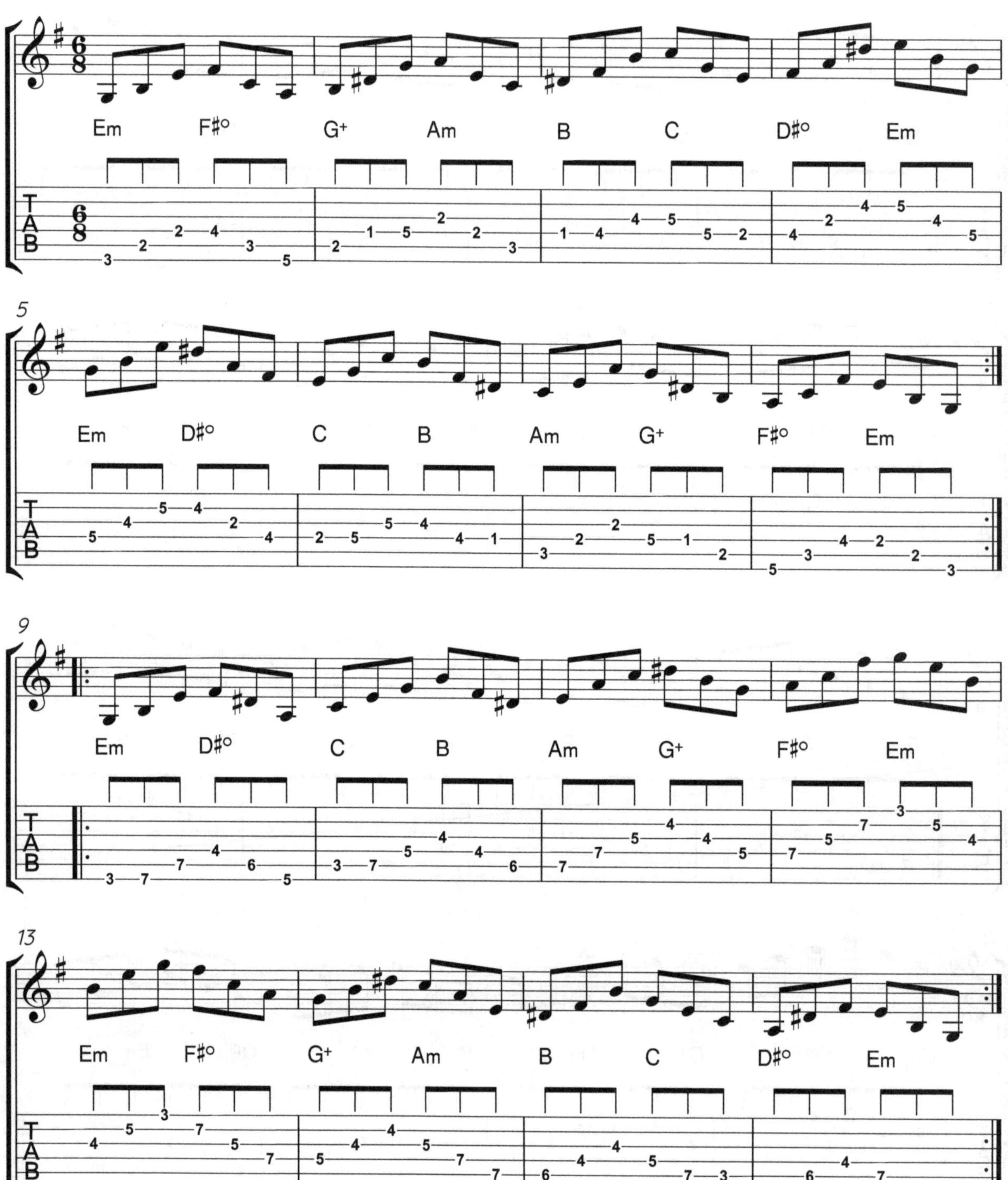

# E Harmonic Minor Scale 6/8 Sequence ③
## First Inversion (Alternative Position)

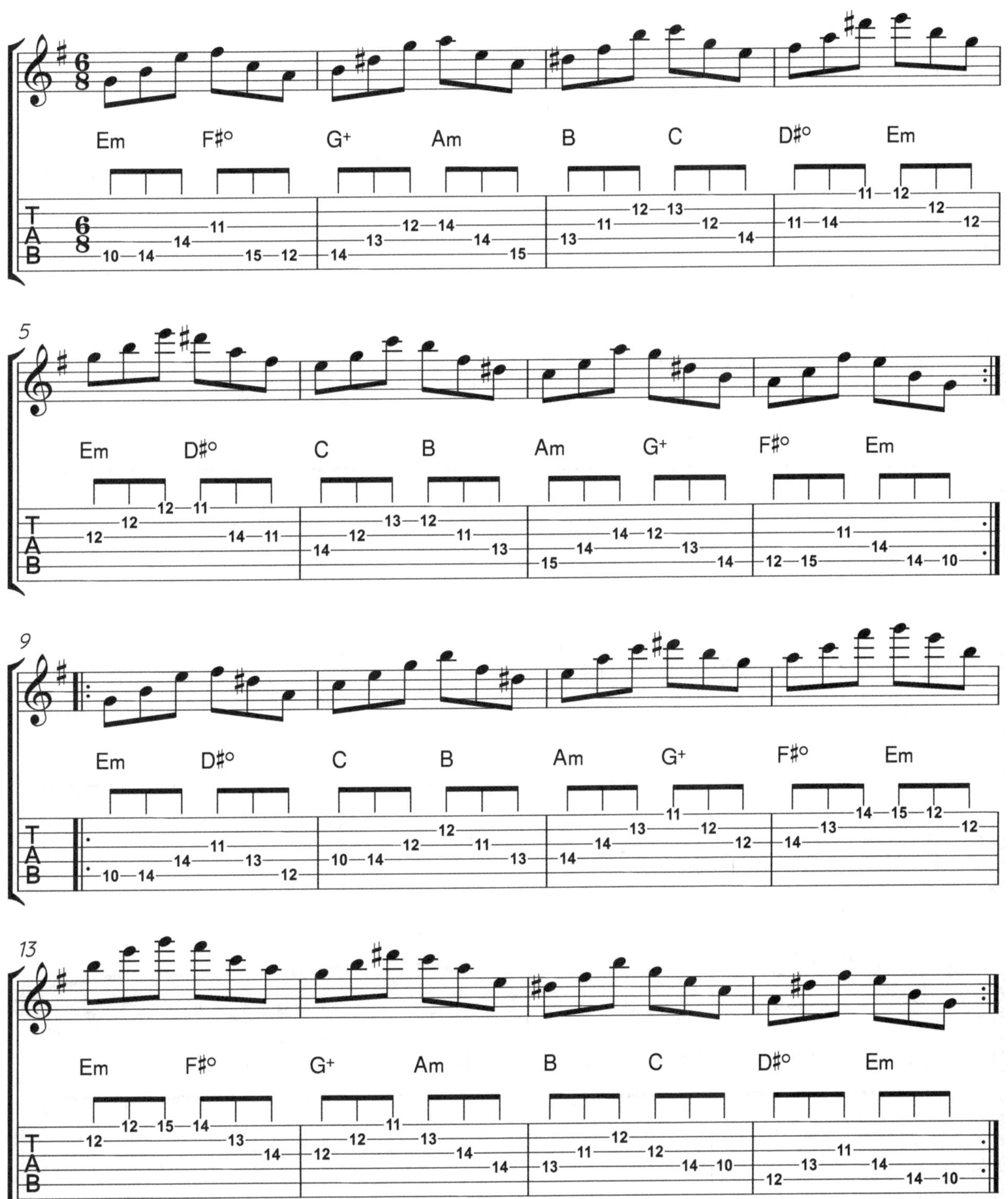

# E Harmonic Minor Scale 6/8 Sequence ③
## Second Inversion

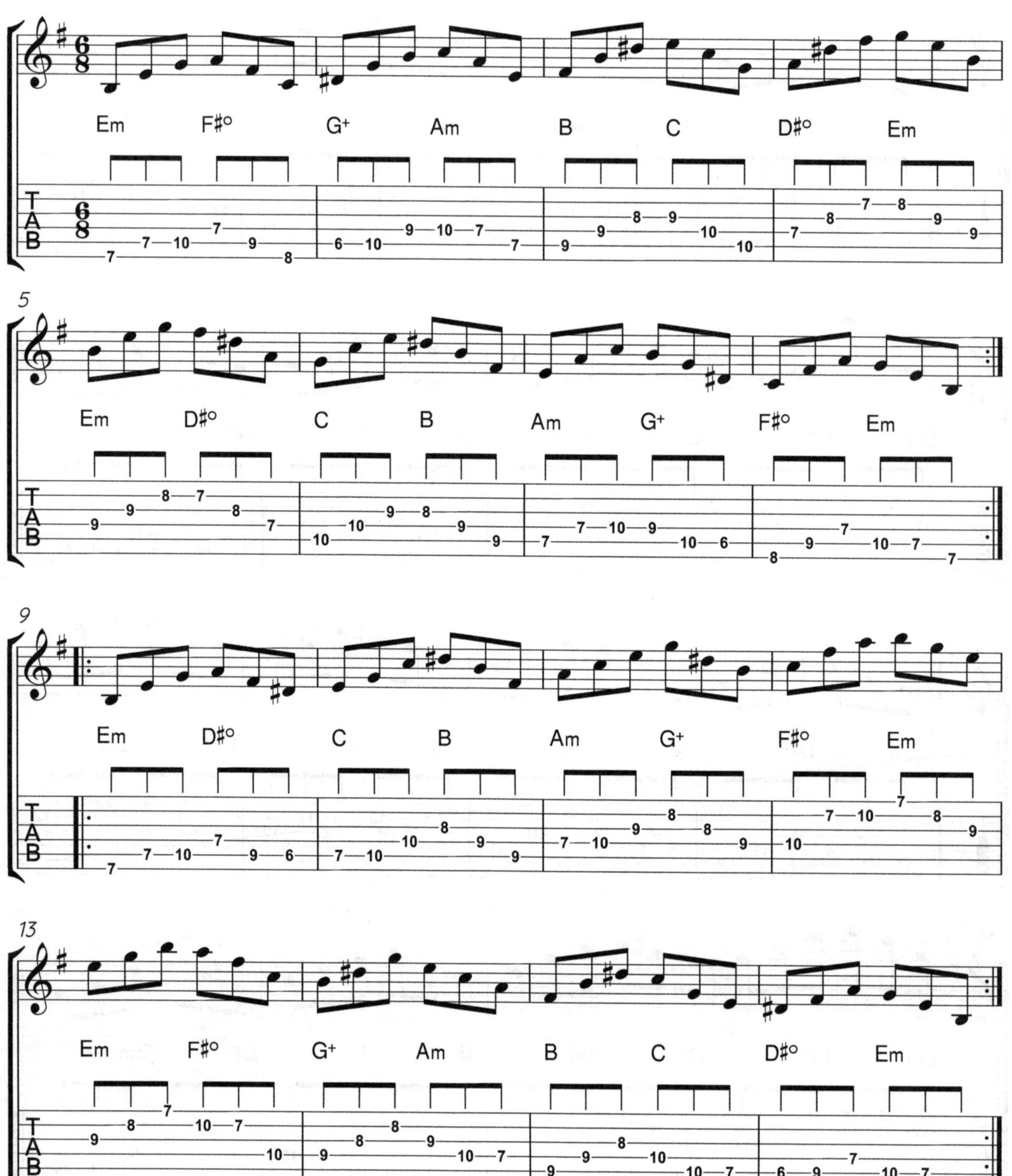

# E Harmonic Minor Scale 6/8 Sequence ③ Second Inversion (Alternative Position)

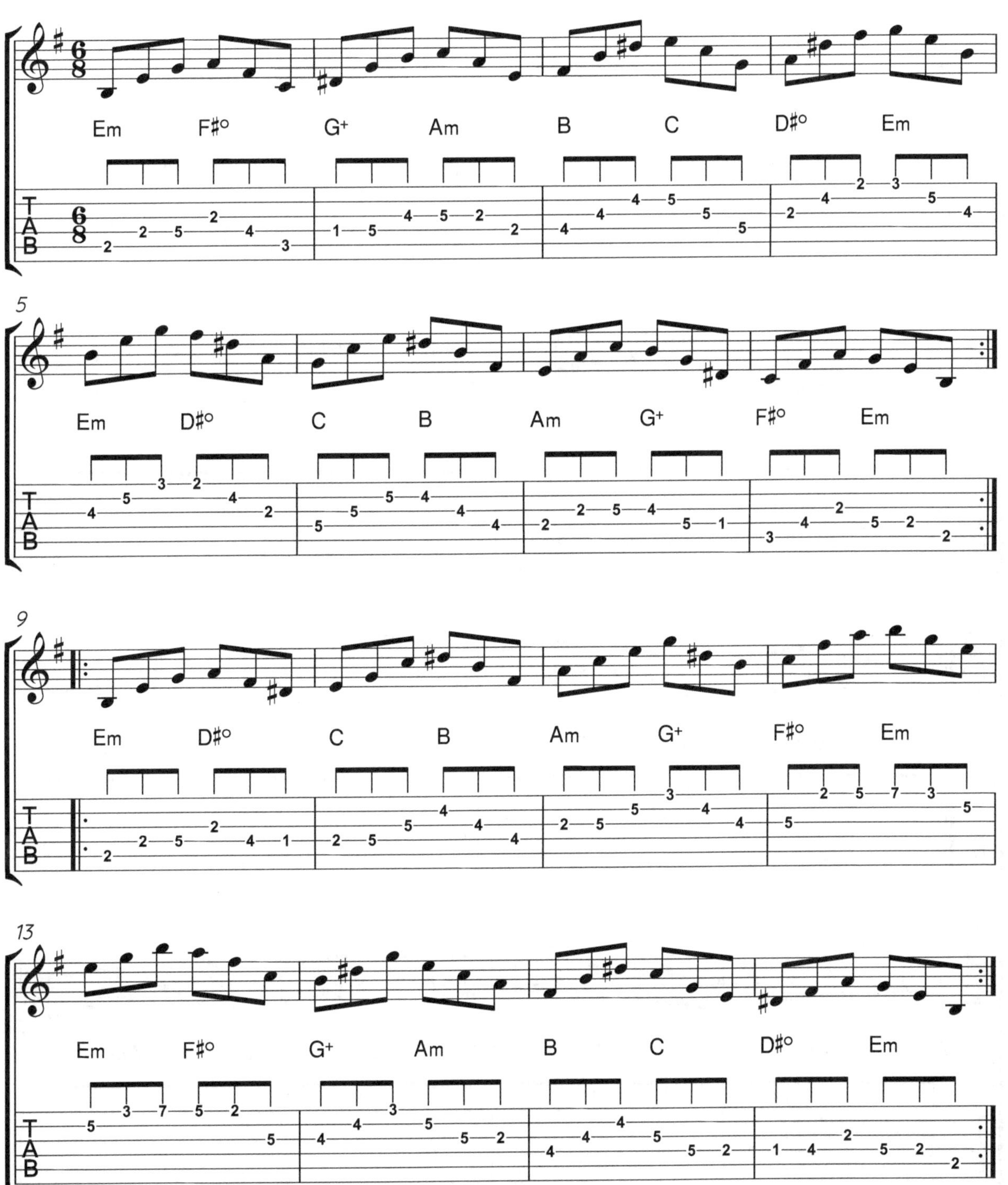

# A Melodic Minor Scale 6/8 Sequence ③
# Root Position

# A Melodic Minor Scale 6/8 Sequence ③
# Root Position (Alternative Position)

# A Melodic Minor Scale 6/8 Sequence ③
First Inversion

# A Melodic Minor Scale 6/8 Sequence ③
# First Inversion (Alternative Position)

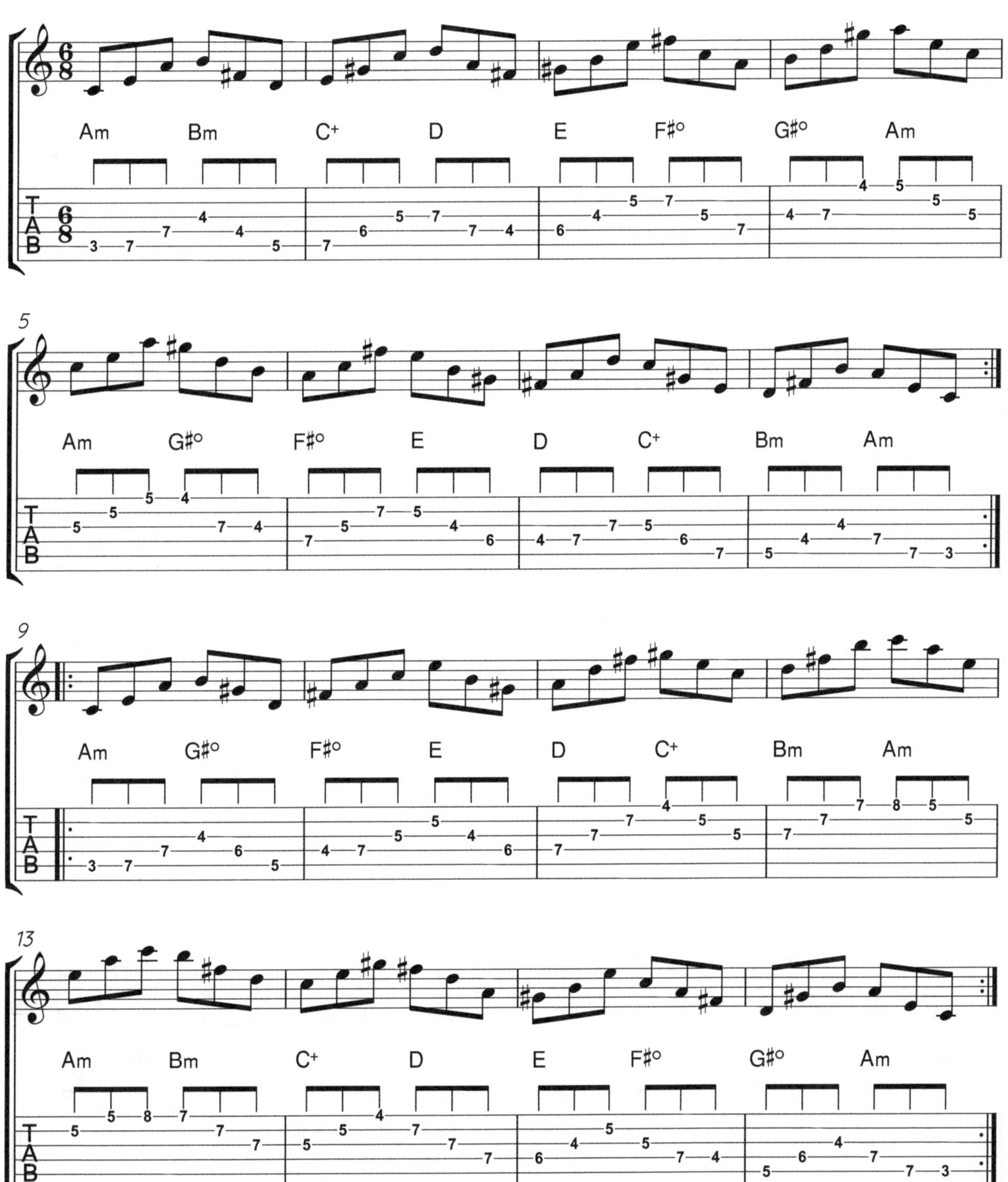

# A Melodic Minor Scale 6/8 Sequence ③
## Second Inversion

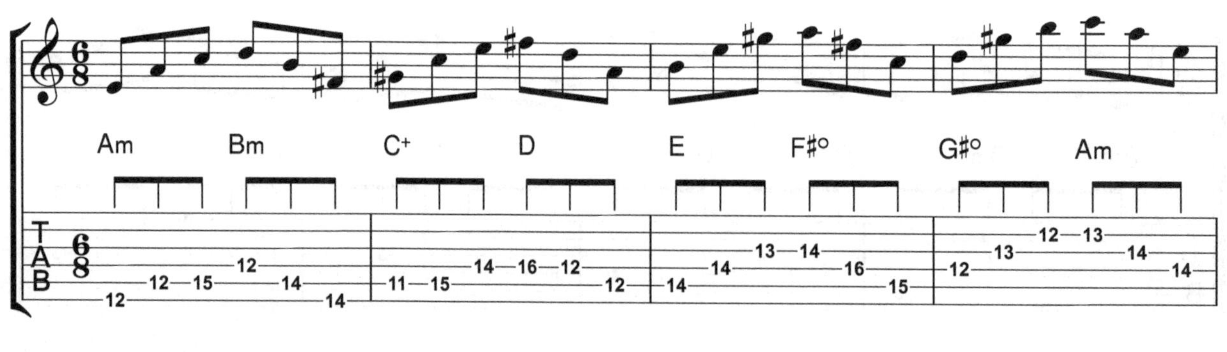


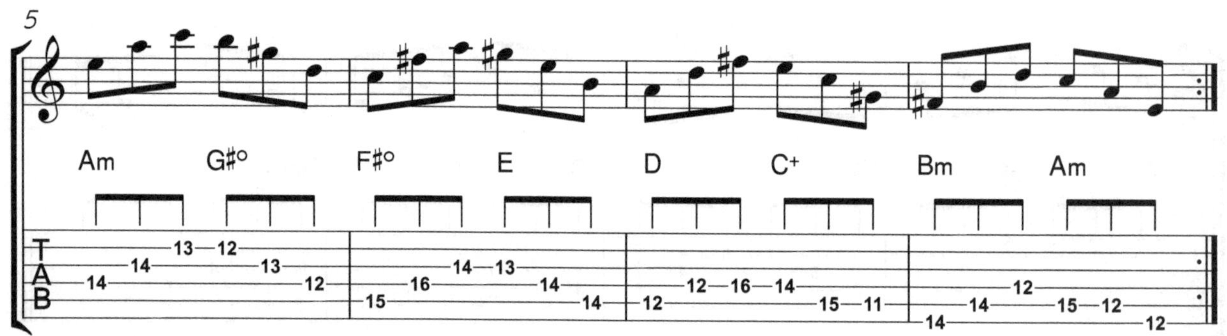


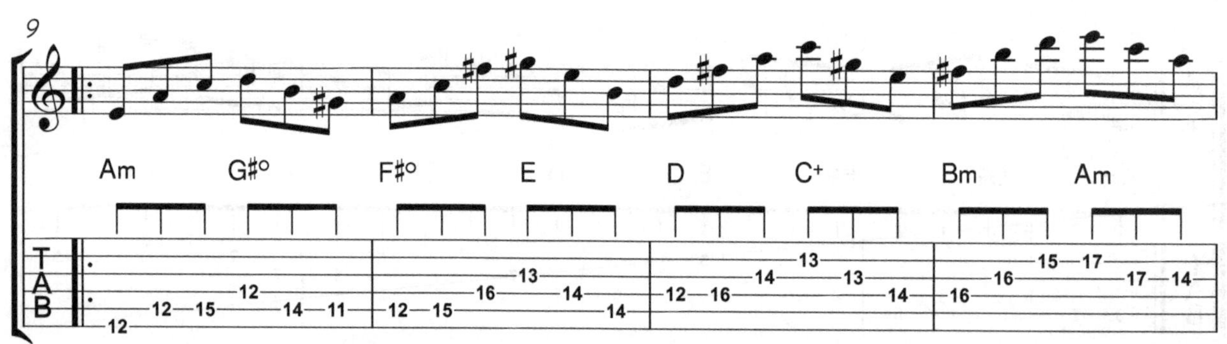


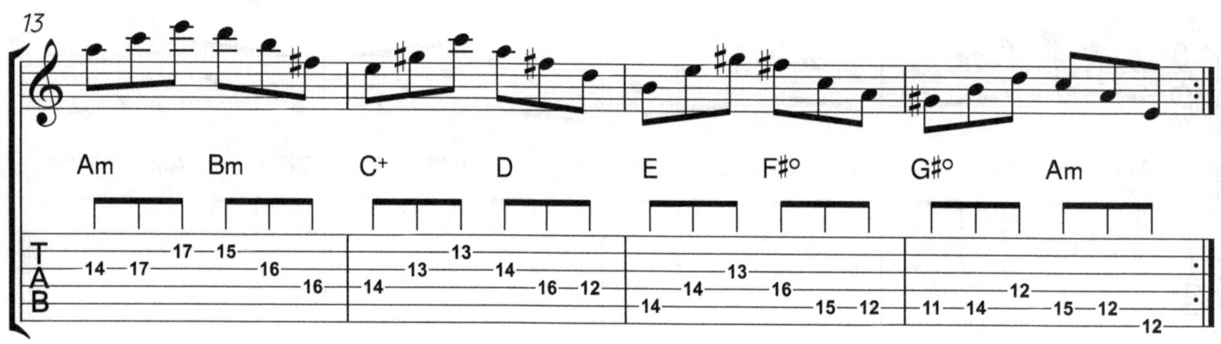

# A Melodic Minor Scale 6/8 Sequence ③
# Second Inversion (Alternative Position)

# D Harmonic Major Scale 6/8 Sequence ③
# Root Position

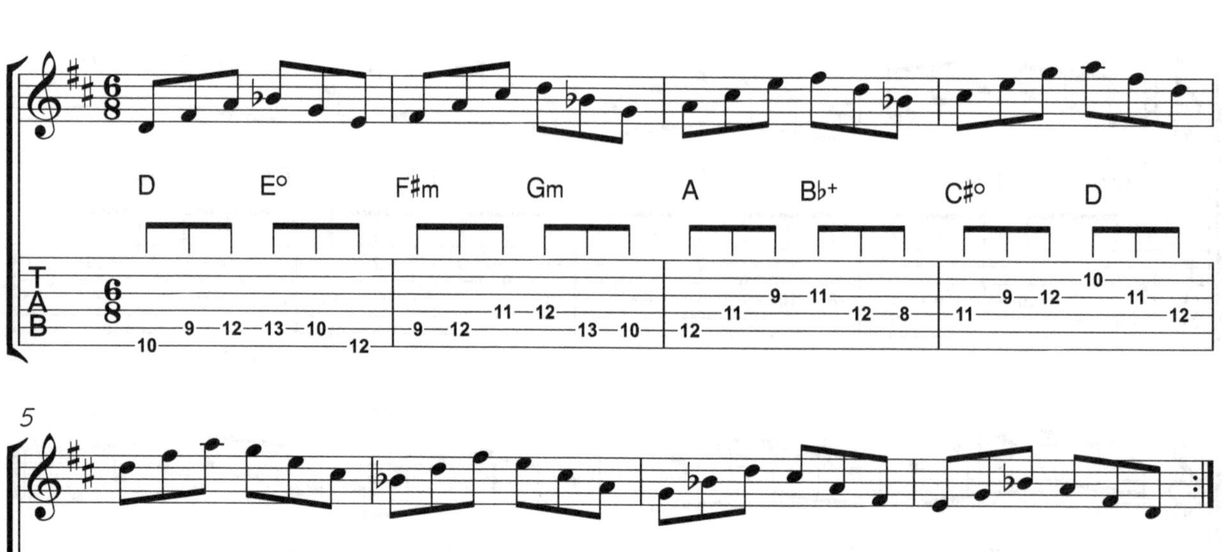


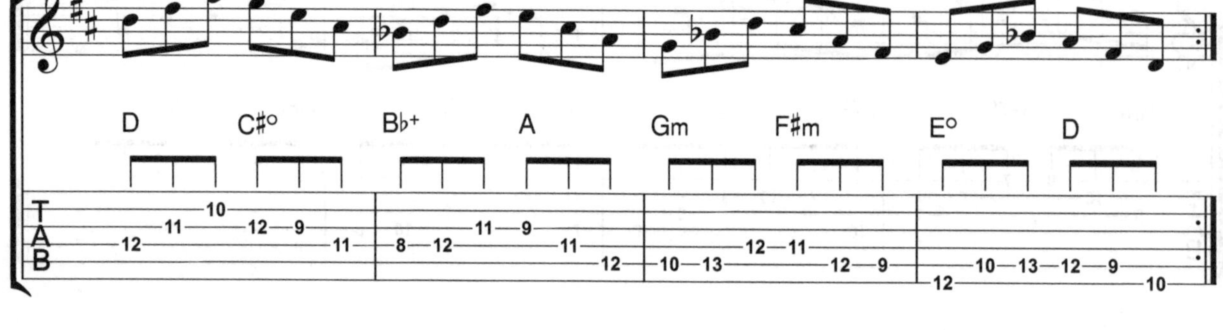


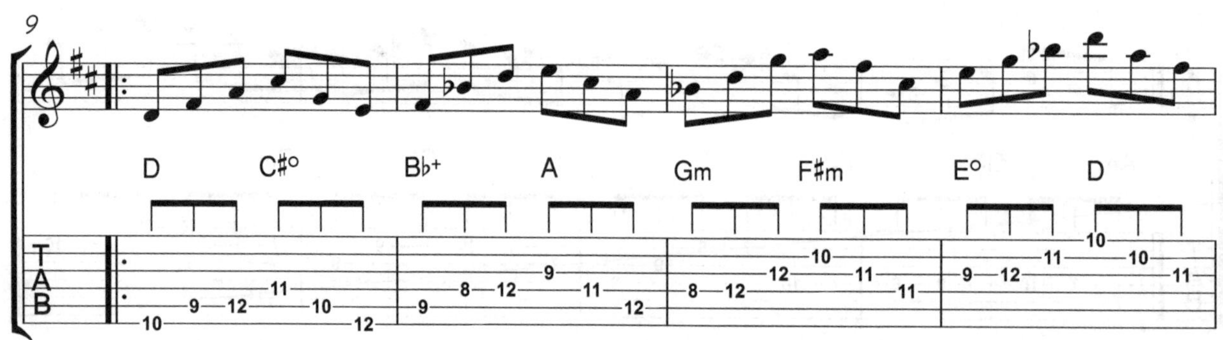


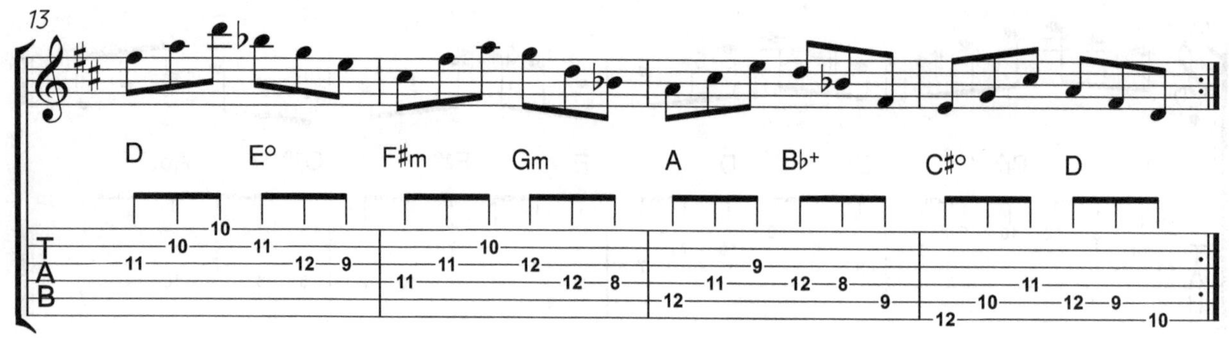

# D Harmonic Major Scale 6/8 Sequence ③
# Root Position (Alternative Position)

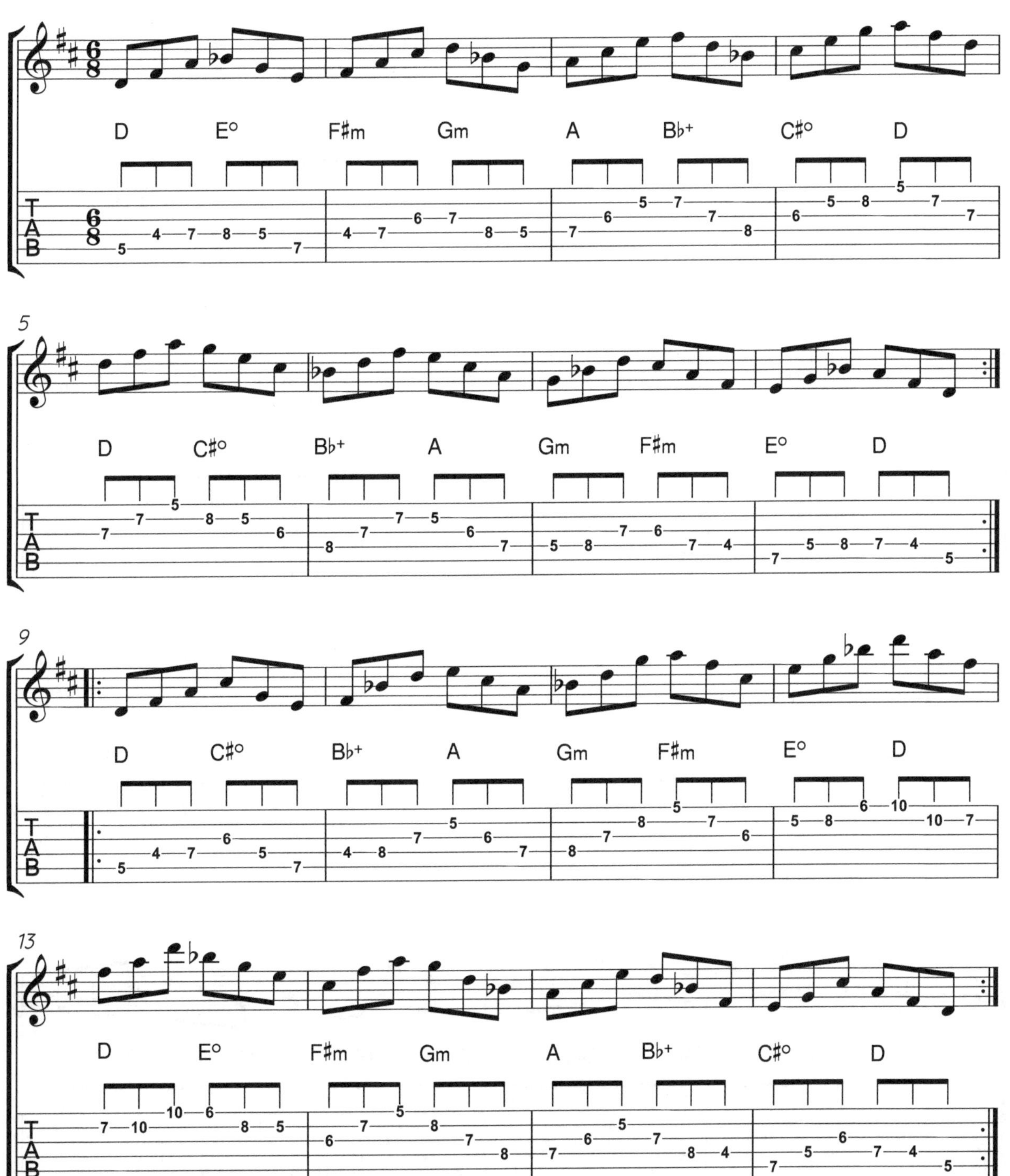

# D Harmonic Major Scale 6/8 Sequence ③
## First Inversion

# D Harmonic Major Scale 6/8 Sequence ③
# First Inversion (Alternative Position)

# D Harmonic Major Scale 6/8 Sequence ③
## Second Inversion

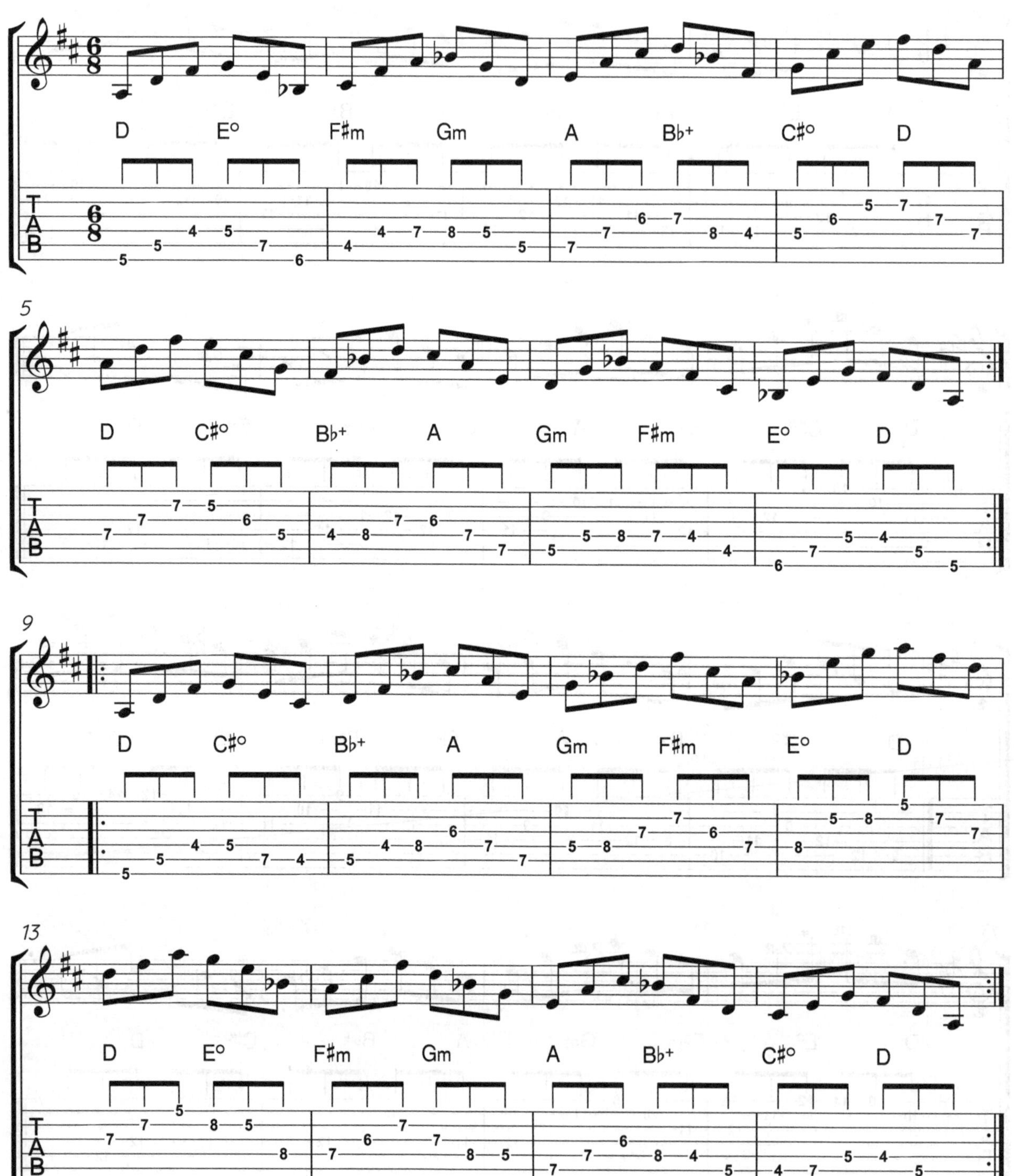

# D Harmonic Major Scale 6/8 Sequence ③
# Second Inversion (Alternative Position)

Made in United States
Troutdale, OR
02/16/2024

17710245R00157